Sun, Steel and Spray

A History of
the Victoria Falls Bridge

About the Author

Peter Roberts is a researcher and writer on the natural and human history of the Victoria Falls. Born in Wales and an ecologist by training, Peter has become drawn to the landscapes, wildlife and human history of Africa and the magic, especially, of the Falls and its surrounds. Following the successful publication of the first edition in 2011, Peter now presents this revised and expanded second edition of 'Sun, Steel and Spray - a History of the Victoria Falls Bridge.'

Also Available

To the Banks of the Zambezi and Beyond -
Railway Construction from the Cape to the Congo (1893-1910).
Life and Death at the Old Drift, Victoria Falls (1898-1905).
Corridors Through Time - A History of the Victoria Falls Hotel.
Footsteps Through Time - A History of Travel and Tourism to the Victoria Falls.

- - -

Sun, Steel and Spray - A History of the Victoria Falls Bridge
Peter Roberts

Copyright © 2021 Peter Roberts. All Rights Reserved
www.zambezibookcompany.com

First Published April 2011, Victoria Falls Bridge Company
Second Edition July 2016, Zambezi Book Company
Third Edition November 2020, Zambezi Book Company
Fourth Edition October 2021, Zambezi Book Company

Cover design and page layout by Peter Roberts

ISBN: 9798487276964

Roberts, Peter (2021) Sun, Steel and Spray - A History of the Victoria Falls Bridge Third Edition, Zambezi Book Company / CreateSpace Independent Publishing

Sun, Steel and Spray

A History of the Victoria Falls Bridge

Peter Roberts

Contents

Foreword

By the Joint Chairmen of the
Emerged Railways Properties Private Ltd.

Emerged Railways Properties (ERP) Pvt Ltd is an inter-state body owned jointly by the Governments of Zambia and Zimbabwe and responsible for managing cross border railway assets including the Victoria Falls Bridge.

It was with great excitement that we first learned of Peter's plans to write a full and thorough account of the history of our most iconic of bridges. Now that we have had time to absorb his text we want to acknowledge him for a job well done, at last a true and accurate account of the bridge is available for all to share and enjoy.

For our part, we see ourselves as nothing more than custodians of the bridge, looking after it for the generations to come, after all, the bridge is for the people of Africa, and so it will be for many years to come.

That the bridge is now a celebrated African icon is of no surprise to us. As the Falls are a natural wonder so the bridge is a man made wonder and they compliment each other perfectly, thank you Mr Hobson for your inspired design and thank you Mr Imbault for your ingenious construction.

Our hope is that this book will be read by many around the world and perhaps inspire them to visit the bridge. We know that those who do will not be disappointed. Perhaps we will meet you there!

For and on behalf of the Board of Emerged Railways Properties Pvt Ltd.
Air Commodore Mike Tichafa Karakadzai and Mr Knox Karima,
Joint Chairmen,
March 2011.

Preface

Welcome to this history of the Victoria Falls Bridge, icon of the Victoria Falls, and a journey through over a century of travel and tourism to the Victoria Falls. This book started life as a research project for the Victoria Falls Bridge Company to support in the development of the Bridge information centre and history tours, but soon outgrew its initial concept and developed into a detailed and comprehensive study on the history of the Victoria Falls Bridge. First published in 2011, this extended third edition builds on the information previously published in the first and second editions, with expanded text and additional images.

In presenting the story of the Bridge, I have, wherever possible, described events directly through contemporary references and descriptions, quotations from which form a key element of the text. Many references have been used to compile this work, and I have referenced as much material as possible as these sources will be of interest to those wishing to know more about the fascinating history of the Bridge.

In some cases I have found conflicting accounts of details or events, and it is interesting to see how, in just over 100 years since the bridge was built, stories have become embellished and in some cases twisted into complete untruths. Most common amongst these 'tales' is that Imbault, the Chief Construction Engineer, committed suicide by throwing himself from the Bridge after finding that the final

An early view of the Victoria Falls Bridge

piece of the arch did not fit. The construction was perfectly executed, and Imbault was in fact widely celebrated for his skill in managing the construction of the Bridge.

The names of places and countries have changed over the years, and old names are first introduced in their original historical contexts, whilst also identified with their contemporary names for clarity, for example Bechuanaland (now Botswana).

For ease of reading the text often refers simply to the 'Railway Company,' rather than the various names of the original construction and operating companies. The Bechuanaland Railway Company was originally formed in 1893 and renamed the Rhodesia Railways Limited in 1899. This company would oversee the construction of the railway to the Victoria Falls and building of the Victoria Falls Bridge. The operating company became the merged Beira and Mashonaland and Rhodesia Railways in 1903, changed to simply Rhodesia Railways in 1927 and becoming Rhodesia Railways, Limited, in 1936. Following nationalisation the company became a statutory body, the Rhodesia Railways, in 1949, and finally evolving into the National Railways of Zimbabwe in 1980.

I have tried to avoid repeated references to ever increasing monetary amounts, however, reference is occasionally made to significant sums in either United Kingdom Pound, or later the United States Dollar, at their contemporary value.
I apologise for any errors, mistakes or omissions in the text, which I hope are few in number and small in nature. Comments and criticisms are welcomed, as are contributions; especially information, stories or key photographs missing from this account. Additional information, amendments, updates and notification of future revised editions will be published online at www.zambezibookcompany.com.

I hope you enjoy reading this history of the Victoria Falls Bridge, covering the story of its inception, erection and continued vital role as road, rail and footbridge high over the Zambezi. Readers interested in the wider history of the development of tourism to the Victoria Falls during the twentieth century will also be interested in the companion publication 'Life and Death at the Old Drift, Victoria Falls (1898-1905),' (first published 2018, third edition 2021), as well as 'Corridors Through Time - A History of the Victoria Falls Hotel' (first published 2015, third edition 2021); and 'Footsteps Through Time - a History of Travel and Tourism to the Victoria Falls' (published 2017, second edition 2021).

Peter Roberts
October 2021
www.zambezibookcompany.com
peter@zambezibookcompany.com

Introduction

The Victoria Falls Bridge is widely acknowledged as a man-made engineering marvel to rival the natural wonder of the Falls themselves. Crossing the Batoka Gorge a short distance downstream of the great waterfall, high over the Zambezi River, the Bridge provides a vital transport connection between Zambia and Zimbabwe. The attractive yet simple design, and unforgettable location, make the Victoria Falls Bridge an instantly identifiable global icon.

Opened in 1905 as a landmark link in the proposed 'Cape to Cairo' Railway, the Bridge was the brainchild of Cecil John Rhodes, who dared to envisage his railway crossing the river just below the Falls so as to have 'the spray of the water over the carriages.' Its construction, however, was not without controversy, with Cecil Rhodes' own brother, Colonel Frank Rhodes, protesting against its location.

The spanning of the Zambezi required a bridge that would push engineering knowledge and construction techniques of the time to new heights, literally, for at the time the Bridge was the highest of its kind over water. Celebrated with typical colonial fanfare as a great British engineering achievement, the connecting of the Bridge and opening was publicised across the English-speaking world.

The arrival of the railway and building of the Bridge, only fifty years after Dr David Livingstone had first announced their sublime grandeur to the world, opened the Falls to tourism and development. The Railway Company quickly erected a temporary Hotel overlooking the rising spray of the Falls and site of the Bridge.

Originally known simply as the 'Zambezi Bridge' (and spelt 'Zambesi' before becoming 'Americanised' in the 1950s), the Bridge has become commonly known as the Victoria Falls Bridge after the construction of further bridges downstream. Today the Bridge carries a roadway together with the railway and pedestrian walkways, and is not only an economically important transport crossing, but tourism attraction in its own right. Tourists can view a unique perspective on the Falls from the Bridge, and can even experience it upside down on the end of a bungee cord if they dare!

The Bridge has well and truly passed the test of time, reaching its centenary in 2005, and now looking forward to the 125th anniversary of its opening in 2030. Tribute indeed to all those involved in its conception and construction, and whose efforts have made a significant and lasting contribution to the growth and development of the region. Their stories are an integral part of the history of this great engineering achievement.

To the Victoria Falls

Known to the local inhabitants of the region for centuries, the majestic natural wonder of the Victoria Falls was first brought to the attention of the wider world by the famous Scottish missionary and explorer Dr David Livingstone (1813-1873).

In mid-1851 Livingstone and his travelling companion William Oswell were exploring north into the unmapped interior, eventually reaching a large river which the inhabitants living along its wide reaches called the *Liambai* and which Livingstone correctly identified as the Zambezi, previously known only to Europeans by its lower stretches and great delta on the east coast. Befriending the Makalolo chief Sebetwane, who held power in the region, they were told of a great waterfall some distance downstream, although they did not travel to visit them. Livingstone later recorded:

> *"Of these we had often heard since we came into the country; indeed, one of the questions asked by Sebituane was, 'Have you smoke that sounds in your country?' They* [the Makalolo] *did not go near enough to examine them, but, viewing them with awe at a distance, said, in reference to the vapour and noise, 'Mosi oa Tunya' (smoke does sound there). It was previously called Shongwe, the meaning of which I could not ascertain."*

It was not until 1855, after first exploring upstream and a route across to the west coast, that Livingstone returned to the Zambezi with his Makalolo porters and finally journeyed downstream, escorted by Sebetwane's successor, Chief Sekeletu. Travelling by canoe and then walking along the north bank to avoid the Katambora Rapids, Sekeletu arranged a canoe and local boatman to take Livingstone the final distance downstream to the waterfall.

Dr David Livingstone (1813-1873)

On 16th November 1855 Livingstone was guided to a small island on the very lip of the Falls. Scrambling through vegetation to the sudden edge Livingstone struggled to understand the dramatic scene which unfolded before him:

"I did not comprehend it until, creeping with awe to the verge, I peered down into a large rent which had been made from bank to bank of the broad Zambesi, and saw that a stream of a thousand yards [915 m] broad leaped down a hundred feet [30.5 m]... the most wonderful sight I had witnessed in Africa."

Livingstone was perhaps deliberately cautious in his estimates, adding: *"Whoever may come after me will not, I trust, have reason to say I have indulged in exaggeration"* (Livingstone, 1857). He seriously underestimated the scale of the Falls, which span 1,708 metres (5,604 feet or 1,868 yards) and drop up to 108 metres (355 feet).

On his explorations Livingstone carefully recorded local names for geographic landmarks. Here, however, he also named them in English in honour of his monarch, the reigning British Queen Victoria.

"Being persuaded that Mr Oswell and myself were the very first Europeans who ever visited the Zambesi in the centre of the country, and that this is the connecting link between the known and unknown portions of that river, I decided to use the same liberty as the Makololo did, and gave the only English name I have affixed to any part of the country." (Livingstone, 1857)

Livingstone continued his epic journey following the Zambezi downstream to the east coast, again supported by his Makalolo porters, and completing a 3,000 mile (4,828 km) trek from the west to east coasts of the continent in the process. Returning to England Livingstone's accounts of his African travels caught the imagination of Victorian Britain. His first book, 'Missionary Travels and Researches in South Africa' was published in 1857 and became an instant best-seller. Livingstone envisioned the Zambezi River as the transport route by which the central regions of Africa would be opened up to Christian values and trade, describing the Zambezi as 'God's Highway.' But his dreams of 'Christianity, Commerce and Civilisation' - his personal motto - were dashed by the impassable gorges and rapids of the Middle Zambezi sections below the Victoria Falls.

Many followed in Livingstone's footsteps to the Falls. Yet few predicted that within fifty years of Livingstone first setting sight on the great waterfall that they would be connected to the Cape by rail and the gorges below traversed by the highest railway bridge in the world.

Legends of the Leya

The wider regions of the Upper Zambezi floodplains are inhabited by the Barotse (now more commonly known as Lozi, after their language, SiLozi), the 'people of the plains,' their kingdom known as Barotseland and controlled under the Paramount Chieftainship of their king, or *Litunga* - the 'Lord of the Land.' At the time of Livingstone's visits, however, the region had fallen under the control of the Makalolo, led by Chief Sebetwane, who had invaded from the south in the mid-1830s. Makalolo dominion was eventually crushed by the Barotse uprising of 1864 (Mubitana, 1990).

The local Toka and Leya people have inhabited the region of the Falls and river upstream for several centuries or longer, their closely related language and traditions collectively known as the Toka-Leya. The Toka are one of the largest cultural groups inhabiting the wider districts on north bank of the Zambezi in the region of the Falls, under the hereditary title of Chief Musokotwane.

The immediate vicinity of the Falls is home to the Leya under the leadership of Chief Mukuni, whose village is still located close to the Falls on the north bank. Upstream of the Falls are the Leya of Chief Sekuti, whose people traditionally lived on the islands and northern bank.

Skilled boatmen, fishermen and hippopotamus hunters the Leya have rich cultural traditions linked to the Falls which they call *Syungu Namutitima,* 'the Mist that Thunders,' (Hang'ombe *et al*, 2019) translated by Livingstone on his later visit as 'the Place of the Rainbow' (Livingstone and Livingstone, 1865).

"The Leya name for the waterfall was 'Syuungwe na mutitima,' which can be translated as 'the heavy mist that resounds,' although the term 'Syuungwe' itself also implies rainbow, or the place of rainbows." (McGregor, 2003)

On his way downstream to the Falls Livingstone was told of local belief in a powerful mythical river 'spirit-serpent:'

"The Barotse believe that at certain parts of the river a tremendous monster lies hid, and that it will catch a canoe, and hold it fast and motionless, in spite of the utmost exertions of the paddlers." (Livingstone, 1857)

Livingstone recorded that the islands on the edge of the Falls were used by local chiefs for traditional ceremonies and as places of worship to the ancestors. The French Christian missionary François Coillard, who visited Barotseland some thirty

A etching by Thomas Baines (1862) showing the view of the Falls from where the Bridge would subsequently be built

years after Livingstone, similarly noted:

"[Local inhabitants] believe it is haunted by a malevolent and cruel divinity, and they make it offerings to conciliate its favour, a bead necklace, a bracelet, or some other object, which they fling into the abyss, bursting into lugubrious incantations, quite in harmony with their dread and horror." (Coillard, 1897)

Royal Dynasty

Mukuni N'gombe, the first Mukuni chief, is said to have originated from the region of the present day Democratic Republic of Congo. Believed to be the son of one of the Mulopwe kings of the Lunda-Luba Empire, he migrated south with his followers during a period of instability and turbulence that engulfed the region during the 17th century. N'gombe eventually settled at Gundu on the north bank of the Zambezi close to the Victoria Falls, marrying the residing female ruler, the Bedyango, and establishing a dual monarchy with separated powers of responsibility and independent lines of succession. The Bedyango bestowed upon Mukuni the title of Munokalya Muchelwa, the 'Lion King,' with Gundu becoming known as Mukuni village after its new chief (Munokalya, 2013).

Chief Sianyemba Mukuni, the 15th Munokalya Mupotola, oversaw what must have been a period of great change for his people, ruling from 1900 until 1918, witnessing the arrival of the railway and construction of the Bridge. The current incumbent, Chief Munokalya Mupotola Siloka Mukuni, was enthroned in 1986 and is the 19th successive holder of the male title, and the Bedyango Ann Siloka the 18th in the female line.

Rhodes and Rail

Cecil John Rhodes (1853-1902) arrived at the Cape Colony in September 1870 at the age of 17. After a short unsuccessful stint cotton farming, he followed his older brother Herbert to the newly discovered diamond fields in Kimberley, where he was to have slightly better luck. Rhodes made his fortune at Kimberley, founding the De Beers Consolidated Mining Company in 1888.

Rhodes was an ardent believer in British colonial imperialism, and as the vehicle for his ambitions he formed the British South Africa Company (B.S.A.C.), seeking British Royal approval for its activities in southern Africa. The Royal Charter, granted by Queen Victoria in 1889, gave the Company authority to administer an unspecified area of southern Africa on behalf of the British government.

The Charter bestowed wide-ranging powers to the Company, including:

"The right to make and maintain roads, railways, telegraphs, harbours; to carry on mining or other industries; to carry on lawful commerce; to settle territories and promote immigration; to establish or authorize banking companies; to develop, improve, clear, plant and irrigate land; to establish and maintain agencies in Our Colonies and Possessions, and elsewhere; to grant lands in terms of years or in perpetuity." (Strage, 1974)

These powers, however, were conditional on the agreement of appropriate, and legitimate, treaties with local rulers - but merely a paperwork exercise for a man of Rhodes' means and methods.

Rhodes became Prime Minister of the British Cape Colony in 1890 and championed the railway as the essential means by which to achieve his political and business

Cecil John Rhodes (1853-1902)

ambitions. He is recorded as saying: *"Pure philanthropy is all very well in its way, but philanthropy plus five per cent is a good deal better"* (Hensman, 1901).

Rhodesia was officially named after him in May 1895, a reflection of his popularity as the territory had already become widely known as 'Zambesia.' The less appealing 'Charterland' had also been in widely used. Rhodes is quoted to have said to a close friend: *"To have a bit of country named after one is one of the things a man might be proud of"* (Rotberg, 1990).

The name of Southern Rhodesia (known as Zimbabwe since independence in 1980) was officially adopted in October 1898 for the territory south of the river. The territory north of the Zambezi was originally divided into North-Western (adopted 1899) and North-Eastern Rhodesia (1900), before being amalgamated to form Northern Rhodesia in 1911 (and known as Zambia since independence in 1964).

Cape to Cairo

After initial successes at Kimberley, Rhodes briefly returned to Oxford to complete his studies, becoming friends with Sir Charles Metcalfe (1853-1928). In 1878 Sir Charles joined the firm of Sir Douglas Fox and Partners and later travelled to South Africa as their consulting engineer for the developing Cape railway system, where he renewed his friendship with Rhodes. Sir Charles would spend three decades as the company's chief representative in southern Africa and be the leading figure in the development of the railway into the interior.

As early as 1888 Sir Charles had envisaged an 'African Trunk Line' - a rail and communications route traversing the length of the continent. The grand concept soon became popularly known as the 'Cape to Cairo' railway, the 'iron spine and ribs of Africa.' At the time several European powers were competing in their rush to claim African territories, and the Portuguese and German powers in particular looked towards the regions of the Upper Zambezi in order to connect territories on the east and west coasts. Sir Charles advised in an article he co-authored and published in London *"there is positively a race for the interior, and that nothing but a firm policy will maintain British interests and keep open the way for the development of British trade in Africa"* (Metcalfe and Richarde-Seaver, 1889).

Rhodes quickly became convinced of the importance of the railway in developing the 'British sphere of influence' in southern Africa. Although the Cape to Cairo scheme never materialised in its entirety, this period saw the rapid spread of a interconnected web of 'pioneer railways,' penetrating the subcontinent from the south and east coasts and opening up the interior to development.

Pauling and Company

George Craig Sanders Pauling (1854-1919) was the man Rhodes entrusted to build his railway. Born in England, George Pauling followed his father to the Cape in November 1875, aged 20, quickly establishing himself as an able worker and skilled engineer.

A giant in stature and personality, he was a forceful and colourful character, noted for his drive, capacity for hard work and physical strength. His favourite show-piece was to lift his Basuto pony on his shoulders and carry it around - until one night he tried to climb some stairs and man and beast came down in a heap, after which the animal apparently would no longer co-operate in the trick.

George Pauling (centre), with Harold (right), and Mr A L Lawley (left)

In 1891 Rhodes invited George Pauling to Cape Town to discuss plans to extend the railway from Vryburg to Mafeking (now Mahikeng). The Bechuanaland Railway Company was formed in May in 1893 with the backing of the Chartered Company, and with Cecil Rhodes as chairman Pauling was invited to bid for the contract. Costs were eventually agreed and the contract signed, with Pauling's cousin, Harold, as chief construction engineer, a role he would assume all the way to the Victoria Falls.

The contracting firm of Pauling and Company Ltd. was formed in 1894, consisting of brothers George and Henry, and cousins Harold, Willy and Percy. Prior to this Pauling had operated under various company names, earning a solid reputation constructing several branch lines, and the Company can trace its origins to 1877.

Successive contracts followed for the extension of the line to Bulawayo, and eventually the Victoria Falls, and over a period of 18 years Pauling and his men constructed over 6,000 kilometres of line in southern Africa.

Bulawayo and Beyond

The arrival of the railway line at Bulawayo in 1897 was a landmark event in the colonial development of southern Africa. The railway established a vital communication and transport route and promised to bring an end to the pioneer town's isolation. The first construction train, the same engine that had been used for the plate-laying of the line from Vryburg, arrived at Bulawayo on 19th October 1897. Decorated with flags it carried the banner 'Advance Rhodesia' on the front, surmounted by the arms of the Chartered Company.

The official opening was an event to be celebrated. The day was declared a public holiday and for the following week of celebrations businesses closed each afternoon to enable the townsfolk to attend the many functions, dinners and parties. Hundreds of guests were invited and a special medallion struck to commemorate the event.

> *"For the opening ceremony on the 4th November 1897 the temporary railway station was decorated with flags, bunting, greenery and a variety of slogans considered suitable for the occasion. These included 'Our Two Roads to Progress, Railroads and Cecil Rhodes' and 'Change here for Zambesi.'"*
> (Croxton, 1982)

Four special trains run by the Cape Government Railway arrived carrying guests from all parts of the British Empire. The first train, with passengers travelling from the Transvaal, Orange Free State, Port Elizabeth and East London, arrived at seven in the morning. The second, with passengers from Kimberley, and including

The first construction train arrives at Bulawayo

the De Beers director's coach, arrived half an hour later. Unfortunately the third train, with passengers from the Cape, derailed on route. No-one was injured, but it did block the line for some time and delayed the forth train, carrying many distinguished visitors from England. The four hour delay, after the five day and 1,360 mile (2,176 km) journey from Cape Town, was a major disappointment for the guests, who missed the opening ceremony and lunch, but arrived in time for the speeches. Luckily the new High Commissioner of the Cape, Sir Alfred Milner, who performed the opening ceremony, had arrived two days previously - although his train had also been delayed, ensuring a long wait for the welcoming committee.

Mr (later Sir) Henry Morton Stanley, on his last visit to Africa and having arrived late on the delayed fourth train, commented:

> *"In any other continent the opening of five hundred miles of new railway would be fittingly celebrated by the usual banquet and after dinner felicitations of those directly concerned with it; but in this instance there are six Members of the Imperial Parliament, the High Commissioner of the Cape, the Governor of Natal, scores of Members of the Colonial Legislatures and scores of notabilities, leaders of thought and action, bankers, merchants, and clergy from every Colony and State in the southern part of this continent."* (Stanley, 1898)

But one man was noticeable by his absence - Rhodes had not travelled due to ill health, although some claimed he was sulking after political setbacks in the Cape. He sent a telegram to the opening ceremony announcing:

"We are bound, and I have made up my mind, to go on to the Zambesi without delay. We have magnificent coalfields lying between here and there, which means a great deal to us engaged in the practical workings of railways. Let us see it on the Zambesi during our lifetime. It will be small consolation to me and to you to know it will be there when we are dead and gone." (White, 1973)

The official opening of the line to Bulawayo

To the Banks of the Zambezi

Rhodes promoted details of his grand scheme to extend the railway to the Zambezi and beyond at a meeting of the Chartered Company's shareholders in London on 21st April 1898, selling his dream of a railway connecting the length of the continent:

> *"I want two million pounds to extend the railway to Lake Tanganyika - about 800 miles... Look at the matter. You get the railway to Tanganyika; you have Her Majesty's Government's sanction for a railway to Uganda, and then you have Kitchener* [and his railway] *coming down from Khartoum* [in the Sudan]. *This is not imaginative: it is practical. It gives you Africa... the whole of it!"* (Strage, 1974)

Many in London were shocked by his ambitious plans and the Government did not respond positively, possibly because more than half of Africa was already under the control of rival European nations across whose territory it would have to travel. City investors however were more interested, although Rhodes would have be a major investor in his own railway schemes. Not everyone shared Rhodes' enthusiasm for the project.

> *"Sir William Harcourt, who thoroughly detested Rhodes, thought the scheme hair-brained, and never hesitated to say so. He was staggered, therefore, to find a Welsh steel mill hard at work manufacturing rails for the Cape to Cairo railway."* (Rhodesia Railways Magazine, November 1957)

With the extension of the railway to Bulawayo the board of the Bechuanaland Railway Company, under the chairmanship of Cecil Rhodes decided to rename the construction company the Rhodesia Railways Ltd, and on 1st June 1899 the 'Rhodesia Railways' were born (Croxton, 1973).

The consultant railway engineers Sir Douglas Fox and Partners had originally envisaged the route north would cross the Zambezi River over the Kariba Gorge, some 350 kilometres downstream of the Victoria Falls, before continuing north to the east of Lake Tanganyika. Sir Charles Metcalfe surveyed a possible route to the river in 1898. However the country between Kariba and Lake Tanganyika was found to be unfavourable for the railway, and an alternative, less challenging and less expensive route was needed.

Large coal deposits had been identified in the Wankie region (now known as Hwange) in 1893 by a German prospector, Albert Giese, who had heard reports from Africans of 'black stones that burn.' At the time coal was essential to the development of the railway, which had until then survived on imported coal from the south, and cutting of timber from forest reserves along the route of the line, to feed the engine furnaces. Located only 200 miles (320 km) north-west of Bulawayo, it was claimed that the coalfield held sufficient high quality coal to last hundreds of years. A sample consignment was tested by a locomotive on the line to Bulawayo and declared to be 'equal to the best Welsh coal' (Rhodesia Railways Magazine, July 1955).

An extension of the line from Bulawayo, via the coalfields, and terminating at the Victoria Falls was planned and surveyed from 1899 to 1900, and Sir Charles Metcalfe soon looked to the possibility of the continuation of the line to the north.

The Old Drift

Prior to the building of the Victoria Falls Bridge, the Zambezi River was crossed above the Victoria Falls at several established ferry points.

Giese's Ferry was the closest to the Falls of the three main ferry points, but suitable only for small craft. After selling his stake in the Hwange coalfields, Giese had established a series of trading stores between Hwange and Victoria Falls. Further upstream where the river bends significantly was the Palm Tree Ferry, which portered travellers across the river to two points on the north bank.

The most important crossing was nine kilometres upstream of the Falls, where the river was at its narrowest, about a kilometre in width, but also at its deepest.

The Old Drift crossing

Known as the Old Drift, a small European settlement of the same name slowly established itself on the north bank to await the arrival of the railway.

Mr Frederick J 'Mopane' Clarke arrived at the banks of the Zambezi in late 1898, charged with operating the crossing and associated forwarding services on behalf of the Chartered Company. A skilled carpenter, 'Mopane' Clarke established what would become the core of the new settlement, a small 'hotel' built of wood and mud, and adjacent bar. Within a couple of years several trading stores and bars had sprung up, including a Mission Station founded by an Italian, Giovanni Daniele Augusto Coisson (under the auspices of the Paris Missionary Society) and associated school. Clarke operated the crossing using an iron barge transported in sections to the Zambezi in mid-1898, and later also a steam launch. Passengers were taken in the barge, paddled by eight Barotse men, whilst wagons and goods were towed by the launch.

> *"Life in this predominantly male settlement centred on the bars. On any given evening it often happened that virtually the whole population congregated in one bar, so the others closed. Gambling was the central attraction at Clarke's bar, notably a roulette wheel with two zeros run by a loud-voiced American. The bar-owners had their staff sieve the sandy floors each morning for coins dropped by the previous night's revellers."* (Phillipson, 1990)

However, his choice of site was not ideal - close to the high water level, it became

The Old Drift Mission Station

a flooded marshy quagmire in the wet season and proved extremely unhealthy. The death rate among the early pioneers of the small settlement was extremely high. If they did not die from malaria they succumbed to blackwater fever (a malaria complication). Many of the early settlers were interred in a small cemetery close to the Old Drift - the cemetery is now all that remains of the settlement.

On the Wagon Trail

From 1898 successive wagon roads were opened north to the Zambezi, eventually bypassing Kazungula, the main crossing point 75 kilometres upstream of the Falls, and following progressively more direct routes to the Falls. Trade wagons, carrying between three and four tons of goods, and often pulled by sixteen to eighteen oxen (or sometimes mules), ferried supplies north to the Zambezi. The Old Hunter's Road to the north, forming the modern day border with Botswana and Zimbabwe, fell into disuse during this time.

"Most people travelled at night to spare their oxen and themselves the pain of moving in the heat of the heat of the day. Nocturnal journeys also reduced the risk of cattle being bitten by tsetse flies and infected with trypanosomiasis - sleeping sickness. The Old Hunters' Road was supposed to be free of fly at least as far as Pandamatenga. Oxen were temperamental creatures, with their own names and characters - lazy or hardworking, good-natured or bad-tempered. A good transport rider knew how to train them, match them in pairs and encourage them to work without undue coercion. Even so, individual oxen sometimes went on strike, sat down and refused to move. Stories were told of wagon 'boys' resorting to a variety of strategies to make then get up - from biting their tails to lighting fires under them. Not all travellers used oxen and wagons. Some people used carts drawn by donkeys, which were unaffected by tsetse flies, but unable to draw such heavy loads." (Macmillan, 2005)

Mr Stanley Portal Hyatt, a 'transport rider' based in Bulawayo during the days of the wagon roads, recorded the difficulties of transporting loads on the rough roads:

"Our greatest terrors on the mud flats were what we used to call 'graves' the pits formed by the digging out of other wagons. Sometimes, these were of huge size, quite sufficient to contain the whole fore-carriage. The men who had dug them had left them open - it was worse than useless to try and fill them in again with soft mud - but the recent rain had filled them, and there was nothing to warn you. Even if your cattle managed to avoid them, one of your wheels might plunge in, perhaps resulting in the capsize of the whole wagon. Even when I had plenty of cattle available, I have spent two days getting one wagon out of

Travelling on the wagon road

a 'grave.' Now and then, you came across 'graves' which were, literally, large enough to contain a wagon, huge pits dug with infinite labour, and having a gradual 'pullout.' You know, at once, what these mean - someone with a load all in one piece, a boiler, a mortar-box, an engine casting, has had a capsize, and the only method of reloading was to sink the wagon to the ground level, and roll, or lever, the load back on to it." (Hyatt, 1914)

Hyatt recalled the road north from Bulawayo to the Falls was not favoured by the transport riders, the 475 kilometre trek taking three weeks or more depending on season and conditions.

"The road which had the worst reputation in every way was that leading from Bulawayo to the Victoria Falls. In winter, it was quite impossible, owing to lack of water, neither man nor beast could get up it; whilst in summer, when the few wagons did go up, conditions were very nearly as bad. There was too much water then, wholly appalling stretches of black mud alternating with terrible stretches of rocky track; there were unlimited lions to eat your cattle, and any amount of 'poison veld' to kill those which the lions spared." (Hyatt, 1914)

Getting to the banks of the Zambezi was only part of the challenge. Mathilde Keck Goy, wife of Auguste Goy, a Paris Missionary based at Sesheke, recorded her first crossing of the Zambezi at Kazungula in 1889.

"Everything must be carried over in canoes, box after box, even to the smallest parcel. The wagon must be taken to pieces, and the parts separately ferried to the other side. It was an interesting sight to see the tent of the wagon resting on four or five canoes and the men rowing with all their might, trying to cross the river. But what terrible loss it would be if the canoe should capsize and one of the precious parts of the wagon should go to the bottom! To get the oxen across is a difficult matter. Each ox is caught by the horns with a strong 'riem' or leather thong. One man in the canoe holds it, while three of four others are rowing, and so the poor animal is dragged to the opposite bank quite exhausted. To carry a wagon and its load, together with a span of oxen... across usually takes two or three days when it is calm, but when there is wind, the work goes very slowly. It took us a whole week for all to cross, and to again put our waggon together and repack." (Goy, 1901)

The explorer Captain (later Lieutenant-Colonel) Alfred St Hill Gibbons, who travelled extensively in the region between 1895-6, recorded that trek oxen from the south were more reluctant swimmers than the local Barotse cattle.

"In such cases each ox is secured with a riem passed over the horns. A boy sitting in the centre of the canoe holds on to the other end, while the beast is driven, sometimes with much difficulty, into deep water. He is then drawn to the side of the canoe, and his head held and secured so as to render his struggles powerless to upset the unstable craft, and in this position he remains until his feet strike the shallows of the opposite bank." (Gibbons, 1898)

Zeederberg Coach Company

Christiaan Hendrik Zeederberg, or 'Doel' as he was known, together with his three brothers Dolf, Louw and Pieter as partners, established Zeederberg and Company, Coach Proprietors in 1887, later popularly known as the Zeederberg Coach Company. Their first mail-coach route, between Johannesburg and Kimberley, began operating in the same year. In 1890 Cecil Rhodes commissioned Doel to survey the new Rhodesia territory and suggest likely transport routes, and their first regular service was opened the same year. Doel was a shrewd businessman and superb horseman, surveying most of the routes himself over the next three years, and would become known as the 'coaching king' of southern Africa.

The coaches were of American manufacture, lightly built and wheeled but remarkably robust. They carried up to twelve passengers with room on top for mail and baggage and were usually drawn by ten mules, which were changed at regular coaching stations at 10 to 15 mile (16-24 km) intervals, allowing the coaches to

Zeederberg Mail Coach

travel continuously without delays. The transport road from Bulawayo to the Victoria Falls was completed in 1898 under the direction of Captain (later Major) Jesser Coope. Trade wagons pulled by upwards to twenty oxen ferried supplies from Bulawayo north to the Zambezi. This 475 kilometre trek often took up to a month or more depending on season. The old hunter's road, forming the modern day border with Botswana and Zimbabwe, fell into disuse during this time.

In 1901 Zeederberg introduced a regular mail coach service from Bulawayo to the Victoria Falls, with journeys taking 10 to 12 days.

"About 1901 the first rough survey of a coach route from Bulawayo to the Victoria Falls was undertaken jointly by Sir Charles Metcalfe and [Doel Zeederberg]. A weekly service was opened to the Wankie coal fields and the Falls, chiefly for facilitating the exploration of the mineral and other resources of the country. This... was eventually extended to Broken Hill, and later was replaced by the advancing Cape to Cairo railway." (Beet, 1923)

The Zeederberg coaches ran for a number of years across the Rhodesias, opening new routes and hailing the coming of the railway, before the advancing rails made their services redundant. Rhodes himself said that no other individual had done more to open up Rhodesia.

"In his own sphere of activity Doel may be said to have been among the few who played a leading part in the development of Central South African resources. In conjunction with Cecil Rhodes, this sturdiest of pioneers recognized the potentialities of the great North Land." (Beet, 1923)

Legacy in Steel

Cecil Rhodes died in April 1902, aged 49, from the heart-related illness which had limited much of his latter years. He is buried in the Matopas Hills at a place he named 'World's View,' his estate bequeathed to the nation and now the heart of the Matobo National Park.

At the time of Rhodes' death, the line from the southern Cape to Bulawayo had been operating for several years and Bulawayo itself had grown to become a significant town, with a population of six thousand. The line from the east coast port at Beira (in Mozambique) to the capital Salisbury (now renamed Harare) was also open, and the extension from Salisbury progressing towards Bulawayo - with the connection of lines into the interior only a matter of months away. Plans for the northern extension to the Victoria Falls were well advanced, with the first contracts for the line from Bulawayo finalised in mid-1901 and work having started in October 1901. In the same year Rhodes had also approved the preliminary design and location of the railway crossing over the Zambezi. Sir Charles Metcalfe later commented that Rhodes had also planned to build a house nearby (Muskett, 1957).

A few years later, whilst the Victoria Falls Bridge was being built, Sir Gilbert Parker wrote in the Daily Mail (March 1905):

> *"It was this gift of imagination which made Cecil Rhodes say, 'Build a bridge... where the trains, as they pass will catch the spray from the falling Zambezi.'"*

Colonel Frank William Rhodes, Cecil's own brother, expressed doubt that he had ever stated this desire, deploring its location and accreditation to his brother, writing in the same month of 1905:

> *"I have always taken the deepest interest in everything connected with the Victoria Falls, and much regret that the present site should have been chosen for the railway bridge. It cannot be denied that the step was taken in a hurry, and without that careful consideration which should be given when dealing with one of the grandest things in the world. In any case I must protest most strongly against the selection of the site for the Zambesi bridge bring attributed to my brother Cecil. It is true that he once said that the railway would pass close to the Falls, but he himself never saw them; had he done so everyone who knew him will admit that the bridge would not be where it now is."* (Hutchinson, 1905)

George Hobson, engineer and designer of the Bridge expands:

"That he ever gave this direction has been doubted, and even denied by some people, including one, at least, of his own relatives; but I have it on the authority of one who, better than any other man living or dead should know the facts of the case, that the record is true." (Hobson, 1923)

Indeed Cecil Rhodes had committed pen to paper in September 1900, when asked to write a forward for the book 'From Cape to Cairo; the first traverse of Africa from south to north' by Ewart S Grogan and Arthur H Sharp:

"We propose now to go on and cross the Zambesi just below the Victoria Falls. I should like to have the spray of the water over the carriages." (Grogan and Sharp, 1900)

The crossing of the Zambezi, immediately downstream of the natural wonder of the Victoria Falls, where the river is trapped within the narrow zig-zagging Batoka Gorge, required a bridge that would push engineering and construction knowledge of the time to its limits. Rhodes' plan was ambitious, as the writer Strage describes:

"It was the concept that was bold, to the point of arrogance: to build a modern steel bridge supported by a single slender span here, in the middle of deserted jungle... Only fifty years earlier, David Livingstone had been the first European to describe them... and even now a simple visit to behold their grandeur required a carefully planned expedition. Even counting missionaries and curious officials, it is doubtful that more than a hundred or so white men had ever seen them. And this was not just a bridge, but the highest bridge in the world." (Strage, 1973)

Rhodes has always been a polarizing figure, dividing opinion in his day, and even more so when judged by modern standards and perspectives. The railway into the interior and the Bridge over the Zambezi are, however, his lasting legacy to the industrial and economic development of southern Africa. Construction of the Bridge would begin in 1904, two years after Rhodes himself had passed away, and it was left to Sir Charles Metcalfe to realise his dream of a rail crossing over the Zambezi within sight and sound of the Falls.

Through the Wilds to Hwange

In mid-1901 the route of the railway extension covering 280 miles (450 km) to the Zambezi was agreed, the line travelling from Bulawayo to Wankie (now Hwange) and then on to the Victoria Falls, which it was hoped would be reached by the end of 1903. The surveys for the line were undertaken in late 1899 into 1900 and the work was contracted in three successive sections, each awarded to Pauling and Company, with Harold Pauling again overseeing the work and Mr Stephen F Townsend as Chief Resident Engineer for the Railway Company. Mr Townsend had been appointed personally by Rhodes on the early sections of the line north and would work on the construction to the Zambezi and beyond.

The first part of the route, the 161 mile (259 km) of line from Bulawayo north to Mambanje, was agreed in July 1901 and work commenced in October. Construction progressed at a comparatively relaxed rate, opening to traffic in March 1903. The railway ran through sand veld, well wooded with mopane (*Colophospermum mopane*) and teak (*Baikiaea plurijuga*) trees, and with the exception of two river crossings was fairly easy going for Pauling and his men. The country, however, would steadily become tougher for the construction gangs.

In April 1903 the second contract was agreed for the construction of a further 46 miles (74 km) of railway terminating at the Hwange coal mine. Reporting on progress of the line was Mr Charles Beresford-Fox, Assistant Resident Engineer for the Railway Company (and nephew of Sir Douglas Fox). Mr Beresford-Fox would be involved with the development of the line to the Falls and preparations for the Bridge.

Mr Edward Rosher, surveying engineer for the line, recalled that the section from

Railway construction gangs at work

Dete to Hwange travelled through some of the toughest country he had ever encountered - believed to be Livingstone's infamous 'Valley of Death.' The country also teamed with wildlife, from small antelope to giraffe and elephant, with lion causing much anxiety amongst the railway labourers.

"It was often a case of crawling on hands and knees along game trails to get through the bush and forest to reach a suitable spot where the bush could be cut back enough to allow instrument work to be done for the next traverse. No easy job in a country abounding with lion, elephant and other game... all of which made camp life far from enjoyable." (Croxton, 1982)

The advancing rails reached Hwange, 212 miles (341 km) from Bulawayo and 2,448 ft. (746 m) above sea level, in early October 1903. Such was the demand for coal that the first train loads were dispatched south later the same month, with the line still under construction conditions. The line was officially opened for traffic on 1st December with onward passengers and mail transferred to the Zeederberg coach service for the remaining 68 miles (109.5 km) to the Victoria Falls. Construction on the third and final section of line to the Falls started in late 1903, with a bonus for Pauling and his men in the event of the rails being suitable for the passage of trains by 1st April 1904.

Mr Clark Stakes His Claim

In 1903 Percy Missen Clark arrived at the Victoria Falls from Bulawayo with the intention of starting a photography business. Clark records that he reached the Falls in May 1903, before crossing the river at the Old Drift:

"I made my headquarters at the Old Drift for the time being, but my intention was to settle at Victoria Falls as soon as the railway was completed, for I believed that there would be great opportunities for those who got in early at the railhead. At the end of the year I engaged a man to build a hut for me near the spot where the railway station would be pitched, and where the hotel would be built, but I had no mind to cross the river until the railway did come up.

"While I lived at the Old Drift I spent a lot of my time at the Victoria Falls taking photographs, and I got together quite a good collection. I would camp out for a couple of days at a time in the hut... When that was completed I lived in it, but for most of the time I was over on the other side at the Old Drift. I liked the older haunts, and the old crowd." (Clark, 1936)

Despite claiming to be the first resident of what would become Victoria Falls town, Clark kept one foot on the north bank and still thought of himself as 'Old Drifter.'

He lived in the Falls area until his death in 1937 - but was buried, however, in Livingstone Cemetery.

Clark's primary trade was photography, and he sold many postcards and a popular portfolio of photographs of the Falls. He also published his own guide book to the Falls and traded in African curios and souvenirs.

Towards the end of 1904 Sir Charles approached Clark with a contract to photograph the building of the Bridge during its various stages of construction, thus leaving us with a valuable pictorial record.

"During the building of the bridge Sir Charles Metcalfe stayed at the Falls hotel and he commissioned me to photograph the structure at varying stages of its erection. He often came to my place, and if there were any visitors he was sure to bring them over. He rolled up one day with two of the Coats brothers, the cotton-spinning millionaires, and introduced them with: 'Here you are, Clark - two gentlemen with plenty of money. See what you can get out of them.' He then went off laughing. Sir Charles was very popular with the men, who called him 'Uncle Charlie,' and he was a very good friend to me." (Clark, 1936)

Percy Clark was made Fellow of the Royal Geological Society for helping Henry Balfour, on the visit of the British Association, find stone-age axe heads close to the Victoria Falls. He exhibited his photographs of the Falls at the Royal Geographical Society and was elected Associate of the Royal Photographic Society in 1925.

Percy Clark outside his photography hut

Crossing the Zambezi

The original examination and selection of the bridge site below the Falls was carried out by Sir Charles Metcalfe in June 1901, who reported that it would not present any insuperable engineering problems (Rhodesia Railways Magazine, November 1965). Sir Charles later recorded *"on my first visit... I decided that an arch bridge was right both from the engineering and the artistic point of view"* (Metcalfe, 1923).

Rhodes, despite never visiting the Falls, had been clear where the Bridge was to be built. Mr G A Hobson, the man who designed the Bridge, recorded in his final report on the construction of the Bridge to the Institute of Civil Engineers in 1907:

> *"In 1901... he was shown at his office in London a sketch of the bridge it was then proposed to build. Although he had never visited the locality, he was sufficiently familiar with it from travellers' descriptions and engineers' surveys to indicate in a general way the point of crossing. He determined that passengers in the trains going over the bridge should have a view of the Falls; and as the site on which the bridge now stands is practically the only one which could fulfil this purpose, it may be said to have been chosen by him. The preliminary design of the bridge above referred to was prepared to meet Mr Rhodes's views, and it received his approval."* (Hobson, 1907)

The final choice of site was governed by the natural formation of the rock walls of the Batoka Gorge, advantage being taken of the minimum distance to be spanned, combined with the soundest foundations obtainable. Sir Charles returned to England to raise funds for the project, but as news of the site selected for the Bridge reached London there were strong voices of opposition.

> *"The site chosen had given rise to much adverse criticism both in England and in Africa, the critics saying that such a natural wonder as the Falls should not be allowed to be desecrated by any of man's handiwork - that the bridge ought not to be within sight of the cataract."* (Prince, 1906)

The Bulawayo Chronicle Christmas Annual of 1901 contained an artist's impression of the Bridge, in full colour and with the caption 'a glimpse into the near future,' which provoked much local disbelief, partially due to the artistic licence taken with the subject matter (Rhodesia Railways Magazine, July 1955).

> *"There were not wanting people who suggested that to bridge the gorge at all would be an act of vandalism, and Sir Charles Metcalfe and his assistants,*

when this scheme was elaborated and presented to the authorities, came in for a great deal of unpleasant criticism. Quite a commotion was raised by the fact that a correspondent writing in the columns of The Times expressed the belief that the bridge, when completed, would be found to greatly distract from the magnificence of the scenery in the midst of which it was to be placed: and he strongly urged upon the Company that they should reconsider the exact site with special reference to the generally picturesque character of the locality, and to the regret which would be universally felt if the most stupendous Falls in the world were deprived, by obtrusive structures of stone and iron, of any of the magnificence which Nature had lavished upon them." (South Africa Magazine, April 1905)

Sir Charles would later write *"no part of the railway was made for sentimental reasons,"* but the Victoria Falls Bridge is the one exception to his statement. As Frank Varian, an engineer who joined the team building the Bridge and who would work with Pauling extending the railway line north later observed:

"The choice of its site was more for sentiment than for practical reasons... A simpler crossing could have been achieved six miles [9.5 km] further up, [near Kandahar Island] where the longest span need only have been 150 feet [45.72 m]." (Varian, 1953)

Hobson maintained that the site chosen was the best possible for the Bridge.

"I am of the opinion that it is the best possible position for a bridge near to the Falls. The very beauty of the spot has, however, created objections to its selection. The situation is briefly this: The scene is laid within the tropical zone. At a place where the river is

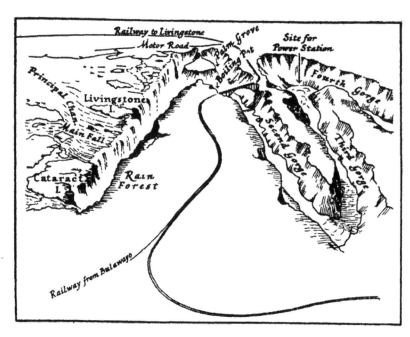

Sketch of the Victoria Falls showing position of the Bridge (From 'Some African Milestones', Varian 1953)

a mile in width, the bright and lovely Zambezi, whose gentle rippling waters flow sparkling in the sun, is precipitated suddenly into a dark chasm which lies square across its path, and through only one constricted outlet down below the whole body of water forces its agitated way into a narrow deep and sinuous gorge beyond. The bridge crosses this gorge." (Hobson, 1923)

Perhaps perversely his main argument against the alternative site, at the Old Drift crossing point, was that it would mar the beauty of the river upstream of the Falls:

"It has been contended that there is another and a better site some few miles above the Falls, near Livingstone drift; there is, it is true, an alternative site which I have examined. For the most part the piers of a bridge, if built there, would stand upon a rocky shelf in shallow water, and there would be only two deep and broad channels to cross. It would be a long straggling structure of no great beauty, and it would mar, to a large extent, the attractions of the broad, shining Zambezi, which presents at this spot a river scene of unparalleled beauty, scarcely inferior in its own way to that of the Falls. If we can descend to sordid considerations, the cost of its construction, which I have taken the trouble to count, would be three or four times that expended on the present bridge, and it would entail, in addition, the making of about eight extra miles [nearly 13 km] of railway. I may, therefore, venture to say that if there are a sufficient number of persons who hold the pure aesthetic view, and are willing to subscribe towards its fulfilment the necessary capital, without expectation of any return, no one will object, and there is a firm of engineers able and willing to give them satisfaction." (Hobson, 1923)

An early artists impression of the Bridge, with the Main Falls in the background

Designing the Bridge

The credit for designing the Victoria Falls Bridge goes to Mr George Andrew Hobson (1854-1917), a partner in the London based engineering consultants Sir Douglas Fox and Partners. In 1907 he was awarded the George Stephenson Gold Medal by the British Institute of Civil Engineers for his account of the design and construction of the Bridge.

In designing the Falls Bridge Hobson was assisted by Mr (later Sir) Ralph Freeman, the engineer who went on to design the famous Sydney Harbour Bridge, opened in 1932. At the time of the designing of the Victoria Falls Bridge Freeman was still only a junior assistant in the firm (having joined in 1901), although he was employed in calculating the stresses within the steelwork design. He later recalled:

George Andrew Hobson (1854-1917)

"It is about twenty-five years since, as an assistant to the late Mr G A Hobson, I first undertook the design of an arch bridge, that crossing the Zambesi River just below the Victoria Falls. At that time we regarded this as a large bridge, though it is a very small affair compared with Sydney Harbour Bridge." (Sydney Morning Herald, March 1929)

The design of the Falls Bridge required certain special considerations, not least including an appearance that would compliment the natural beauty of the site. Then followed the more practical engineering problems of strength and rigidity (to permit railway traffic), economy in building (to keep within the financial limits of the contract) as well as finally a method of construction that dispensed altogether with scaffolding, which would have been impossible to erect.

"Several kinds [of design] *were considered, but the nature of the situation and the purpose of the work made it obvious that a two-hinged spandrel-braced arch was the only one worth considering, as it completely and satisfactorily answered all the requirements of the case... A steel arch of this character was therefore designed to spring from the rock walls of the Zambezi chasm, to be*

erected cantilever-wise simultaneously from both sides. The best, though not the earliest, example of this type is the bridge which... carries the Grand Trunk Railway over the Niagara Gorge." (Hobson, 1907)

A final consideration was the effect of the Falls themselves, specifically the spray from the waterfall on the steel structure:

"Care was exercised in designing the details to ensure simplicity in all sections, and the avoidance of enclosed parts or hidden spaces anywhere in the structure... There are no cavities for holding water, nor any surfaces where moisture can condense, the air being free to circulate everywhere. All the parts, in fact, are designed to be visible to the eye, and easily accessible to the painter's brush." (Hobson, 1923)

The final design chosen is known as a trussed arch and is comprised of three distinct sections; the main central arch, a graceful parabolic curve with a span of over 150 metres and supported by two feet at each end with foundations embedded in the steep sides of the Batoka Gorge, and two supporting side span sections braced to the walls of the gorge on either side. The horizontal upper deck, or chord, is linked by verticals to the arched lower chord and braced diagonally, creating the characteristic and appealing structural design.

"The bridge consists of three spans. The end span on the left bank of the river is 62 feet 6 inches [19.05 m], and that on the other bank 87 feet 6 inches [26.67 m]. These spans are composed of braced girders of ordinary type, 12 feet 6 inches [3.81 m] deep, with horizontal upper and lower chords, and divided into square panels. The girders are fixed 20 feet [6.1 m] apart. Connected with the end posts of the central span, they unite it with each bank of the river in a direct and simple manner. The deck is horizontal, and is laid on the top chords throughout the bridge... The cross girders, spaced 12 feet 6 inches [3.81 m] apart, rest on the top chord. The central span is 500 feet [152.4 m] from centre to centre of bearings, with a rise of 90 feet [27.43 m]. The curvature of the arched rib is parabolic. The panels, twenty in number, are 25 feet [7.62 m] in length." (Hobson, 1907)

The Bridge was designed to be constructed simultaneously as cantilevers from each side of the gorge and meeting in the middle. Hobson explained:

"The uninitiated, looking at pictures of the half-completed bridge, with its great arms projecting from the sides of the chasm, apparently supported by nothing at all, wonder how it is done. Owing to the immense depth of the chasm and

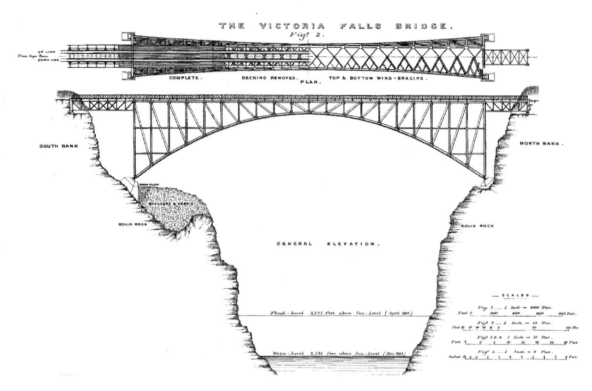

*Technical design drawing of the Victoria Falls Bridge, by George H Hobson
(From Institution of Civil Engineers Report on the Bridge, Hobson, 1907)*

*of the water below, the idea of supporting the work during erection by means
of scaffolding was not to be thought of, and happily it was not necessary.
The engineer never for a moment contemplated calling scaffolding to his aid,
for he well knew that he could do better without it. The design of the bridge
when completed is that of a pure arch, self-supporting on its abutments; but
throughout the process of its erecting, commencing from opposite sides, each
half is a cantilever, and cantilevers they remain until, their end reaching out to
each other, they join in mid-air.*

*"Now, a cantilever is simply another name for a bracket, and a bracket requires
to be well fixed to the wall, or whatever it may be that holds it. The strength of
the attachment must be equal to the weight exerted by the projecting portions of
the bracket, with a sufficient surplus for safety. In the present case the means of
attachment were provided by a series of steel wire ropes. These were secured
at the top of each cantilever, and carried to a point some distance to the rear,
where they entered holes bored in the solid rock, and their looped ends were
buried therein. It was simply a matter of calculation how many ropes were
necessary, what their united strength should be, and how much of Northern and
Southern Rhodesia respectively it was necessary to lay hold of...*

"The process of erecting the individual parts of which the bridge is composed - it may be called the subsidiary process - was performed by means of electrically driven cranes, which, securely resting on the portions of the bridge already completed, projected their long necks sufficiently far forward to place in position the members composing the next panel.

"The moment the two ends of the cantilevers met each other and were properly joined together... the function of the cantilevers ceased entirely, and the anchorage ropes were slackened and could have been removed completely. They were nothing them but contractor's plant, which had served their purpose and were no longer needed." (Hobson, 1923)

A key element of the design are the pin-bearings at the base of the main arch, with the four 'feet' of the Bridge hinged to steel bearings mounted on concrete abutments. Under the hot African sun the steelwork of the great arch is designed to expand and lift slightly, turning on these hinged bearings, but at the same time retaining its rigidity without buckling or becoming distorted.

"An essential feature of the design is the uniform distribution of the load over the various parts which compose the bearing. The load must be placed uniformly upon the length of the pin, and in like manner the pin must be supported in its bearing, so as to avoid bending. The load having thus been transmitted to the pin, it must be equally distributed through the pedestal and thence to the baseplate which rests upon the concrete, so that the load on the latter may be uniform per square foot of bearing-surface." (Hobson, 1907)

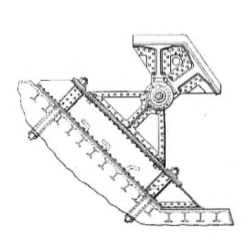 

Technical design drawings of Bridge bearing joint,
showing side elevation and perspective view, by George H Hobson
(From Institution of Civil Engineers Report on the Bridge, Hobson, 1907)

Contracting the Work

With the design finalised tenders were invited to undertake the work of manufacturing the steelwork and erecting the Bridge. Hobson recorded:

"The contract was divided into two parts, namely, first, the construction of the steelwork in the makers' yard and the delivery of it on board ship in a British port; and secondly, the erection of the steelwork on the site. Tenders were invited from British, American, and German firms - the majority of whom ventured only to quote a price for the first part of the work."

Several leading firms tendered for the manufacture of the steelwork sections but most were daunted by the scale of the task involved in erecting the Bridge. In the end only two English firms, Dorman, Long and Company and the Cleveland Bridge and Engineering Company, were in the running.

"As was to be expected from the completeness of the design and the information laid before the parties tendering, the offers received for the first part of the contract were fairly close; whilst as regards the two firms referred to there was hardly any difference between them. They, however, differed a good deal in their estimate of the cost of erection on the site, or it would be more correct to say, of their proposed plant for that purpose." (Hobson, 1907)

Hobson later described the process in an account published in 1923, several years after his death in 1917.

"To go back to the time when one's mind was almost wholly occupied in the work of design, and in the preparation of the specification and contract, there is a recollection of a haunting fear that some German or American firm would secure the contract...

"I may here observe that the fear of British firms shrinking from the task in the present case was well grounded, for one of the best known and highly reputed among them, after having expressed a desire to compete for the work, and having obtained all the needed information, turned craven at the last moment and failed to tender. This in spite of the fact that much thought had been given by the engineers to the idea of eliminating from the situation, as far as it was possible to do so, all the unknown, doubtful or incalculable factors associated with work of this nature...

"Fortunately, all our British firms were not broken reeds; but it is a fact that only

two of their number, by submitting a complete and reasonable offer, evinced any keen desire to participate in the undertaking. To the honour of the Cleveland Bridge and Engineering Company, of Darlington, personified by Mr Charles F Dixon, their managing director, who succeeded in getting the contract, and Messrs Dorman Long and Company, of Middlesbrough, who were equally bent upon it and ran their rivals fairly close, that the saving of our British reputation for enterprise was due." (Hobson, 1923)

The contract specified a construction period of fifty-five weeks (Girouard, 1906). The cost of the work was identified in the specification for thee works as (£):

Steelwork	21,000
Transport	12,700
Erection	27,000
Cableway	4,000
Spare rope, conveyor and tires	750
Excavations, exclusive of railway cutting (estimated)	6,550
Total	72,000

The railway contractors, Pauling and Company, also tendered for the contract. A handwritten note in the paperwork files of Sir Charles Metcalfe, held in the archives of the Bulawayo Railway Museum, records his enthusiasm. Undated and written on a correspondence envelope of the Mount Nelson Hotel, Cape Town (and presumably the text of a telegram) the note indicates that Sir Charles thought Pauling was at the time very keen to build the Bridge:

"George Pauling visited site of Victoria Falls Bridge with me - with view to tender for Bridge and erection. If his tender is satisfactory can depend on him carrying out work. He really wants to do it." (Metcalfe, c.1902-3)

In May 1903 the Cleveland Bridge and Engineering Company was awarded both contracts, to construct and erect the Victoria Falls Bridge, for a price of £72,000. Pauling was disappointed to loose the contract to the Cleveland Bridge Company and wrote in his autobiography 'Chronicles of a Contractor:'

"My firm had sent in a tender but it was too high; their tender, on the other hand, was too low, and I hardly think they made a profit on the work. I had had so great a connection with railway work in Rhodesia that I was sorry we had not the honour of building the bridge, but honour of that kind can be purchased at too heavy a price." (Pauling, 1926)

Steelwork Sections

To ensure accuracy in manufacture the Bridge was assembled in sections at the Cleveland Bridge Company yard in England before being disassembled and prepared for shipping. The contract specified that parts were to be accurate to within 1/32 of an inch (0.8 millimetres).

Hobson describes the process:

"In order to check the accuracy and completeness of the work done in the bridge-yard, the erection on the contractor's premises of the whole of the work in sections was determined upon, and it may be here stated that this was so effectively performed that... when the steelwork was erected at the Victoria Falls, all the members met accurately together in their respective positions."

The rolled steel used to construct the Bridge sections was manufactured by the Consett Iron Company, Durham, weighing 490 pounds (222.2 kg) to the cubic foot (30 cubic cm).

"With few exceptions the bridge is constructed of rolled steel manufactured in England by the Siemens open-hearth acid process. All the plates and the principal angles were made by the Consett Iron Company, Durham. Material and workmanship were subjected to rigid inspection and proved to be of uniformly high character. The breaking stress of the tested pieces averaged 29.6 tons per square inch, the elongation being 24-6 per cent in 8 inches [20.3 cm], and the limit of elasticity 60 per cent, all within a 2 per cent margin of variation. The exceptions referred to consisted of steel forgings. No cast iron or cast steel was

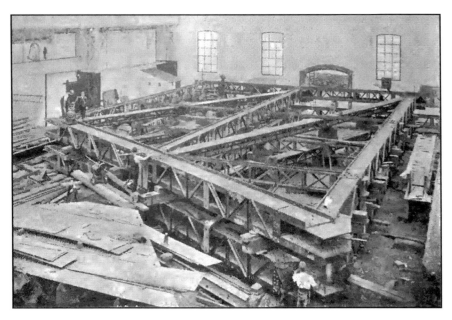

Sections of the Bridge assembled in the Cleveland foundry

Section of main arch assembled upside-down in the Cleveland yard

employed in the work." (Hobson, 1907)

Once prepared the steelwork sections were thoroughly cleaned and painted with red lead primer and a final protective linseed-oil coating, ready for transportation from industrial England to the heart of Africa.

From Middlesbrough to Mozambique

After testing and preparation in the manufacturing yard, the bulk of the steelwork was shipped from Middlesbrough to Beira (Mozambique) on the *S.S. Cromwell*, departing port on 5th March 1904. The parts were then transported on the Beira and Mashonaland Railway via Salisbury to Bulawayo, and eventually on to the Victoria Falls, a total distance of close upon 9,500 miles (over 15,000 km). With a view to hastening the arrival of the steelwork and its erection, Sir Charles Metcalfe co-ordinated the arrangements, favouring delivery to the Beira, to be then transported on their own railway system, rather than Port Elizabeth and transportation on the Cape rail system. This was despite the possibility of floods affecting the line at that time of year and Sir Charles emphasising that he 'could not afford any delays' (Metcalfe, 1903).

Delays in the construction of the line to the Falls would be the ultimate factor determining arrival of the steelwork to the site. Hobson noted:

"It was then anticipated that the construction of the railway up to the Falls would be completed by the end of that year [1903] *or the beginning of the next, but unexpected difficulties were met with on the route, which caused a delay of 4 months. The rail-head actually reached the site at the end of May, 1904. Until then the transportation of the bridge-material was impossible."* (Hobson, 1907)

Indomitable Imbault

In 1903 Mr Georges Camille Imbault (1877-1951), a gifted young French engineer was appointed by the Cleveland Bridge Company as their Chief Construction Engineer for the project. Imbault would direct the construction of many significant global engineering projects, including the Middlesbrough Transporter Bridge (England), the Blue Nile Road and Railway Bridge (Sudan) and the famous Sydney Harbour Bridge (Australia).

Georges Imbault

Colonel Frank Rhodes, Cecil's brother, expressed strong displeasure when he heard that a Frenchman was to erect the Bridge. *"Cecil would never have allowed anyone but a British engineer"* he is recorded as saying. Imbault, aged 27 at the time, had been selected because of his experience with overhead electric conveyors, an essential element in the construction of the Bridge.

Imbault excelled in his role as Chief Construction Engineer, notably designing the cranes which moved outwards with the construction of the Bridge arches and facilitated installation of the steelwork sections. He was described by one commentator as *"an explosive Frenchman, ...[who] was always at loggerheads with his men and he had many escapes from falling spanners etc. when he had occasion to go down below on inspection work"* (Bulawayo Chronicle, November 1950). Arthur Davison, one of the team of engineers sent out by the Cleveland Bridge Company to construct the Bridge, later recalled:

> *"[Imbault] was a great engineer, otherwise he would not have been there, but he was never liked as I have seen other engineers on other bridge jobs. He was respected, yes, but not loved."* (Northern Rhodesia Journal, January 1952)

In July 1903, having visited Sir Douglas Fox and Partners in London and agreed the final design for the electric cableway which would span the gorge, Imbault set sail on the Union Castle Line Royal Mail Steamer 'Saxon' for the Cape. He then caught the Train-de-Luxe to Bulawayo where he was met by Sir Charles Metcalfe who escorted him the final distance to the Falls (Sir Douglas Fox and Partners, July 1903).

Visit of Colonel Frank Rhodes and Friends

Colonel Francis ('Frank') William Rhodes (1851-1905), younger brother of Cecil, visited the Falls for the first time in mid-August 1903 in the company of friends, Sir George and Lady Farrar - who later wrote a detailed unpublished account of their journey. After travelling on the Train-de-Luxe to Bulawayo they completed the final section of their journey by horse and wagon.

"Col. Franky was in a great state of excitement, and kept riding on ahead, determined to have the first view of the Falls. We soon reached the top of a hill, and could now clearly see the vast volume of vapour over the Falls, and could distinctly hear the thunderous roar of the falling waters. It caused a feeling of the wildest exhilaration, and with one impulse we all broke into a gallop, Col. Franky as usual leading. At last we came to a rather open space, and we heard the noise of the cataract on our right front, only a few yards off. This was where we had been advised to camp."

Whilst camped at the Falls Sir Charles and Imbault arrived, having also just travelled to the Falls from the railhead at Mambanje.

"The next morning the party of Engineers came over, and we had a long talk with them... We made bold to criticise the position they had selected for their projected railway bridge, but of course their Railway Engineer, a Frenchman, who was evidently pleased at getting the bridge to construct, said it would be the highest and finest bridge in the world, so he wants to get the best position to show off its mechanical perfections.

"I could not help, however, feeling that the position selected would mar the beauty of the view, and freely expressed my opinion. In making the line, also, it will be necessary to cut down many of the beautiful trees. Col. Franky warmly supported me: however I am afraid they will have their way... [although] there are many other points in the gorges over which they could put their bridge. The Engineers, however, say it is impracticable.

"Sir Charles Metcalfe is going to build a fine large hotel here, with five hundred bedrooms, in the Egyptian style of architecture, and has great hopes of its being quite a success, and he thinks that with railway facilities the Falls will soon be quite an attraction to globe-trotters, especially Americans, who will journey up here in great doubt that we have Falls actually wider and higher than Niagara. I am only too pleased that we visited the Falls before this stream of tourists has set in, with their sandwiches and orange-peel." (Farrar, 1903)

Connecting the Gorge

On 2nd September 1903, soon after arriving at the Falls, Imbault and Sir Charles Metcalfe, together with Mr S F Townsend (Chief Resident Engineer for the Railway Company) and Mr Beresford-Fox (Assistant Resident Engineer), visited the proposed site of the Bridge to confirm the final positioning and measurements of the gorge.

Mr A Prince, Chief Engineering Assistant to Imbault, later recorded:

> "On their arrival at the Falls, Mr Imbault at once took steps to open direct communications with the opposite side of the river, for intercourse up to this time was by boat at Livingstone drift some four miles [6.4 km] up the Zambesi. The whole country round the Falls was quite undisturbed. Game abounded. Sir George Farrar, who was there at the time, shot a fine buck within a few yards of the Bridge site... My first impression was that it looked a fairly awful place to build a bridge over, though, of course, this feeling wore off after one grew used to the problem." (Prince, 1906)

In order to measure the exact width of the gorge, and at the same time establish communications with the north bank, cables needed to be installed across the chasm. Initially attempts were made to fly the line across the gap by means of a kite, but this ingenious effort was foiled by the eddies and currents of air from the Falls which tossed the kite in every direction but the right one. Undeterred a small rocket system was used to fire a line across - although this took three attempts before landing on the opposite side.

> "The method adopted by Mr Beresford Fox, the assistant engineer-in-charge, was to fire a rocket across the river at the spot selected - which is just below the 'Boiling Pot,' as the entrance to the twenty-mile canon is called - and to the rocket was attached a thin string. Next, a stouter string was sent across, and, finally, a telephone wire."

After communications with the north bank had been achieved, a specially marked line was pulled across to measure the width of the gorge.

> "Next a marked steel wire was passed across, and a strain put on it; the strain was measured by means of a spring balance in order to compute the sag of the wire." (Page, 1905)

Finally a basic winch-system was erected to transport men and materials across

Tower's Camp

the gorge, on the downstream side the Bridge site. A steel-stranded rope three-eighths of an inch (9.5 mm) in diameter was pulled across the gorge. This was passed over a 12 inch (30.5 cm) pulley firmly embedded in the rock on the north bank. The tactics were then reversed, with the free end of the pulley rope dragged back to the south bank, before it was pulled tight and taken twice round the barrel of a windlass.

A small camp of huts had been established on the south bank of the Falls, a short distance from the Bridge by Mr William Tower, Resident Engineer for the Railway Company, and known as the Bridge Engineers or Tower's Camp. Mr Tower had overseen the surveying for the line north from Vryburg and was Resident Engineer for the early part of the line to the Falls, before being transferred to work on the construction of the Bridge. As his assistants were Mr C Everard and Mr Charles Beresford-Fox, who was the son of Sir Francis Fox, one of the founding partners of the civil engineering company in London (Varian, 1953).

Missionary Memoirs

Ms Catherine Winkworth Mackintosh, niece and biographer of the distinguished French missionary, the Rev. François Coillard ('Uncle Frank'), made the first of two trips to the Zambezi in 1903, arriving at the Falls in late August 1903. Coillard was the first missionary to visit Barotseland, in 1878, and established the first mission station in 1885 at Old Sesheke (now Mwandi).

"We stopped in our walk at the site where the bridge is to be. At present it is crossed by four wires, and a copper telephone wire at a slightly different angle, glittering in the sun. I believe these wires had just that morning been laid...

"We had returned to the camp for a rest, when Uncle Frank came up with three official personages, politely craving tea. One of these was Mr Beresford-Fox... and another was the engineer himself, M. Imbault, a Frenchman, from Marseilles, in the service of the Cleveland Bridge Company of Darlington, which has the contract. You may be sure it was a very agreeable surprise to Uncle Frank to find a Frenchman charged with the task of spanning the gulf, in a material sense, which he has been trying to span morally and spiritually for so many years; and it is very nice to think that French and English are joining hands over this part of the work as well as the other. M. Imbault seems very young for such an important responsibility."

Mackintosh described the wagon journey back to the advancing railhead.

"At the outspan there is no time to cook, not even at night. We unload the cart while the 'leader' makes the fire and fetches the water. Then we make tea, coffee or soup in ten minutes, tear open a tin and divide the contents (first setting out our tablecloth on a box with plates and saucers), wash up and perform a hasty toilette. It was not nearly so hot on the return journey, a cool wind meeting us all the time; but we had so little luggage there was no ballast for the cart, and oh! how we were thrown about!

"We saw quite a different country from that coming up, as now we passed places by daylight that previously we had traversed in the dark and vice versa. When the scrub widens out, vast prairies of tall grass look like fields of red wheat against the forest background. We saw no wild creatures except locusts; the traffic on the road frightens them away. We crash over all obstacles, nobody ever takes anything out of the way; young trees, e.g, lie right across the road for the next trekkers to pick up. We met many natives either coming back from the mines or coming up in gangs to work on fresh sections of the railway. But we saw none hastening south to take the places of those returning home. The latter were mostly in very poor condition, some quite starving and emaciated, with wolfish eyes, others hardly able to walk." (Mackintosh, 1922)

Passing back through Hwange on their return journey south the party would later meet again with Mr Beresford-Fox:

"Our engineer friend, who has been out since 1898, told us that he had calculated the span for the bridge by triangulation for the Railway Co, and when M. Imbault did it for the Bridge Building Co. with a chain and rocket by actual measurement, there was only six inches difference between their estimates.

The exact distance is 580 feet [177 m]; the bridge is to be an arch with girders resting on rock buttresses which Nature has conveniently placed on either side, rising half-way up the cliff." (Mackintosh, 1922)

An Interview With Imbault

In September the Bulawayo Chronicle printed a short interview with Imbault, who was returning south after his visit to the Falls.

"The steel girder bridge which is to span the Zambesi below the Victoria Falls, is the subject of considerable interest. The following notes obtained by a representative of the Bulawayo Chronicle from Mr Georges C Imbault, of the Cleveland Bridge and Engineering Co, Darlington - the firm that has the contract - will, therefore, be worth perusal. Mr Imbault said he went up to the Falls, accompanied by Mr S F Townsend, Chief Resident Engineer of the Rhodesia Railways, and Mr Beresford Fox, for the purpose of obtaining an exact measurement of the length the bridge would require to be...

"The final length of the bridge will be 650 ft. [198 m], and this result coincides closely with the length measured two years ago. There will be three spans, two short ones of unequal length, and the big central or main span of 500 ft. [152.4 m]. The southern span will be 87½ ft. [26.6 m] and the northern one 62½ ft.[19 m]. From the two main pins of the bearings attached to the masonry foundations of the central girder to the level of the railway will be 110 ft. [33.5 m]. These pins are the points from which the booms of the central girder or arches spring...

"The width of the bridge will be 80 ft. [24.4 m], sufficient for a double line of rails. The central span will be supported by steel main posts and the big arch is to be braced throughout with steel ties. The erection of the bridge will take place simultaneously from both sides of the river, the weight being carried by steel cables until the two halves of the central span abut and are connected. A net will hang under the bridge until finished for the purpose of catching boys and tools should they unwittingly drop during construction.

"The structure, the total weight of which will be 1,600 tons of steel, is nearly finished in England now, and will be shipped about December. As soon as the rails reach the Falls construction will commence, and this is expected to be about the 1st of May next year. During its erection a cable-way will be arranged for the purpose of passing across material required for the bridge, and also for conveying railway material needed for the line north of the river. Asked if he thought the bridge would impair the appearance of the banks in any way, Mr

Imbault said he did not think so, when once it was finished and the construction works cleared away.

"Mr Imbault leaves Bulawayo on the 18th inst to consult with his firm on various details, see the bridge finished and arrange for the special machinery required in its construction." (Bulawayo Chronicle, September 1903a)

A Blot on the Landscape

Also returning to Bulawayo after visiting the Falls were Sir George Farrar and Colonel Frank Rhodes, who both felt that the railway line and Bridge would detract from the natural beauty of the surrounding landscape.

"We understand that both Sir George Farrar and Colonel Frank Rhodes consider that the proposed line of the railway is much too near the Victoria Falls, destroying, as it must do, a great deal of timber and undergrowth in close proximity to the Falls; from all we hear one of its greatest charms is its loneliness and grandeur. This will be entirely destroyed by the shriek of the railway engine."

Mr Townsend replied on behalf of the Railway Company, defending the plans.

"Re your paragraph in this morning's Chronicle headed 'The Victoria Falls' the railway will not destroy any of the timber or undergrowth of what is commonly called the 'Evergreen Forest,' but keeps outside through ordinary short scrub all the way. Visitors to, and while viewing, the Falls need not know there is a railway there at all!" (Bulawayo Chronicle, September 1903b)

A few weeks later the construction at the Falls made the national newspapers back in London, a correspondent writing in The Times newspaper in early October 1903 that the finished Bridge would be 'a blot on the unspoiled scenery' of the Falls.

"A correspondent, writing to the Times this morning says that unless something is done by the public at Home to bring pressure to bear on the Chartered Company, the rare beauty of the Victoria Falls will be seriously impaired. For no particular reason the engineers and contractors, the correspondence continues, are preparing to carry the railway across the Zambesi immediately below the Falls, and are ruthlessly cutting down the fine timber and luxurious undergrowth which adds so much to the beauty of the scene."

The Times editors also commented:

"The Times, endorsing the sentiments of its correspondent, depreciates any vandalism at the Victoria Falls. The Chartered Company - the newspaper adds - may legitimately be expected to carefully preserve one of the greatest works of nature from unnecessary disfigurement." (Bulawayo Chronicle, October 1903)

At least one reader agreed, noting in a letter to the paper: *"That man Rhodes,"* is a *"vandal"* and a *"desecrator of all that is beautiful in nature"* (Rhodesia Railways Magazine, August 1955). Sir Charles later recorded:

"We read, therefore, with some amazement, before the bridge was commenced, an onslaught in the Times on the engineers and contractors who were going to ruin the scenic glory of the spot. It is only fair to state that, after the competition of the bridge, the Times, of its own accord, handsomely apologised for its attack." (Metcalfe, 1923)

The criticisms of the planned developments at the Falls, although too late to impact on the planned line of the railway and location of the Bridge, perhaps had some influence on Sir Charles and his plans for a grand hotel.

"On his last trip to the Victoria Falls, Sir Charles Metcalfe laid out the site for a hotel. This will be built on the slope of a sand hill, situated on the southern side of the great cataract and about three-quarters of a mile from its nearest point. The hotel will command a very fine view of the Falls. The scheme is that the hostelry will stand in a natural park of 4,000 acres [16 km²], which will be enclosed.

"It is probable that the township of Livingstone, if it be decided to establish one, will be placed on the northern bank of the river, and all the busy clamour of a tourist station will be a mile and a half away, so that the environment of the Falls will be preserved in all its pristine beauty. The railway bridge will be a mere detail in the scenery, like a spider's web or thread of filmy gossamer stretching across the chasm. Only a glimpse of the Falls will be discerned from the train, as the river leaves the seething whirlpool obliquely, and the 'rain-forest' obscures the view...

"We understand that previous to any work of bridge construction, a substantial wire fence, confining the workmen to their own area, will be erected, so that the work will not interfere with the grandeur of the scenery in the vicinity of the Falls." (Bulawayo Chronicle, September 1903b)

The Bosun's Chair

Passengers were taken over the gorge one at a time on an improvised 'bosun's chair' suspended from small pulleys running on the cable which was worked by the hand winch. More for reassurance than safety a canvas bag was attached into which the passenger climbed and which was strapped round the legs and across the chest. Mr Beresford-Fox was responsible for setting up the cable system and made the first passage across the chasm in November 1903. In a letter to his father Sir Francis Fox he described the experience:

"Well, I am crossing the gorge almost daily now by the wire rope: it is such a saving of time and trouble; but the first sensation is almost terrific. I was the first to cross, and did so from the north to the south side... As they tied me into the 'bosun's chair' I must admit to feeling a bit strange in relying absolutely on my own calculations for my safety. The chair is a piece of wood suspended by four ropes, with a canvas back and a sack and board as a foot-rest. Of course one is so tied in that were you to lose consciousness you could not fall out; this precaution, for some people, is advisable.

"All ready, so they gave the signal to the windlass on the south side, and I felt the endless rope tightening and pulling up the slack, and slowly out the pulley ran... After the first few moments there is a real charm in looking down; nothing but space between you and the water, save for the 'sag' of the returning endless wire; the small trees and even the large ones on the south ledge bearing such a different appearance below.

"Of course the predominant thought is, what would one feel if the pulley broke, whether you would really be unconscious after the first 100 ft. [30.5 m], and whether that last jerk you felt isn't the cable snapping; and you hurriedly look down to see if the water and rocks are not rushing up to meet you in your downward flight, and are relieved to see the cable still intact and stretching in a graceful curve to either side of the gorge.

"Such a comfortable sensation too, on a sagging rope - a smooth, gliding motion, and but for the slight vibration caused by the pulley running over the separate strands, more like that of a boat, with a steady rise and fall, and perhaps a slight swinging of the chair from side to side. This journey of 800 yds. [731.5 m] through the air saves a detour of 9 to 10 miles [14.5 to 16 km] by land and river, and gives a good idea of the splendid view which will be obtained from the bridge, when completed, of the superb scenery."

Beresford-Fox during his first crossing of the gorge, November 1903

Beresford-Fox also summarised the technical specifications and shortcomings:

"The cable is a ⅝ in [1.6 cm] diameter steel wire rope, 900 ft. [274.5 m] in length, and is supported at each side by a solid post 2 ft. [60 cm] in diameter, let down into the rock some 7 or 8 ft. [2.1-2.4 m] Then a ¼ in. [0.6 cm] stranded wire acts as an endless hauling rope round a windlass at one side and a pulley on the other. The running pulley is, however, not quite satisfactory, as we could not obtain a trolley in Bulawayo, and so, temporarily, have to do the best we can; the present arrangement is safe, but not good mechanically." (Fox, 1904)

Edwin Verner, a surveyor with the Railway Company employed on planning the line north crossed the gorge in early 1904, recalling that the 'seat' was a re-purposed bacon crate and that during his first trip across the African labourers pretended the mechanism had jammed, leaving him suspended half-way across the gorge - but at least giving the opportunity to take a photograph (Leen, 2018). Varian, one of the engineers working on the Bridge, later recorded in his memoirs 'Some African Milestones' (published in 1953):

"It was a primitive mode of transport. The supporting wire sagged ominously in the middle of the gorge, and if one disliked heights, there was plenty of time to brood in transit as the flimsy box jerked its way across." (Varian, 1953)

Prior to establishing the cable system the shortest route to the north bank was to cross the river was above the Falls at the ferry point known as Giese's Drift, a short distance upstream on the south side of the river. From here a canoe could cross to the Maramba River mouth, a tributary on the northern bank above the Falls. To get from one side of the Bridge site to the other was a distance of several kilometres and took a couple of hours. By means of this simple system foodstuffs and material were transported to the northern side, and engineers and workmen crossed the chasm daily during the construction of the Bridge. Tourists brave enough could travel across in about 10 minutes, paying 10 shillings for the privilege. The system was also used to transport the mail across the gorge.

> *"It was not until a bag containing the mails was jerked off the hook into the gorge that it dawned on the engineer in charge that the crossing had its dangers. The bag, of course, was light compared with a man, and so was the more readily jerked off. After this accident the hook on the cable was provided with a safety catch which prevented the loop of any burden working off it."* (Clark, 1936)

Crossing the gorge by means of the bosun's chair

Christmas Party

The earliest recorded rail tour from Bulawayo to the Falls was arranged in December 1903, six months before the railhead actually reached the Falls. The group travelled by train as far as the railhead at Hwange before transferring to a coach service for the remaining distance to the Falls:

> *"Travellers to the Zambezi were informed that the round trip from Bulawayo would take twelve days. The management of the Grand Hotel, Bulawayo, packed attractive baskets of food, but as fresh meat would not keep indefinitely, tourists were counselled to shoot giraffe and hippo... Arrived at the Zambezi, enterprising fishermen could add to the larder by catching tigerfish - 'an appetising dish.'"* (Rhodesia Railways Magazine, December 1954)

The Bridge Builders

The first group of specially selected engineers were sent by Cleveland Bridge and Engineering Company in early 1904 to prepare for the construction process. Including Imbault and his chief assistant engineer, Mr A Prince, they travelled by steam-liner from the United Kingdom to Cape Town in March 1904, and then by passenger train to Bulawayo.

"In the first week of March 1904, Mr Imbault, who had returned to England in October... and the first detachment of English workmen, started from England for the Falls. We travelled from Cape Town to Bulawayo in the train de luxe, which is wonderfully comfortable and rather upsets the ideas of those who come to Africa expecting to have to rough it. There are many trains in Europe which would suffer badly in comparison."

This was followed by an uncomfortable journey to Falls that included travelling on construction trains to the railhead and the remaining 56 kilometres by Zeederberg coach.

"The post cart trip of about thirty-five miles [56 km] *occupied two days instead of ten hours, as we had expected and provided for."* (Prince, 1906)

A second group of about 30 construction engineers travelled to the Falls via Beira on the east coast. One of the group, Arthur Frederick Davison, recalled travelling through Umtali and Salisbury before arriving in Bulawayo, where they appear to have spent some time, no doubt awaiting the completion of the railway line and transportation of the steelwork sections of the Bridge to the Falls. Mr Davidson was among a handful of men who remained after the completion of the Bridge to work on the continuation of the railway line north and eventually settled in Northern Rhodesia. Davison later recalled:

"The story of the Falls Bridge should be written for the benefit of the thousands of visitors... Mr Prince, second engineer in charge, a fine and honest man, Charlie Beech, Charlie Brooks, Longbottom, are all names that should be preserved. If they had been in a cricket team or soccer team they would have been, but since they were only a crowd of hard-working and hard-drinking bridge builders who created a vision of Rhodes into reality and gave access to Northern Rhodesia and the Katanga, they have had no write-up. They put up with conditions that were, to say the least, very primitive, and it says wonders for all the men engaged on the construction - quite a lot of men were later engaged in Africa, mostly in Kimberley - that they remained to see the job

finished." (Northern Rhodesia Journal, January 1952)

The handful of engineers named in references and reports include Mr Charles (Charlie) Albert Victor Beech, foreman for the construction; Mr Howard Schofield Longbottom, responsible for all the plant equipment used during construction (electrical, mechanical, hydraulic and pneumatic) and who also later took over as Bridge foreman; Mr Chalmers, who operated the specialist electrical transporter known as the Blondin; Mr E D Peile, who was involved in a tragic accident during construction whilst operating one of the construction cranes; and Mr Charles Friel who unfortunately died in the same accident. Pauling's Italian sub-contractor, Giacomo D'Alberto, who was contracted by the Railway Company to excavate the Bridge foundations, was also employed by the Bridge Company to prepare the concrete foundations of the Bridge.

Mr Beech, who also later settled in the country, is recorded travelling north after the construction of the Bridge with *"Freddy Binloss, Big Charlie Osborne (there were two Charlie Osborne's) and another fellow who died en route and was buried in some lonely spot"* (Northern Rhodesia Journal, July 1953a).

Others whose names have been recorded include Mr J A Powell, Mr Rutherford and Mr McEvoy, who were all also involved in the rebuilding of the top deck and reinforcing of the Bridge in 1929 (Powell, 1930). Mr Powell also refers to a Mr Perch, involved during the original construction of the Bridge. They were a rough and ready bunch and no doubt accurately described by a visiting hunter, Mr J W B White, as *"the most extraordinary collection of cosmopolitan toughs I have encountered anywhere."*

Imbault established his base of operations on the north bank, known alternatively as the Bridge Engineer's, Imbault's or Salmon's Camp, and where the majority of the Cleveland Bridge engineers and workmen were also based. Captain Ernest Harry Lindsell Salmon was the Rhodesian government transport officer and responsible for ensuring the camp was prepared to the necessary standard. Accommodation was also provided for the African labourers, but before being occupied one source recorded that they *"unfortunately burnt down, owing to the fusing of some electric wires, and had to be re-built... they are of a highly inflammable nature, and were burnt to the ground in a few minutes, together with all they contained."* (The Engineer, April 1905)

Conditions for the construction workers must have been difficult, with the European men unaccustomed to the temperature and humidity. Several of the workmen had to leave on account of bad health, suffering from malaria, fever, and dysentery.

The construction engineers pose for a group photograph. The child in the front centre of the image is possibly Mr Arton-Powell, who was recorded as the first child to cross the Bridge.

"During this work the spray was very heavy, sometimes falling all day with the force of a heavy shower. In consequence, with perhaps a little help from other causes not water, several of the workmen we brought out from England had to leave the country on account of bad health. Malaria, fever, and dysentery were the chief evils from which the men suffered." (Prince, 1906)

One visitor to the Falls in June 1904, Mr George Pallet, recorded:

"The men here have to work under great difficulties, owing to the continual spray from the Falls. Sometimes it is falling over them continuously, and they have to work in oilskins. Their pay is £18 per month and rations - not much for this part of the world - and considering the hardships and sickness they have to put up with. They all say that as soon as the time they signed on for is up, they will get back to England." (Bendigo Advertiser, September 1904)

The engineers were assisted by an estimated 400 African labourers over the period of construction, although the average number working on the Bridge was about 200. Labourers were paid from £3 to just 10 shillings a month.

Construction Camp

Mr Beresford-Fox was charged with the preparation of the camp for the construction engineers and labourers on the northern bank. In a letter to his father he recorded:

"I am putting up some fifteen or twenty huts for the railway company, or for the men and boys, e.g. a bedroom hut (all circular), 13 ft. or 14 ft. [3.95-4.25 m] diameter inside, about 7 ft. or 8 ft. [2.1-2.4 m] walls, and a sloping conical roof; another 12 ft. [3.65 m] high. It is made of poles cut out of the bush, and placed close together all round save for doors or windows. The roof is then thatched with good grass, and the walls and floors 'darghad,' i.e. plastered with clay, hiding the poles completely; and then you have a delightfully cool and waterproof dwelling. Then, again, a mess hut is 15 ft. to 18 ft. [4.6-5.5 m] diameter inside, and has a 5 ft. [1.5 m] verandah all round, with perhaps a light trellis-work balustrade. The floor inside and on the verandah is dargha; but the main walls are poles 12 in. [30.5 m] apart, and covered inside and out by long ½ in. [1.27 cm] diameter reeds, placed side by side perpendicularly, so that the air, cooled by the verandah, filters through these reed walls, and keeps the whole place delightfully fresh." (Fox, 1904)

The Fall and Rise of Mr Beresford-Fox

Together with his claim as being the first to cross the gorge by cable, Mr Beresford-Fox was soon to have another tale to add to his African adventures - one from which he was lucky to escape with his life and resulted in his premature return home. There are several different accounts of this story, each with its own errors and variations. Clark placed the story in early 1904, Hobson (1907) states it occurred in April, and other accounts place the accident in October. The Bulawayo Chronicle detailed the rescue in a report published in late February 1904, although they were perhaps behind on the news, as two weeks before they reported *"Mr Beresford Fox has almost completely recovered from the effects of his fall."* (Bulawayo Chronicle, February 1904a)

Mr Beresford-Fox appears to have been quite an adventure seeker, Mackintosh recording that when they met he was planning to lower a canoe and men down into the gorge in order to ride the rapids (Mackintosh, 1922). Together with Percy Clark he also enjoyed a joint passion for photography, as well as fishing, and the two men decided on an adventure exploring the gorges below the Falls.

"I got into the way of stopping with Fox at his camp, and in his spare time we

wandered about a good deal together, exploring and taking photographs. One day we determined to descend to the bottom of the gorge. It was a descent that had not been done from the southern side by anyone previously... We started from the point where the work on the foundations had begun, using the ladders that went down to the base of the working. From here we clambered along the face of the gorge wall, looking for some place that might afford a relatively easy descent the rest of the way. The way, however, that we finally did choose was not to be easy. It was, indeed, perilous going, with thick and thorny undergrowth, but eventually we got down to within twenty feet [6 m] or so of the bottom. Thereafter came a sheer drop, which we successfully negotiated by tying the rope we had with us to a tree and sliding down. So far, so good. We were actually the first to get to the bottom of this wonderful gorge from the southern bank."

This, however, was only the beginning of their adventures. Proceeding up around into the Boiling Pot they reached a point with only the narrowest of ledges to walk along. Beresford-Fox went ahead alone and Clark slowly retraced their steps, expecting his companion to catch up with him on his return.

"I did not think it wise to remain in the gorge after sun-down, and after a while I thought it time to return. Now, the men working on the opposite side of the gorge had a habit of doing all their blasting at the end of their day's operations. It was plain that they had not seen me on the gorge bottom, for as I clambered back to where we had left the rope a whole lot of charges went off with a terrific uproar, throwing tremendous rocks in all directions about the gorge. One huge piece that looked to me to be as big as a hut came sailing over as if to land on my head. I threw up my arm to ward it off. It landed, however, about fifty yards [45.7 m] from me with a terrific crash. My relief was immense, for I had thought my last day was come. There was no sign of Fox. I shinned up the rope and began to climb to the top. Half-way up I sat down for a rest, when it occurred to me that Fox could not have returned or I should have seen him; it was clear that I must go back and look for him. So once again I descended."

Returning to the bottom of the gorge Clark records 'a workman on the other side of the gorge making urgent signals to me' and directing him back to where the two adventurers had separated. This time Clark proceeded further ahead, negotiating the dangerous ledge, but only to find his way blocked again by a 50 metre wall of rock which he could not climb.

"It was becoming dusk, and I though there was nothing for it but to go back by the way I had come and get help from the workmen's camp. I again safely

negotiated the ledge and reached the hanging rope. There was no great length of rope to climb, but I failed in several attempts to get over the top of the rock. I was too exhausted. Willy-nilly I must spend the night in the gorge. I tied myself on to a ledge and settled down. My bed was a wet one, for water condensed from the spray fell on me in rivulets. As I lay there I kept wishing that I had some whisky to go with the spray. Dawn broke at last, and once again I essayed to climb the rope. This time I managed it, and clambered to the top of the gorge. There I found Flossie [his loyal dog] *waiting for me. My little pal had not moved from the spot where I had left her the previous afternoon.*" (Clark, 1936)

As Clark was clambering out of the gorge he was still unaware of the fate of his friend. Mr John F Sharp was part of a small crowd of men on the north bank to who word had reached the previous evening that Beresford-Fox had been seen falling whilst climbing in gorge, and part of the rescue team sent to the scene.

"Sergeant Major Sykes of the police took charge and we started to rig a derrick to swing out over the gorge to lower someone down to... Beresford who had been caught on a ledge over 100 feet [30.5 m] *down. At the first attempt it was found that the wire rope was too short. A little Cornish blacksmith, Jack Whitten by name, who had volunteered to go down in a bosun's chair had to come back and we had to splice another fifty feet* [15.25 m] *on to the rope so that Whitten could reach the body. I helped with the splicing.*" (Northern Rhodesia Journal, July 1954)

The delay had done nothing for Whitten's (spelt Whitton according to Davison) nerves, who eventually only agreeed to go down a second time after a 'good drink of whisky.' Suitably emboldened Whitten was again lowered into the gorge. According to an account published in the Bulawayo Chronicle Mr Whitten was lowered down three times into the gorge.

"It was due to the efforts of Messrs J Whitton, C Bissett and J H West, who, with some 15 boys, eventually hauled up and carried Mr Fox to camp. Mr Whitton was let down by a rope a distance of about 100 ft. [30.5 m] *no less than three times... in pitch darkness and by the light of lanterns, before Mr Fox's position was located, and he remained down while the injured man was hauled up, and had most difficulty in finding the rope when finally thrown down to him.*" (Bulawayo Chronicle, February 1904b)

At about half-past three in the morning, after a rescue operation of over six hours, Mr Beresford-Fox was pulled out of the gorge *"very much broken but still alive."*

"As far as I remember his right thigh and arm and one of his collar bones were broken and he had a lot of head injuries. It was thought most of them were caused by his fighting to get out of the cactus he had lodged in when he fell." (Northern Rhodesia Journal, July 1954)

Sharpe details the date of the accident as 7th October, and the rescue the 8th. Meanwhile Percy Clark was still missing, having also spent the night in the gorge.

"I staggered the half mile or so to the men's camp and found them at breakfast. 'Where's Fox?' I asked. 'We've got him,' they said. 'Where's the whisky?' was my next question, and they gave me a stiff tot. I will say that I needed it... I asked what had happened. Fox had got to the top of the mound which I failed to climb, but had been unable to get down again. Nor could he climb up from it. His shouts had been heard by the workmen before they knocked off work for the day, and they had gone along and lowered a rope to him. Instead of tying himself to it and letting them haul him up, he had started to climb it hand over hand. Towards the top the rope was slippery with mud from the spray and damp earth; his hands slipped and he fell about a hundred feet [30.5 m], but had a miraculous escape from death. Fortunately he landed on the branch of a tree, and toppled from that on to a ledge of rock. No bones were broken, but he had an awful shock, from which I believe he never fully recovered... In the meantime I had been reported dead and missing, and somebody had already departed south to Bulawayo with the news." (Clark, 1936)

Beresford-Fox later described a lighter side to his six hour ordeal in a letter to his father:

"I had often wished to experience a long swing - suggested by the movement of candelabra suspended from the roof of a cathedral: and I attained my desire - a pendulum 110 ft. (33 m) long with an oscillation of 40 ft. (12 m) from side to side, with a period of about 10 seconds; moreover I enjoyed it." (Fox, 1904)

Sir Francis Fox, father of the adventurous Beresford-Fox, recalled in his memoirs:

"Beresford was seriously injured in arms, legs, and back, but his life was saved, and in a letter to me he said he attributed his escape to the direct intervention of God, as nothing else could have saved him."

Mr Beresford-Fox sustained severe injuries and no doubt some fractures, and after several months recovering in Bulawayo and several more re-cooperating at the Falls, he was eventually invalided back to England in October 1904.

Some sixteen years later, Sir Francis managed to track down Mr Whitten to thank him personally for saving his son's life.

"At last I was enabled to write to Mr Whitten, and thank him for saving my son's life; to which he replied, April 4, 1920: 'As to what I did at the Falls for your son, it is, or was, only what any Englishman would have done under the circumstances, and I thank you for your kind reminder.'" (Fox, 1924)

Mr Whitten received an inscribed gold travel clock for his bravery, which he treasured until his death in 1947. Arthur Davison, one of the Cleveland Bridge company engineers, was also present at the rescue and recalls:

"We took it for granted that he had been killed and Jack Whitton, the blacksmith, volunteered to go down on a rope with a sack to bring up the bits. But [Beresford-Fox] had been caught on a tree part way down and had nothing worse than a broken ankle and a great fright. So Jack Whitton was hauled up and he went down again with more ropes to bring up Fox. Jack was presented with a beautifully engraved gold travelling clock, and when he died in the Old Men's Home at Ndola... this clock was the only possession he had. He died in 1947, a pauper, like so many grand old men of the Territory, but he never tried to raise money on the clock which is now with his sister in the United Kingdom." (Northern Rhodesia Journal, January 1952)

Mr Beresford-Fox's replacement, Mr H F Varian, reported for duty in August 1904. Charles Beresford-Fox died in Toronto, Canada in 1912 following complications after an operation, aged 37.

A view of the Main Falls, from a postcard by Percy Clark

Gone Fishing

The two friends also shared a passion for fishing, with Beresford-Fox observing during the excavations of the Bridge foundations:

"All these boulders and debris falling into the water have attracted enormous tiger-fish, which from time to time play on the surface of the swirling backwater directly below the bridge: bream about 18 in. [45.7 cm] long, and awful-looking barbel about 4 ft. 6 in. to 5 ft. [1.4-1.5 m], like serpents. I've written off to Bulawayo for some especially large hooks and strong cord; and before long I hope to have some fun fishing from the ledge below, or from the cable above, as it is as yet impossible to get down to the water's edge." (Fox 1904)

Undeterred by Beresford-Fox's accident, Clark soon set off back down into the gorge, lured by the prospects of landing himself a record breaker.

"Controversy was great at the bridge camps and the Old Drift as to whether or not there were fish in the gorge. There were those who said they had seen what looked like fish from the top. It was a controversy that interested me, and I made my mind to try and settle it. A fortnight after my night at the gorge bottom I made a second descent. This time I took my native servant with me and some stout fishing-tackle. This consisted of thin rope borrowed from the bridge works. Attached to it were three great shark-hooks bound with wire, much in the manner of those attached to spoon bait in trolling for pike or tiger fish. I put a large chunk of raw meat on each of the hooks, and slung the line out into the rushing waters of the gorge. Presently the line ran out and I hauled in a fish about four feet [1.2 m] long. It looked like a cross between an eel and a barbel, with a softish fin running right along its back and down its belly.

"The second cast resulted in what appeared to be a catch-up on a rock. My boy and I put out combined weight on the line to pull it free. For a it seemed to be stuck for good; then suddenly it gave. We hauled in, and a huge head, as big as a human being's, appeared on the surface. It was like a gargoyle. We put all our weight on the line but failed to haul the monster in. At length we wound the line round a large rock, trusting to the stoutness of the line and the strength of the hooks to prevent Leviathan from getting away. But suddenly there was a terrific jerk, and the brute was gone. And in going, as we saw when we pulled in the line, it had straightened the two hooks it had taken into its mouth. I am quite convinced there are enormous fish in the gorge!

"I skinned the barbel-eel, intending to send it to the British Museum. But a

Bulawayo man who was on a visit to the Falls suggested that, as a Rhodesian, I ought rather to send it to the Bulawayo Museum. He offered to take the fish to Bulawayo himself and I agreed. Some time later I received a letter from the curator of the museum, who said that the fish was of a new unclassified species and that further information would be sent on. A few months later I had occasion to go to Bulawayo, and naturally I went to see how my capture looked in the museum. There had been some sort of spring-cleaning there, and specimens were lying around in heaps. Of my fish, however, there was no trace, and no trace of it has been found to this day." (Clark, 1936)

The Engineers Entertain

Miss Constance Thwaits visited the Victoria Falls with her sister in May 1904, at the invitation of Mr Townsend and Mr Beresford-Fox. The party travelled by rail from Bulawayo and stayed at the construction camp on the south bank. Miss Thwaits recorded in her diary:

"There was a row of grass huts - each of us had one. They had no doors but grass mats hanging over the doorways. I thought a lion or other wild animal might walk in, so pushed a cupboard in front of my curtain. In the morning an African brought in a tray of tea with quinine which I had to take to keep malaria away. It was lovely in the morning and there was a hammock near the huts which I liked. Mr Townsend was in the next hut, then Mr Fox and then the dining hut. Mr Fox had everything arranged well, and had ordered wild flowers or grasses to be in the vase on the dining table always, and nice silver and glass which his mother sent to Africa for him.

"We... eventually got to the Bridge site, where there was just a skip for the men to cross by. It is like a child's swing with iron ropes instead of ordinary rope. They had promised me that I could go across the gorge on this, but when I saw it I wondered! They held the swing over the land while I got in and I was wound over in seven minutes about. The sight of the Falls was glorious and I took a photograph of that with Mr Fox's camera, which he had lent me." (Thwaits, 1904)

Crossing in style

The Railway Arrives

Construction of the final 68 mile (109.5 km) section of the railway line from Hwange to the Victoria Falls began in late 1903, again financed by Rhodesia Railways Ltd, who were also responsible for the funding of the Bridge.

The first 47 miles (75.5 km) of line from Hwange was particularly challenging for Pauling and his construction gangs, and included very heavy work through difficult country covered in dense bush and supporting a full complement of Africa's 'Big Five.' Percy Clark had travelled to the Falls whilst the railway was still under construction, recording that the workmen slept in the trees for fear of attack from lion and other dangerous wild animals.

"The sixty-eight miles [109.5 km] of line from Wankie to Victoria Falls included forty-seven miles [75.6 km] of very heavy work through difficult country... Two severe banks were encountered, one from Deka siding up the Katuna valley and the other from Matetsi to a point later named Fuller. These climbs were both on maximum grade against northbound trains and the Katuna bank was aggravated by a horseshoe bend, which was to cause endless trouble to enginemen over the years to come. Two major river crossings were involved, one over the Deka, nine miles [14.5 km] from Wankie, with a water tank sited not far away to top up supplies before tackling the Katuna bank, and the other was the Matetsi, about half way to Victoria Falls." (Croxton, 1982)

River crossings on the line were initially traversed with temporary bird-cage trestle bridges, sufficient to carry the construction train and necessary materials forward. The trestle bridge at the Matetsi, 260 feet (79 m) long and 43 feet (13.1 m) high, was the largest bridge of this type on the line and was supported by substantial rock ballasting.

Trestle Bridge, Matetsi River

The construction company were also responsible for erecting semi-permanent masonry and steelwork bridges, built to basic requirements but suitable for passenger traffic, before handing the line over to the Railway Company for operation. Permanent bridges were erected along the line in the years that followed.

Pauling's Italian stone-masons at work

Pauling subcontracted the work of preparing the earthworks ahead of the construction gangs to experienced Italian engineer Giacomo D'Alberto, who had worked on mining and railway contracts in southern Africa since the early 1880s (Museo dell'emigrante, Roasio, 2021a). The skilled work of constructing the supporting stonework piers and abutments for the temporary bridges was also undertaken by a group of specialist Italian stone-masons.

The line to the Victoria Falls was completed on 24th April 1904, several weeks after the target date of 1st April - for once Pauling and his men had been unable to deliver to a deadline. As the last rails were laid the supporting construction train slowly rolled to a stop within sight of the rising spray of the Falls. Celebrations were held including a sports-day and feast for all the construction workers.

"Harold Pauling was once more in charge of this contract and, as usual, the work was speedily pushed ahead to reach Victoria Falls, where the site for the famous bridge had already been selected. On 24th April 1904, only seven months after work began, the first construction train pulled in at the site of Victoria Falls station... The train was hauled by RR 7th Class No.22 and for the last lap was driven by Harold Pauling's daughter, Blanche, with the locomotive flying a Union Jack and bearing the board below the headlamp reading 'We've got a long way to go.' This referred to Cairo, as the target of Cecil Rhodes was still very present in men's minds. Blanche Pauling had already travelled on the first engine to reach Bulawayo in 1897, so she could well claim to be a pioneer

engine driver. In wide-brimmed felt hat, high collared white blouse and dark skirt down to her ankles, she made an unusual figure on the footplate. As soon as the last sleeper was laid and the train came to rest, celebrations began, with native sports, mock battles by the tribesmen, and a feast for all the staff, white and black, engaged on the work." (Croxton, 1982)

In his autobiography Percy Clark proudly tells of his success in selling photographs of the arrival of the first train to all the engineers, contractors and railway staff, recording that he *"did a roaring trade in prints at five shillings a time"* (Clark, 1936).

A temporary station building was quickly improvised, with Pauling operating two trains a week between Hwange and Victoria Falls from 10th May 1904, before the line was handed over to the Railway Company for official opening on 20th June 1904 (a permanent station building was erected in the first half of 1905 with Mr John Fairlamb as Station Master). The Zeederberg mail service to the Falls stopped soon after, although they continued to run a short linking transportation run from the Falls the Old Drift on Thursdays and Sundays to coincide with the train timetable (Shepherd, 2008).

From the Cape it took three days by train to Bulawayo and a further 22 hours to reach the Falls. In advertisements it was stressed that passengers must provide their own blankets and food for their journey as there were no dining carriages, and no intermediate stations where refreshments could be obtained. Mr Pierre Gavuzzi, Manager of the Bulawayo Grand Hotel, provided hampers for the adventurous train travellers.

In May 1904 Mr Gavuzzi would have been packing his own hamper for the journey north, travelling by train with several truckloads of building materials for the construction of a small hotel overlooking the rising spray of the Victoria Falls and to which he had been appointed as general manager.

Celebrating the first train to arrive at Victoria Falls

The Victoria Falls Hotel

With the line to the Falls complete the Railway Company arranged in early May 1904 for the transportation of materials for the construction of a 'temporary' hotel at the Falls. It has previously been recorded that the Victoria Falls Hotel opened on 8th June 1904 (Creewel, 2004). A notice in the Bulawayo Chronicle of 4th June, however, appears to indicate that construction of the Hotel was still ongoing, with a party of workmen departing for the Falls on Monday, 30th May. A notice from the Railway Company appeared in the same issue indicating a three week delay in construction:

> *"A telegram has been received from Mr S F Townsend, of the Rhodesia Railways, notifying that visitors would do well to defer their trips for about three weeks in consequence of delay in the hotel construction."* (Bulawayo Chronicle, June 1904)

A simple wood and iron structure, construction of the Hotel was speedily effected once construction materials and men arrived at the Falls. The main building consisted of a cast-iron frame, wooden panels and corrugated iron roof, all raised above the ground and fronted with a wide open veranda overlooking the Batoka Gorge, the view extending down to the rising spray of the Falls.

The Hotel was initially capable of hosting up to 20 guests, with twelve single and four double rooms, together with a dining room, bar and administrative offices, and was equipped with modern luxuries including electric lights and fans and running hot and cold water. Bridge engineer Howard Longbottom assisted with the installation of the electrical fittings.

The Railway Company leased the operation and management of the Hotel to the partnership of Mr G Estran and Mr W Scott-Rodger, who were already running the Grand Hotel in Bulawayo and who sent their Manager, Mr Pierre Gavuzzi, to oversee the establishment of the new Hotel (Roberts, 2021a).

The early Hotel staff were cosmopolitan in origins - Mr Gavuzzi was an Italian, the chef was French, and the barman from Chicago, with service supported by Indian waiters. The young chef, Mr Marcel Mitton, known as 'the Frenchman who became a Rhodesian,' was a well-known character in early Rhodesian history, trying his hand as a hunter and miner as well as a chef.

Many of the Hotel's early guests would have been linked to the Railway Company and construction of the Bridge, as well as the occasional adventurous traveller. Sir

Charles Metcalfe made the Hotel his base of operations, overseeing the Bridge construction from the veranda and utilising the telegraph at the neighbouring Post Office to communicate progress to London and across the world.

The lowest all-inclusive tariff was twelve shillings six pence per day, and such was the demand for accommodation that within a month of opening an advert had to be placed in the Bulawayo Chronicle notifying visitors intending to stay at the Hotel that they should advise the management in advance of their arrival *"in order to ensure accommodation and to avoid disappointment"* (Bulawayo Chronicle, July 1904a).

The rising numbers of visitors to the Falls did not go unnoticed by the Railway Company, Sir Charles Metcalfe and others soon referring to the Hotel in terms of accommodating guests rather than engineers:

"The line has been open right up to the Victoria Falls since June 20th, and the Hotel we have built there for the accommodation of visitors is a very comfortable one. It possesses every modern convenience, and from it there is obtained a beautiful view of the Zambezi Gorge." (Metcalfe, 1904)

Guest lists from 1904 show people arriving from England, the United States and the Cape Colony. It soon became clear that the Hotel needed increased capacity to accommodate the growing number of guests, with visitors often having to use train carriages as extra accommodation at busy periods. In September 1904 two old railway sheds were relocated to the site, with one converted into a large dining room, and the other into bedrooms. Soon after further railway buildings were added, re-purposed into accommodation with en suite bathrooms and becoming known as the Annex or Honeymoon Suites.

Front view of the first Victoria Falls Hotel

The Victoria Falls Hotel

"The Hotel, at the beginning, was simply a long structure of wood and iron containing a dining room and bar, bedrooms and offices. Later on it was enlarged by the addition of two large engine sheds removed from railway headquarters. One of these was converted into a dining room and the other into bedrooms. Later still two annexes of wood and iron were put up, complete with bathrooms. In the hot weather the rooms were ovens, and in the cold, refrigerators - but nobody grumbled much. After all, what could one expect in the heart of Africa?" (Clark, 1936)

The British travel agent, Thomas Cook and Sons, as official passenger agent for the Cape Government and Rhodesia Railways, followed the progress of the railway and construction of the Hotel and Bridge in its magazine, the Travellers' Gazette (9th April 1904) and began offering excursions from Cape Town in the same year. The company anticipated a rapid expansion of business at *"nature's greatest spectacle"* where the traveller could *"enjoy European luxury even here in the heart of Africa"* (McGregor, 2009).

The Hotel's first logo included the African lion and Egyptian sphinx, symbolising Rhodes' dream of a railway connecting Africa from the Cape to Cairo, and fittingly readopted by the Hotel in 1996.

The Iron and Timber

An outside bar, known to the railway workers and engineers as the 'Iron and Timber,' was provided at the Victoria Falls Hotel, and soon became the social hub of the transitional community, and many an evening was described as 'lively.' Percy Clark expands in his autobiography:

"While the Bridge was still in course of construction an outside bar was put up for the workmen. They were a rough lot, even for the wilds, and they made the hotel very uncomfortable for sedater guests in the main building, especially just after they got their monthly pay. At this time the Hotel was run by private management. The lessee was an Italian, and the antics of his customers, both heads and hands, kept him scared almost out of his wits... Whenever he came in sight of the workmen using the outside bar he was at once chased round the premises. If caught he was hauled into the bar and made to stand drinks all round. He did not relish this rough handling and had not the knack of taking it easily. He therefore gave the outside bar a wide berth, though he must have made a pile from it.

"For two or three days after the men received their pay the bar would be packed. Drinking and gambling went on continuously, with free entertainment day and night for anyone who cared for that sort of thing. There was always a fight going on outside the bar - and the workmen certainly could scrap. Fortunately for the management it had secured the services of an ex-prize fighter as barman. He was not a very big chap, but he stood no nonsense from the crowd." (Clark, 1936)

Despite his stage fright, Mr Gavuzzi appears to have fancied himself as an entertainer, it being recorded that for the opening of the Bridge *"Gavuzzi added to the gaiety by singing Italian arias"* (Green, 1968). This may have accounted for his popularity among the engineers.

"On one occasion when the whole gang was having a vary hilarious night of it in the Hotel bar Gavuzzi, who was small in stature, was hoisted up on the mantelpiece and obliged to sing a song." (Croxton, 1982)

High-risk High-jinks

Powell, writing in 1930, recalls an incident involving Mr Perch, the compound manager on the north bank, and two early visitors to the Falls, identified only as 'Lady L' and 'Lady F':

"When the railway reached the Falls visitors flocked to see it. Among others were Lady L and Lady F the wives of two Rand magnates. They were brought over by the small ropeway and remained on the north side, as the guests of the chief engineer [Imbault], while they explored the north bank of the river. During the dinner hour a note was brought from the chief engineer stating that the ladies luggage had not been brought over, and would Perch, the compound manager, get in touch with the south bank, and ask the people there to send over the two suit-cases.

"Attempts to gain attention to the telephone having failed, Perch decided to pull himself over, hand by hand. I tried to dissuade him from this mad adventure, but he was the son of a British Naval Captain, and his forbears had been sailors for generations. In addition to the boatswain's chair, that was fixed to the travelling wire, there was a second chair that could be secured to the wire by means of clip pulleys. This was used when required. Perch decided to use this chair, let himself down by gravitation to the centre of the wire - which had a sag of thirty feet [9 m] - and pull himself up, hand over hand, to the other side. He took a candle lamp with which he was to signal when he reached the opposite cliff. The chair started down the grade with a tremendous rush and the swaying of the lamp showed when he was hauling himself up. Suddenly I was horrified to see the lamp drop into the gorge. I at first thought Perch had gone with it, but after a while the rope began to oscillate again. Then it came to rest but there was no signal. After about a quarter of an hour, movement again in the rope, followed by a long period of rest. The raw of the Falls prevented any answers of the calls being heard and the darkness of the gorge on a starless night is Cimmerian.

"When the rope came to rest for the third time, I waited fully half an hour and was sorrowfully walking towards the office to telephone the news to the chief's house, when the telephone bell from the south bank was heard - it was Perch. In a strangely subdued voice he told him story. Twice he had nearly reached the bank when the muscles of his arms could haul him no further. At the third attempt he landed but over-come by exhaustion he had to lie down and rub the cramp from his arms."

It turned out Mr Perch had risked life and limb on a wild goose-chase - the ladies luggage having already been sent over that afternoon.

"Asked if he was coming over that night he replied 'Not for any money. I am going to the Hotel for the stiffest drink they can give me, and then straight to bed.' When the chief was told of Perch's adventure, he merely smiled and said, 'You know he always was a little mad.'" (Powell, 1930)

Unfounded Foundations

The start of the Bridge construction experienced significant delay when it was discovered in mid-1904 that the south side provided no solid foundation rock until a depth of about 15 metres below that which had been expected.

> "The start of the erection was greatly delayed... by the deceptive appearance of the surface rock of the foundations on the Cape side. Instead of being practically solid rock, as was anticipated, it proved to be almost anything else. A depth of fifty feet [15 m] below the first estimated depth had to be reached before the required solidity of foundation rock was reached." (Prince, 1906)

The oversight had been made during the initial surveys of the site and as a consequence the Bridge had to be lowered from the position originally intended:

> "The rock being very hard, the bridge was designed to fit the profile of the gorge with as little expenditure on excavation as possible; and it would have done so, but for a mistake made by the surveyor in concluding that the rock on both sides was solid. The mistake was perhaps excusable, and was not discovered until the vegetation which thrives in the hot sun and the spray from the Falls had been removed, and the work of clearing the ground and the excavation of the rock had proceeded for some time. It was then found that the shelf on the right bank on which it was intended to rest one end of the principal span was covered to a considerable depth with debris. By the time the error had been discovered, the preparation of the steelwork was too far advanced to permit of any alteration being made in the structure. The difficulty had therefore to be overcome partly by increasing the depth of the concrete foundations, and partly by lowering the level of the entire bridge to the extent of 21 feet [6.4 m]; but both time and money would have been saved had the true facts of the case been recognized at the beginning, the span designed 25 feet [7.6 m] longer, and the truss increased in depth at the ends by 20 feet [6.1 m]." (Hobson, 1907)

It is not exactly clear where Hobson is pointing the finger of blame - Sir Charles Metcalfe selected and initially surveyed the site and Mr Beresford-Fox later conducted more detailed surveys. Both, together with Imbault, were present in September 1903 when the site was confirmed and final measurements taken. Subsequently several months were lost before the shortcoming was identified, further delaying the start of construction whilst the foundations were prepared.

One sharp-eyed individual at the Institute of Civil Engineers, Mr R J G Read, commented:

"From the section it seemed that the bridge would have looked more comfortable if it had been set farther back into the cliff on the left-hand side. Owing to the lowering of the bridge, the line had to run in a cutting on each side, and probably the view of the Falls had been obstructed to some extent."

Hobson would not accept that the view of the Falls was affected:

"The fact of the bridge being approached in a cutting had made no difference to the view from the line, for owing to intervening ground and forest the Falls could not in any case be seen from the railway except during the crossing of the gorge." (Hobson, 1907)

Hobson later even suggested that the repositioning actually improved the aesthetics of the Bridge.

"The lowering of the level of the bridge, previously referred to, was not a bad thing an artistic point of view. It fits the scenery even better as it is than it would have done at the higher level where it was originally proposed to fix it." (Hobson, 1923)

The work of excavating the foundations for the Bridge and approach cuttings for the line was awarded to Giacomo D'Alberto, Pauling's experienced earthworks

View of the northern bank, showing excavated foundations cut into the rock, with the gorge connected by wires and engineer crossing

subcontractor, and overseen by William Tower, Resident Engineer for the Railway Company. D'Alberto is recorded as working on the excavations from December 1903 to October 1904 (Museo dell'emigrante, Roasio, 2021a).

In January 1904 it is recorded that an Italian, known only as 'Bellinzona' Giacomo, died whilst under Nurse Chapman's care at the Old Drift, the cause of death detailed as a *"softening of the brain."* There is no reference to an accident, although he must have been one of D'Alberto's team working on the foundations (Museo dell'emigrante, Roasio, 2021b). It appears to have been several months into this work before the extent of the problems on the south bank were fully realised, significantly delaying progress and vastly increasing the scale of the work and labour required on the excavations.

Mr James McCarthy of County Kerry, Ireland, was one of six brothers employed by Pauling on the construction of the line to the Falls and later recalled working on the foundation piers of the Bridge, as well as the first station building at Livingstone (Rhodesia Railways Magazine, March 1967).

The unexpected extra task of excavating the foundations proved difficult and dangerous work.

> *"The size of the excavation on the left bank was small, the rock there being sound, but its position on the face of an almost perpendicular cliff rendered work slow and dangerous. On the right bank it was more easily accessible, but was considerably larger owing to the burden of debris which had to be removed."* (Hobson, 1907)

In a letter to his father Beresford-Fox recorded:

> *"Excavation for bridge is getting on slowly only, owing to the impossibility of getting 'boys' [labourers]; there is also such a great deal of cleaning down of the sides of the cliff, to get rid of loose boulders, that the work has been increased in amount. Of course on the north side the debris you clear away falls into the water below, but on this side it falls 80 ft. [24 m] and then rolls, and will mostly have to be shifted again, unavoidably too, owing to the ledge of rock... What erratic courses falling boulders take! You start a large one from the top - probably it breaks, and the pieces go in all directions within 45° of its original course; but often the whole boulder on landing takes an entirely new route, and goes crashing through the brushwood beyond the 60 ft. [18 m] clearing, and away over the ledge at least 100 ft. [30 m] to the right or left of where it started."* (Fox, 1904)

The Blondin

With the arrival of the railhead at the Victoria Falls in April 1904 heavy materials for the construction of the Bridge could finally be transported to the site. Mr Macrae, of Bulawayo, acted as forwarding agent for the despatch of the waiting Bridge materials to the Falls. The first major engineering challenge was the installation of a powerful cable system to transport the large volume of heavy materials needed on the north bank, and varyingly described as the electric cableway or transporter system and known as the 'Blondin' by the engineers.

The idea of an electric cable system across the gorge was conceived at an early stage in the planning for the Bridge, being identified as essential for the movement of the heavy materials needed for the Bridge construction and also for the continuation of the railway north. In order to ease the burden on the Bridge contractors, it was decided that the transporter would be provided by the Railway Company, and a separate contract issued.

"In July, 1903, tenders were invited for a cableway to span a distance of 870 feet [265.18 m] and carry a load of 10 tons net. The conveyor was specified to be capable of lifting and lowering as well as travelling with this load, and to be operated by means of electricity."

The electric transporter system chosen for the task was designed by Mr E A Poole, of Westminster.

"The framing carried an electric motor, and driver's chair, and two drums, motor driven, and having the hoisting ropes wound round them. A pinion on the end of the motor shaft engaged with either one of two spur wheels on the side carriage. The shaft of one of these wheels carried a pinion gearing with teeth on the two travelling wheels. The other wheel operated through the lifting drum, on which the ropes attached to the skips were wound. Each drum being controlled independently by levers, the driver was able to lift, lower, and travel."
(Horner, 1906)

The Blondin

In early 1904 the conveyor and supporting cableway was assembled at the Cleveland Bridge Company's workshops and thoroughly tested.

> *"On January 29th, a large company of engineering experts, contractors, and others met at the works of the Cleveland Bridge and Engineering Company Limited... and inspected a new system of overhead cableway which had been installed for testing purposes before being sent out for use in connection with the Zambesi Bridge... Its span extended from the works across the road for a distance of 870 ft. [265 m]."* (The Practical Engineer, February 1904)

Hobson later recorded that the *"precaution of testing the apparatus was justified in the event, for, in the machine tested, the transmission gear-which was composed of friction-wheels utterly failed, and spur-gearing was ordered to be substituted"* (Hobson, 1907).

The transporter travelled along a single cableway over 265 metres (870 feet) in length, fixed to a tower on the north bank and hinged sheer-legs on the south bank, designed to counter the weight of the machine as it moved along the cable.

> *"The cable was designed to be carried on one bank by a steel tower 36 feet [11 m] high, securely anchored at the rear with guyropes, while on the other side the support took the form of a pair of sheer-legs, 80 feet [24.4 m] long, set*

Crossing the gorge by Blondin

> *at an angle of 45 degrees, hinged upon pins secured to foundation-plates bedded in concrete. One end of the cable was attached... to the end of the sheer-legs, and a counterweight of 60 tons was supported at the same point. The tension of the cable was thus balanced by the counterweight and was practically uniform in all positions. As the load traversed the cable to the centre of the span the counter-weight was raised, and after the load passed the centre it fell... [reducing]*

the power required to drive the load up the incline." (Hobson, 1907)

"Under dead load alone the cable has a deflection of 6½ feet [2 m] at the centre point. Under the 10-ton live load, which is the capacity of the cableway, the deflection is 43½ feet [13.2 m] more." (The Engineering Record, May 1904)

The transporter was capable of lifting loads of up to ten tons (over 10,000 kg) at a lift speed of 20 feet (6 m) per minute, and travelling along the cableway at up to 300 feet (90 m) per minute (Hill, 1911). Electric power was generated by a portable steam-driven engine and electric dynamo supplied by a Newcastle firm and located near the construction yard.

"The driver rode on the carriage, to which current was conveyed by a copper wire stretched from tower to tower, the return current passing through the main rope." (Hill, 1911)

The operator had two separate electric motors to control; one for movement forward and backward over the wire, the other for lifting and lowering vertical weights.

"The hoist is provided with two independent lifting ropes, so that the load can be

The construction yard on the south bank, showing the Blondin sheer-legs

tilted if necessary." (The Engineering Record, May 1904)

Hobson recorded that the design was viewed with some degree of doubt.

> *"The design at the time was comparatively new, and no apparatus of the kind had hitherto been made on such a large scale. It was therefore regarded-in some quarters-with ill-concealed suspicion. In effect the principle of the apparatus is that of an overhead travelling crane in a workshop, but instead of running on a solid rail it runs on a wire rope; the driver sits in the travelling carriage, and from there he controls the lifting, lowering, and travelling movements.*
>
> *"The obvious criticism against this proposition duly made its appearance. No man, it was alleged, could be induced, for wages, to occupy the driver's seat and travel all day long to and fro across that awful chasm for months together. Though many troubles were encountered, it may at once be said that this was not one of them."* (Hobson, 1907)

The transporter and cableway material arrived at the Zambezi in early June 1904, after considerable delays in its manufacture and delivery.

> *"The material for the cableway was unloaded at the Zambezi early in June 1904, considerable delay having occurred in its manufacture and in obtaining delivery out of the hands of the sub-contractors."* (Hobson, 1907)

The confidence of the operator, Mr Chalmers, who was to control it from a small seat perched precariously on its side, must have been severely tested on 19th July 1904, when a chain broke during installation and the heavy machinery crashed down into the gorge. Though badly damaged, it was recovered and repairs were satisfactorily carried out in Bulawayo. An auxiliary cable was subsequently introduced to prevent strain on the main cable.

Before the transporter could be used for the first time it was necessary to clear the cable of various pulleys that had been used in positioning it and which were still lashed to it. They had all gravitated to the lowest position, requiring someone to stand on the top of the Blondin, over the centre of the gorge, to unhook them. Despite a request for volunteers, Imbault, had to undertake the dangerous work himself. Powell recounted the story:

> *"Despite the offer of a bonus, not one of the workers would undertake the job and finally the chief engineer had to do it himself... it was an eerie sensation watching this man standing on a narrow plank in front of the gently swaying*

machine, 450 feet [137 m] in the air, using both hands to undo the steel lashings, and passing the pulleys one by one to the driver at the back. A moment of vertigo, a false balance, and certain death. Truly he was nerveless." (Powell, 1930)

Situated on the upstream side of the Bridge, at a slight angle away from the line of the Bridge itself, the apparatus was finally installed and in working order on the 28th July 1904. The successful crossing was announced in the Bulawayo Chronicle two days later.

"Blondin Conveyor Crosses. Victoria Falls, July 28th... - The Blondin (the electric conveyor weighing 3½ tons) crossed the gorge below the Victoria Falls at 4 p.m. The trial trip occupied exactly four minutes." (Bulawayo Chronicle, July 1904b)

The transporter system became known as 'the Blondin' after the daredevil tightrope-walker Charles Blondin (whose real name was Jean François Gravelet), who had famously crossed the Niagara Falls by rope in 1859.

"The driver of the Blondin, who worked it throughout the whole of the construction period, was one of the coolest men I have ever known, and deserved all credit for sticking to his job. No one envied him, especially on the occasions when permanent way material slipped in its sling in transit, jerking the carrier in a manner terrifying to behold." (Varian, 1953)

The Blondin was used solely for transportation, and not directly in the construction of the Bridge. Two large cranes unloaded the freight from the trains at the yard and connected with the lifting gear of the Blondin. A large steel cage was hung from the winch to transport workers across the gorge, and was used daily at

Bridge sections awaiting transport via the Blondin to the north bank

the beginning and end of each shift. Visitors to the Falls wishing to undertake the journey were charged a small fee, the journey taking about four minutes.

Although essential to the construction of the Bridge the Blondin was not without its problems, in particular affecting the two grooved wheels on which the conveyor was suspended, causing many delays:

"Many difficulties, most of them due to inexperience, were encountered in the working of the apparatus. The system of lubrication was defective. The insulation of the motor gave trouble and finally burnt out. This possibility, however, had been foreseen and a spare motor was quickly substituted. The worst trouble, however, occurred with the tires. With the object of minimizing the wear and tear of the cable, they had been made of a soft-natured cast iron. The load on each travelling wheel of the carriage was 7½ tons, and this heavy weight, running on the uneven surface of a cable made of six strands of hard steel wire, caused an amount of abrasion of the tread which became so serious that doubts were felt whether the apparatus would complete the work... The method of fixing the tire to the wheel-centre was so defective that several days were lost every time the tires were renewed. It was thought, however, that the wearing-out of the tire was the less of two evils: had they been more durable they might have quickly destroyed the cable. The latter, owing to its hemp core, stretched so much that it had to be shortened and re-fixed."

Bridge section being transported via the Blondin to the north bank

The cable itself weighed 5 tons, consisting of six strands of twisted steel wire, 0.125 of an inch (32 mm) in diameter, surrounding a hemp core. In turn each of the six main strands consisted of nineteen twisted steel wires, making a total of 114 individual wires. The resulting cable had a circumference of 8.5 inches (21.6 cm) and an 'ultimate breaking stress' of 270 tons (Hobson, 1907).

The Blondin itself weighed 5 tons, with a carrying a

maximum load of 10 tons and a daily capacity of eight hundred tons. The cable performed admirably but the huge load it carried eventually took its toll.

Hitching a lift on the Blondin

"Towards the end of the work thirty broken wires were discovered in the cable, which represented 13 per cent of its total strength. It was thereupon decided to reduce the loads of railway-material to 5 tons, so as to minimize the wear and stress and save the rope for the completion of the bridge. A spare rope with a steel core was meanwhile ordered of the same size and strength; and, to make assurance doubly sure, an entirely new travelling carriage was ordered as a stand-by in case of need. In the new machine all the defects discovered in the old one were remedied. The tires were made of more durable material, thicker in the tread, and the method of securing them was much improved. Wrought steel was generally substituted for cast-iron in the frames and bed-plates, thus reducing the weight from 5 to 4 tons and increasing the strength and reliability of the apparatus. The erection of the steelwork proceeded with great rapidity towards the close, and it happened that the old conveyor just managed to complete the transportation of the bridge-material before giving out, as it did, entirely...

"The cable had actually stretched about 8 feet [2.4 m], and the elongation had been due no doubt to the presence of the hemp core. The aggregate weight of permanent-way and bridge material carried by the transporter-cable was about 15,000 tons, exclusive of the weight of the travelling carriage." (Hobson, 1907)

Once installed, tested and operational the Blondin was immediately commissioned, transporting steelwork and equipment to the north bank from August 1904.

"The first call on the Blondin was of course the transport of bridge material, the heaviest sections being the lower boom members of the main arch, which were 27' 8" [8.43 m] in length, and 6½ tons in weight." (Varian, 1953)

A separate live wire stretched across the gorge carrying the electric current, which was then picked up by the machine.

Crossing the gorge by Blondin

"Occasionally, when the atmosphere was charged with electricity, the conveyor was to be seen in mid-air enveloped in a blaze of lightning." (Hobson, 1907)

From 3rd September 1904 Zeederberg advertised the sale of tickets for crossing via the Blondin.

"Victoria Falls Electric Cableway. Tickets can be obtained at Zeederberg's Coach Office, Main Street, for passage across the Famous Gorge. Return Fare, 10s." (Bulawayo Chronicle, September 1904a)

Just Hanging Around

In his book published in 1953 Varian describes his 'hands-on' experience with the Blondin. Stranded on the north bank at the end of the day, Varian hitched a lift on the Blondin which was luckily testing new running wheels.

"I waited for its arrival, and the driver offered me a lift back. This meant either hanging on to the hook of the chain sling, or sitting on the lower steel sheave of the hoisting gear. I decided to sit on the steel sheave. The driver accordingly let the gear down, and I took up position on the sharp edges of the block, the three steel ropes of the running tackle on either side of me, all thick with black

grease. It was not a pleasant sensation when the winding gear started, with three steel hawsers around me and three sheaves below, all moving at different speeds. From the driver's seat directly above it was difficult to see exactly what was going on. When the upper sheave approached my hat in very unwelcome proximity, I called out, just before my head was pushed down into my lap. The driver eased down, but could not do much to help as the hook of the chain sling had to be kept as high as possible to clear some temporary work on one of the bridge-erecting cranes. I wound my arms into the three ropes around me - now stationary - shut my eyes, and started praying hard. We left the bank, and as we passed over the crane it was so necessary to avoid, we were brought up with a jerk. The hook had fouled the crane. The praying continued, harder than ever.

"After an eternity, Heaven answered. A native appeared from nowhere on those deserted works, climbed the crane and freed the hook. With another jerk we swung out over the gorge, and began the final journey. At its end, a black and greasy mess descended from the lowering gear, thankful to be on earth again, and also thankful for having screwed up the courage to make the crossing and avoid the long journey round, even under such very trying conditions." (Varian, 1953)

Tragedy Strikes

A fatal incident occurred during the preparation of the railway cutting on the north bank, involving an elderly American traveller, Mr Samuel Alexander, from Honolulu, Hawaii, who was tragically struck by a falling rock whilst walking in the gorge below the excavations.

Hitching a lift on the Blondin

"A fatal accident occurred during the construction of the Bridge, though not directly connected with the work of erection. When the deep railway cutting on the North side was being excavated, adits [shafts] were driven through the walls on either side, and the rock was tipped through them into the Boiling Pot below

the bridge, on the one side, and into the Silent pool on the other. The danger zones were demarcated by a line of 'danger' boards and visitors were especially warned not to go beyond the end board. One day, among the numerous visitors, were an old white-haired American and his daughter. They, like most visitors, went down Palm Grove to take photos of the Boiling Pot, at the water's edge."
(Powell, 1930)

Samuel Alexander was an influential agriculturalist and industrialist in the American sugar industry. Travelling with his daughter, Annie Alexander, tragedy had already struck the small group with the death of their third travel companion and friend, Mr Thomas L Gulick, who had become ill and died in Kijabe, Kenya on 15th August.

"On Sept. 7th, Mr Alexander and his daughter were at Bulawayo, and thence rode to visit the grave of Cecil Rhodes... The air was cool and exhilarating, but Mr Alexander seemed a little depressed, and said that he felt a foreboding of disaster. In the evening, they took the [train] cars for Victoria Falls, and there arrived the following morning. In the afternoon (Sept. 8th) they walked out to take their first view of the Falls... Mr Alexander again spoke of his forebodings, and carefully informed his daughter where to find his letters of credit and the tickets for their voyage on the steamer to leave Capetown for England on Sept. 28th. The next morning, at 9.45 o'clock, they crossed by cable over the chasm of the Zambesi to obtain a better view of the Falls at the opposite shore. They observed that men were constructing a foundation for the Bridge and throwing rocks and earth into the canyon but they thought nothing of it." (Honolulu Advertiser, November 1904)

Annie Alexander recorded details of the incident during her return to Hawaii, published in the Honolulu Advertiser:

"They had just clambered over some great boulders to look up into the terminus of the waterfall, when they observed small rocks falling down the precipice, about 350 feet [106.7 m] high, directly above them. They instantly turned and ran, the daughter ahead... When they had run about 30 yards [27.4 m], and seemed to be out of danger, the daughter set up her camera while her father stood leaning against a rock six or eight feet [1.8-2.4 m] distant observing her. Something caused her to look up, and she saw a boulder, about three feet [0.9 m] thick, bounding toward her. It seemed likely to pass by at a little distance, but striking a rock it veered, and struck her father's foot, and she found him writhing on the ground." (Honolulu Advertiser, November 1904)

High above the gorge, the Blondin operator, Mr Chalmers, had witnessed the accident and blown his whistle to alert the workmen, including Powell.

"A relief party headed by the chief engineer, was hastily got together, and, with a stretcher and first aid appliances, climbed down the gorge. Half way down we met the distracted and exhausted daughter, who said her father had been killed by a falling rock. We found the old gentleman quite conscious; his right foot had been almost severed, and the leg broken above the ankle, He was a plucky old chap! He looked on while the smashed foot was cut away and the stump bandaged, muttering 'I won't get over this, I am too old.' He was carried out and taken to hospital. The leg was amputated, but he died of shock after the operation. It was a sad story... and the unfortunate daughter returned to the United States, bereft and lonely." (Powell, 1930)

Mr Alexander was buried at the Old Drift cemetery, the funeral conducted by Mr Sykes, the District Commissioner on the north bank. His gravestone is one of the handful that survive, although broken, recording: *"Samuel Thomas Alexander. Born of American Missionary Parentage in the Hawaiian Islands, October 29 1836... struck by a falling rock at Victoria Falls and died, September 10 1904."*

A short while afterwards another injury relating to the construction led to the death of an African labourer.

"The work of construction, like all great works, has commenced to exact its tale of human lives. Following the deplorable accident last month, by which Mr Alexander, a visitor from far off California, lost his life, a native got in the way of a heavily laden trolley last week, and was run over, sustaining severe injuries, to which he succumbed the next day. A Government enquiry was held by the District Commissioner in both cases, and verdicts of 'accidental death' returned. Since the accident to Mr Alexander, the Conservator of Forests has wisely decided to close the beautiful but dangerous gorge until the work of construction in its vicinity is completed." (Bulawayo Chronicle, October 1904)

Royal Visitors

Her Royal Highness Princess Helena, fifth child and third daughter of Queen Victoria, and known by her married title of Princess Christian of Schleswig-Holstein, and her daughter Princess Victoria, known as Princess Helena Victoria, were the first members of the British Royal Family to visit the Victoria Falls on 16th September 1904. The first rickshaws were sent up from Bulawayo to convey the Royal guests to and from the Falls.

"The Royal Visit to Victoria Falls. On Thursday, the 16th instant, at 10 a.m, the Royal party arrived by special train at the Victoria Falls Station. By the express desire of H.R.H. Princess Christian the visit was regarded as a strictly private one, much to the disappointment of all loyal residents on the river who were prepared to assemble and do all honour to Royalty and the occasion. This, however, was not to be, as notices were posted up at the hotel, requesting all present to forego their intention of attending at the railway platform. There was consequently no demonstration whatsoever as the Royal train streamed slowly into the station at the appointed time.

"Mr R T Corydon, Administrator of North-Western Rhodesia, Mr F W Sykes, District Commissioner at the Falls, and Mr W Tower, Resident Engineer, were at once introduced to Colonel Edwards, who, in turn, about half an hour later, presented them to Their Royal Highnesses. In the interval between this and lunch a visit was paid to the bridge site, the party proceeding thence by rail.

"On arrival there Mr W Pease, director of the Cleveland Co and Mr C G Imbault, the construction engineer of the bridge, were duly presented. The 'Blondin' motor was then placed at the disposal of the party, a number of whom, including the Princess Victoria, took advantage of the opportunity to travel across the gorge and back, thus obtaining, not only a thrilling sensation in transit, but also one of the finest views of the Falls.

"In the cool of the afternoon Messrs Sykes and Tower had the honour of conducting the Royal visitors to the Devil's Cataract, and afterwards through the Rain Forest. H.R.H. Princess Christian expressed her delight and admiration frequently on seeing the glory of the Falls from some of the best points of vantage, and herself drew attention to the fact that she was the first member of the Royal Family to visit these Falls, called after the later Queen.

"On the following day (Friday) some of the party, of which Princess Victoria was one, visited the Falls on the north bank, again using the Blondin. A trip to Livingstone Island had been contemplated and arranged, but owing to the attentions, not always playful, of a school of hippo just above the Falls, several boats having been damaged recently by them, it was considered inadvisable to run any risks and so one of the most interesting features of a visit to the Falls had to be omitted from the programme...

"At the end of the day Messrs Sykes and Tower were the proud recipients of souvenirs in silver at the hands of H.R.H. Princess Christian, together with photographs inscribed with her autograph. The Royal Party left the Victoria Falls

Station for their return to Bulawayo at 8.30 on Saturday morning." (Bulawayo Chronicle, September 1904b)

Princess Christian recorded that she was *"deeply impressed with the Victoria Falls, and that no one coming to South Africa should miss seeing them"* (British South Africa Company, 1907).

Visit of Lord and Lady Roberts

Lord and Lady Roberts, together with their two daughters, the Ladies Aileen and Edwina Roberts, visited the Falls almost immediately after the Royal Princesses. Field Marshal Lord Frederick Sleigh Roberts, Earl of Kandahar, was at the time one of the most distinguished and celebrated commanders in the British Army, having served in India, Abyssinia (Ethiopia) and Afghanistan (most notably the Battle of Kandahar in September 1880) before leading British Forces in the latter half of the Second Anglo-Boer War.

"In September 1904, the whole family, accompanied by Major Furse as A.D.C. [aide-de-camp], went on three month's tour of South Africa. They landed at Cape Town and went straight up country to see the Victoria Falls. Here they had the incomparable thrill of crossing directly over the gorge in a cage on a wire span. Roberts himself was lost for words of description, as are most who see that fabulous sight. Not so, though, Lady Roberts' old maid, who described them as 'sweetly pretty.'" (James, 1954)

Lord and Lady Roberts and their party were fascinated by the Blondin transporter, and with much anticipation undertook the journey

Lord Roberts and party embark on the Blondin

Lord Roberts and party at the Victoria Falls Hotel

across the gorge. The Director of the Cleveland Bridge Company, William Pease, was present to escort the special group, and it is recorded that once in the middle of the gorge the Blondin slowed to a stop. Mr Pease had sensed an amusing opportunity to persuade to Lord Roberts that he should visit his home town of Darlington to unveil their Anglo-Boer War Memorial - or perhaps find his own way back to *terra firma*. Lord Roberts quickly agreed to his suggestion, visiting the town in August 1905 as guest of honour for the unveiling (Lloyd, 2013).

The British South Africa Company's Directors report dated 6th November 1905 recorded:

"In commemoration of the visit of Her Royal Highness Princess Christian and Princes Victoria of Schlewig Holstein and Lord and Lady Roberts, three of the largest islands just above the Falls have been named 'Princess Christian,' 'Princess Victoria' and 'Kandahar.'" (Northern Rhodesia Journal, July 1953b)

A Sensational Story

In late September, following the visits of the Royal Party and Lord Roberts, a sensational incident was recoded in the Bulawayo Chronicle.

"News is to hand of the discovery of a plot at the Victoria Falls for blowing up, with dynamite, of the Blondin electric carrier which is being used to convey building material for the bridge across the river to the north bank. It is notorious

that there has been disaffection amongst present or former workmen engaged in the bridge construction, the contractors having had, in some cases, to take severe measures, including dismissal.

"It appears that a coloured man disclosed to the authorities the fact that he had been approached by two Europeans with a bribe of £5, for which he was to place some dynamite in position amongst the machinery at night. This communication resulted in the arrest of two men, one, at least, of whom is understood to be a foreigner. It is probable that the men will be put out of the country, as the simplest and most effective way of dealing with the case. Special precautions are being taken to prevent the execution of any such design as was intended, but further trouble of the kind is very unlikely." (Bulawayo Chronicle, September 1904c)

Details are lacking and one wonders if there was more to this than the explanation of dissatisfied workmen. A few weeks later a report on news from the Falls appeared in the Bulawayo Chronicle, by their un-named 'special correspondent,' which suggested dissatisfaction among casual labourers who had travelled to the Falls in the hope of employment.

"Rumours of an attempt to blow up the Bridge were floating about, a short time back. Whether there was any truth in them, or whether, as was more likely the case, they were based upon the drunken vapourings of some of the undesirables who thronged the place, the authorities wisely took such precautions, as will render an attempt of the kind extremely inconvenient, if not dangerous to those concerned. The measures taken by the police were distinctly vigorous and effective, including as it did the deportation of all undesirables. Some of these gentry, to whom a nod was a good as a wink, stood not upon the order of their going, but went to the north side of the river, where, in view of recent proceedings in the High Court, the authorities are, not unnaturally, reluctant to adopt such drastic measures. Those 'unemployed' amuse themselves by making periodical raids upon the various camps, and bluffing the camp boys into parting with their master's belongings. Some of them are, undoubtedly, decent working men out of employment, to whom one can extend such sympathy and help as is possible, but a good many of them are of the 'Weary Willie' type, to whom an offer of employment would come as a painful shock. It cannot be too plainly stated that in the present circumstance, it is most unwise for any working man to come to the Falls unless he has a billet to come to. Many have had a weary tramp up here 'on the chance,' to find disappointment and perhaps destitution awaiting them." (Bulawayo Chronicle, October 1904)

The Railhead Advances

With the transportation of rail equipment to the northern bank the building of the northern extension of the railway to Kalomo could begin. A report from the Falls in the Bulawayo Chronicle, dated 21st October, detailed progress.

> *"On the 25th September the first rail on the north bank was laid by Mr A L Lawley (Pauling and Co's chief representative), assisted by Messrs C V Buchan and W H Beavon, and before nightfall quite a respectable show of sidings had sprung into existence. Since then over 800 tons of railway material and plant, including the first engine, have been transported across the Gorge by means of the Blondin, and the work continues daily, with such intermissions as the exigencies of bridge construction may require."* (Bulawayo Chronicle, October 1904)

Pauling and Company quickly established a base of operation on the north bank.

> *"Pauling & Co established a depot with a small loco shed, coaling and watering facilities, and a permanent way store on the north side of the Maramba river just south of what is now Livingstone. It was the scene of much activity... and adjacent to the locomotive depot the Paulings built quarters for their staff and even had their own guest house which was used by George Pauling and his friends when on tour in what was, at the time, Northern Rhodesia."* (Rhodesia Railways Magazine, July 1967)

The Jack Tar

To move heavy materials and assist with the construction of the Bridge a light shunting engine was required on the northern bank. A small 19-ton locomotive, named the Jack Tar, was dismantled and transported in parts over the gorge by means of the Blondin cableway. The boiler and lighter parts were sent over first. The remaining section, the body frame and cylinders, weighing 12 tons, had to be transported in one piece. Varian described how the cable sagged under this load and dangled over the gulf with a fourteen metre sag in the cable. There it hung for three hours as the engine struggled to cope with the weight, until by boosting the power of the electrical plant and by other means of assistance the carrier slowly reached the other side. The driver, Mr Chalmers, sitting on his little seat with the daunting drop below him is said to have calmly smoked throughout the crossing.

> *"The full capacity of the Blondin was fifteen tons, but this load was only approached once, when the first engine was transported to the north bank to*

continue the construction ahead. The engine was first dismantled on the south bank, to be taken over piece-meal. The boiler and lighter parts went over first, and then the frame - weighing over twelve tons with cylinders attached - was tackled. The sheaves were drawn up to their fullest extent, with the frame suspended below, only just clear of the ground. Soon after the journey began, it was obvious that it was not going to be easy. Slowly the carrier reached the middle of its line over the gorge, where the sag in the cable was at its greatest. There it stopped. The dip was forty-three feet [13 m], and the Blondin was no longer overhead. We could look down on it, as the power was insufficient for it to climb the resulting grade. Preparations were made to run a block and tackle, and wind it up by winch, but that was a long job. In the meantime, extra rails were loaded on to the sling at the sheerlegs, and all possible power boosted up in the plant. After three hours, it slowly began to move again, and with every foot the grade on the sag decreased until eventually it laboriously reached the north bank. During the whole of this ordeal, the driver seemed immune from nervous strain, and sat coolly smoking on his little seat with 350 feet [106.6m] of open space below him." (Varian, 1953)

Once on the north bank the engine was re-assembled by engineer Mr Edward ('Teddy') Layton. The Jack Tar claimed two notable 'firsts' during the construction of the Bridge. Its first claim to fame was to pull the first train north of the Zambezi, over a short track built in a day. It later became the first locomotive engine to cross the Bridge, pulling two trucks from the northern bank across the temporary deck and rails back to the southern side.

"The first engine was brought over in sections, and re-erected by Mr E C Layton, of the Rhodesia Railways, in the creditably short period of 77 working hours. On the 7th [October] a mile of rails being laid, steam was got up and the first trip was made by the engine, driven by Mrs Lawley, with her on the engine being Messrs Layton (R.R.), Beavon (Pauling and Co.) and Powell (Bridge Co.). Afterwards the usual ceremony of 'christening the engine,' the engine was gone through, and it was then abandoned to its useful work of carrying the iron road farther north. The telegraph lines have been erected to the Depot (5½ miles [8.8 km] out), and the rails are expected to reach these shortly, construction being temporarily impeded by the necessity for a 100 feet [30.5 m] bridge over the Maramba River." (Bulawayo Chronicle, October 1904)

Mr William Trayner, editor and publisher of North-Western Rhodesia's first newspaper, the short-lived Livingstone Pioneer and Advertiser, recorded a more romantic version of events.

The Jack Tar

"At sunrise on the level ground above the bridge gangs of men started laying rails in a land where previously no railway existed and went on laying them all through the day, while others gave the finishing touches to a locomotive that had been brought over piece by piece, filled the boiler and lit the fire and then, towards sunset we all had a two-mile ride on a railway that hadn't existed at sun-up that same day." (Northern Rhodesia Journal, January 1963)

The Jack Tar, functionally described as a flat sided 0-6-0 'Saddle Tank' locomotive, was built in 1889 by Manning Wardle & Co of Leeds, Yorkshire and purchased by Pauling and Company in 1896. The engine was shipped to Beira and assembled at Umtali (now Mutare), where it was used on the construction of the line to Salisbury and widening of the Beira line, before being transferred to Victoria Falls in 1904.

After work on the Bridge was finished the Jack Tar returned to Beira for light shunting duties, before being transferred to Bulawayo in 1927 as a workshop shunter. The engine's small size was again an advantage as it could fit on the traverser with a 65 foot (20 m) coach, whereas all other locomotives were too long. In 1935 re-boilering was necessary with resulting changes in appearance, including a brass engine dome, and the open driver's cab was enclosed to give more protection to the driver.

In 1942 the Jack Tar was retired to Umtali for workshop light shunting duties, until finally withdrawn from service for preservation in 1953. The engine was exhibited at the Rhodes Centenary Exhibition in 1953, prior to which the original black livery was replaced with dark bottle green, lined with red, black and yellow for show purposes (Rhodesia Railways Magazine, January 1965). One loss was a little anchor previously fitted to the front of the chimney, a reference to the origins of the engine's name - a term for seamen of the Merchant or Royal Navy. The engine is now fully restored and displayed at the Bulawayo Railway Museum.

The Line North

The line north required an estimated 200 tons of rails and associated material to be transported across the gorge each day in order to advance the railway projected daily target of one mile (1.6 km). Work started in early 1905 and progressed simultaneously with the Bridge construction, with 50 miles (80.4 km) of the 94 mile (151 km) line to Kalomo completed before the Bridge was even open for construction traffic, with all the rail materials transported across the gorge via the Blondin.

Mr P St G Mansergh was again responsible for the surveying of the line (Croxton, 1982). Joining the surveying team was Mr Edwin Earnest George Hamilton Verner, who arrived in time to make an early crossing of the gorge by means of the 'bosun's chair' (Leen, personal communication, 2018).

Mr Townsend remained as Chief Resident Engineer for the Railway Company, with headquarters at Bulawayo (Varian, 1953). Varian replaced Beresford-Fox as Resident Engineer overseeing the ongoing works for the Railway Company, assisted by Mr Everard as Assistant Engineer. Varian also had specific responsibility, as Resident Engineer, for the construction of the Kafue bridge.

Varian established his camp

Railway construction

on the sand ridge which soon after became the new town of Livingstone.

"After a month on the Bridge works, I was detailed as District Engineer to go forward with the construction work that had been started to the north. I accordingly made my camp near the spot chosen by the contractors, Pauling & Co, for their depot. The rails had not yet reached the site, which was on the flat ground surrounding the present Livingstone Station. I camped on the hill just beyond the present township of Livingstone. Several months later, when the Government Surveyor came to lay out the township, I shifted down to the flat near the contractors' depot." (Varian, 1953)

Harold Pauling died suddenly soon after the railway reached the Zambezi, the cause of his death being unspecified by sources. Mr Arthur L Lawley took charge of the railway construction for the contracting company, assisted by Mr Hicks and Mr C V Buchan, who left the construction as the line neared Kalomo (Croxton, 1982).

"The progress of the construction of the 94 miles [151 km] to Kalomo was naturally slow, as all the materials after crossing the gorge either by Blondin or in light loads across the temporary line on the unfinished bridge, had then to be off-loaded, sorted, and re-loaded for transport ahead. This work, together with the re-erection of the engines and rolling stock, was done at Pauling's depot at Maramba, five miles [8 km] north of the river; so there was considerable delay, principally at the river-crossing itself, where transport could only be utilised when it did not interfere with work on the bridge." (Varian 1953)

The terrain was easy country for the track-laying gangs, the only obstacle being the Kalomo river which needed a bridge with three 100-foot (30.5 m) spans. Pauling's men laid an impressive 5¾ miles (9.25 km) of this line within a single working day (totalling eleven hours of uninterrupted track-laying).

"Pauling's workers had laid five and three quarter miles [9.25 km] of this line - in the Pemba area - in the then staggering time of eleven hours. This had arisen as the result of a conversation between Sir Charles Metcalfe, Chief Engineer on the line, and a visiting French engineer [no doubt Imbault], who had asked what length of rails could be laid in one day. 'Guess,' said Sir Charles. The Frenchman hazarded half a mile. Sir Charles spoke to the men and they set to; a quarter of a mile was laid in just 20 minutes. Spurred on by this, they continued the race for 11 hours." (White, 1973)

The then administrative capital of Kalomo was reached in May and the line from Victoria Falls opened to traffic in August 1905.

Construction Begins

The first major challenge in the construction of the Bridge was the setting of the concrete foundations for the Bridge on either side of the gorge. Owing to the problems with the depth of the foundations on the south bank a much larger quantity of cement was required than had been provided, resulting in further delays whilst extra materials were ordered and transported from England.

The preparation of the concrete settings was subcontracted by the Cleveland Bridge and Engineering Company to Giacomo D'Alberto in July 1904, with detailed specifications given on the work (Museo dell'emigrante, Roasio, 2021c).

The concrete was to be made of three parts of broken stone and two parts of sand to one of Portland Cement, to be mixed with minimum water to make the mixture 'gelatinous.' For convenience, all concrete was mixed on the south bank, and transported in batches. Any batch not placed in position within 20 minutes after mixing was discarded.

"All materials for the foundations had to be lowered from the Blondin at both ends. A steel bucket, four feet [1.2 m] in diameter and four feet deep, carried all materials such as sand, cement and water. Visiting that part of the work was another unpleasant little trip. By the time the bucket was lowered to the requisite depth, on some 150 feet [45.72 m] of single rope, it had an unsettling trick of revolving violently one way, then stopping, and revolving with equal violence in the opposite direction." (Varian, 1953)

The four huge concrete foundation blocks, which support the whole structure, were reinforced with old rails and steel rods, the contract specifying that surface layers were to be kept totally clean and free from dust and dirt as the concrete layers were built up day by day.

"The upper surface of the concrete at the conclusion of each days work to be left jagged. The reinforcing steelwork shall be thoroughly bedded in the concrete. Every precaution is to be taken to keep the upper surfaces of any layer perfectly clean and free from dust and dirt. Before proceeding with the next layer, the surface shall be thoroughly well swept, roughened, watered, and covered over with a layer of thin grout composed of one part of Portland cement and one part of sand." (Museo dell'emigrante, Roasio, 2021b).

The plans for the base pedestals specified that all steelwork used to reinforce the concrete foundation were 'not to be dipped in oil, nor painted.'

The greatest possible care was taken to make the positioning of the pedestals and base-plates exact, as it was recognised that the correct setting here would give the position and angle for the bearing pins, and therefore of the whole structure.

"On this account alone these bearings constitute a very important feature in the work; and when it is considered that their duty is also to afford the steel frame of the bridge freedom to respond to wide variations of temperature without distorting itself or causing excessive strain, their importance can hardly be exaggerated." (Hobson, 1907)

The plates were carefully adjusted by means of wedges, and when absolute accuracy of position and elevation had been attained, cement grout was forced, under pressure, through a series of pipes specially located for the purpose.

"The lower part of the concrete was reinforced with old rails, and the upper part with 2 inch [5 cm] steel rods with their ends bent for greater security. The top, for the reception of the baseplate, was strengthened with steel joists 6 inches [15.24 cm] by 45 inches [114.3 cm] by 20 lbs. [9 kg], laid transversely to the joists in the base-plate. Four bolts 3 inches [7.6 cm] in diameter were inserted in each concrete block for holding down the base-plate. In order to allow for a slight adjustment after the concrete had set, the bolts were fitted into tubes

43 inches [109.2 cm] in diameter, the intervening space, after final adjustment had taken place, being filled with cement grout under pressure. Six weeks were allowed to lapse after completion, before any great weight was placed upon it in order to ensure the setting and hardening of the concrete." (Hobson, 1907)

Work having started in May 1904, the concrete foundations for the Bridge were finally ready in October, as detailed in a report from the Falls dated 21st October.

Preparing the 'feet' of the Bridge

"The railway and bridge construction continues to make slow, but sure progress. The main pins of the Bridge are in position and the erection of the end posts commenced. In a fortnight's time, with decent luck, it is expected that the erection of the main arch will have started, and the work of erection will then proceed apace until the structure is an accomplished fact." (Bulawayo Chronicle, October 1904)

Construction of the connecting two side spans commenced in August 1904, anchored to the solid rock and supported by wooden scaffolding fixed to the slopes of the gorge, the one on the south side nearly 100 feet (30.5 m) high.

"The work of erecting the steelwork actually began in August, 1904, and the most difficult and slowest part of it proved to be the operations of fixing the shore spans and connecting them with the end posts of the main girders. The ends of the shore spans were let into recesses cut out of the rock and anchored by their upper corners. They were built out a certain distance as cantilevers, and at a further stage supported by scaffolding fixed on the slope of the cliff. As soon as the end post of the main span was up, the shore span connected with it and the anchorage coupled, a stable platform was obtained." (Hobson, 1907)

Hobson later recorded:

"The really difficult and risky part of the work of erection lay in the end spans, which now look so small as compared with the arch itself that they are scarcely noticed. But once the tall end posts of the main arch were erected, and the short spans were connected with them and the shore, thus affording a stable platform to start from, the rest was easy and rapid work. This stage was actually reached during the last days of 1904." (Hobson, 1923)

The end span and first section of the main arch

Double Fatality

On 31st October disaster struck the construction work with an accident which resulted in the death of a European and an African worker. The Bulawayo Chronicle reported:

> *"A serious accident occurred during the progress of the work on the Bridge at Victoria Falls at eleven o'clock this morning, resulting in the death of a European named Charles Friel, a workman from Anderson, near Glasgow, and that of a native boy.*
>
> *"While a gang of workmen were engaged in lifting into its position a large sections of the main post on the north side of the gorge, the holdings slipped - for some reason at present unknown - and the heavy girder, weighing several tons, fell sideways on to Friel and the native, instantly killing the latter and pinning Friel by the thighs to the cross girder. Assistance was immediately rendered, and, as soon as possible, Friel was released, when it was found that both his thighs were broken, and that he had received severe injuries to his chest.*
>
> *"Dr Sweetlove was at Livingstone, but he rode rapidly to the spot, and was in attendance within an hour of the accident. The case, however, was hopeless, and Friel died within a few minutes of the doctor's arrival. The District Commissioner opened an enquiry immediately. Friel will be buried tomorrow morning in the Livingstone Cemetery."* (Bulawayo Chronicle, November 1904)

Unable to be moved, the Mr Friel's simple last request to the doctor was *"send me down one of my pals and a bottle of whisky"* (Thornhill, 1915).

The official enquiry returned verdicts of accidental death in both cases.

> *"An official enquiry has been held into the circumstances of the recent accident at the Victoria Falls, which, as already reported by the special correspondent of the Bulawayo Chronicle, resulted in the death of Charles Friel, European, and Chunega, a native. The following verdict and rider have been returned, and agreed to by the British Resident:- 'Death in both cases was caused by the accidental breaking of part of a crane, but as to the causes of the breakage there is no direct evidence.' The District Commissioner at the Falls added:- 'I desire, however, to add the following: I recommend that, having regard to the evidence at the inquest (1) further precaution should be taken to insure that no unnecessary addition should be made to the legitimate strain the crane is*

required to carry; (2) some arrangement to be made to prevent the 'surging' referred to, and (3) if possible, some mechanical contrivance to be adopted to indicate to the crane driver at any time the weight his is controlling.'

"Amongst the evidence taken at the inquest was that of John Borough, foreman in charge of the ironwork on the north bank, who said that at noon on October 31st the electric crane was lowering a piece of steel, weighing over five tons, and 20 feet [6 m] in length, being part of the main post on the land span. When the piece was nearly in place the main wheel of the crane broke in two and fell into the gorge. As the steel column fell he saw it pin down the European and the native.

"E D Piele, the crane driver, deposed that the post was almost in position when he was asked to raise it an inch. The wheel, in breaking, struck him on the head, rending him unconscious and preventing him applying the brake.

"The evidence of Mr G C Imbault, engineer in charge, who did not witness the accident, was that the piece of steel had been partly fixed when an order was given to raise it slightly. The crane driver would not known the steel was not free. On this account the crane developed greater power than it was intended for, which led to its breaking.

Work progresses

"J W Chatterton, inspector of bridge work, expressed the opinion that the cranes in use were too light. He had from time to time recorded breakages in them, and considered that they had a bad record. A J Evered gave similar evidence. Several witnesses spoke as to a certain 'surging' in lowering weights, due to the rope not having being would tightly on the drum of the crane. This, by a series of jerks, would put undue strain upon the machine." (Bulawayo Chronicle, December 1904a)

The accident delayed construction on the north bank for several weeks. A report from the Falls, dated 1st December, appeared in the Bulawayo Chronicle:

"The construction of the bridge on the north side was thrown back several weeks by the accident, the fallen girder and other pieces of the steelwork having to be taken out and re-straightened. On the south side the land span is completed and the first bay of the main arch is nearing completion. On the North side the land span is finished and a start is about to be made on the main arch." (Bulawayo Chronicle, December 1904b)

Developments at the Depot

The Bulawayo Chronicle's report from their special correspondent, dated 1st December, also included updates on developments at 'the Depot,' Pauling's base of operations on the north bank.

"The Maramba bridge was finished on the 29th and the work of 'linking-in' to the depot is now proceeding and will probably be completed before these notes are published. The Depot (Pauling & Co's base Camp) is growing daily. Situated on a grass-grown plain, at the foot of the sand-belt, this second 'Raylton' promises to expand into a centre of trade activity in the near future. Already numbers of houses, for the officials, have been erected, and most, if not all, of the Bulawayo houses doing business in North-Western Rhodesia, have opened branches...

"There are to be high-jinks at the depot on Boxing Day and the day following. Quite a creditable programme of sports has been drawn up, including one day's horse racing (December 26th) and flat races and athletic sports on the second day... A race course, eight furlongs in length, has been prepared and a paddock and enclosures are being erected. Two tennis courts, a croquet lawn, a cricket pitch and a fair sized recreation ground are being laid out, and refrigerator and electric light plants are under contemplation or in course of erection. Altogether it looks as if 'The Depot!' has come to stay." (Bulawayo Chronicle, December 1904b)

Christmas Festivities

Christmas at the Falls in 1904 would have seen a significantly different scene to the one the previous year, with the railway now at the Falls and the Hotel six month's old. Construction of the Falls Bridge was well underway, the gorge connected by means of telegraph and transporter system, with electric conveyor, and a large number of European engineers and railwaymen based both sides of the Falls.

"That tourists are now making their way to this spot in Central Africa to see for themselves the eighth wonder of the world, as the Victoria Falls have been rightly termed, is made clear after a chat with the present hotel proprietor. Last Christmas there were considerably over a hundred persons staying at the hotel, many of whom had to sleep in tents and temporary annexes, so crowded was the building itself." (Scientific American Magazine, July1905)

To entertain the crowds a Christmas sports day was held, with live music provided by a band from Bulawayo and a lunchtime picnic under the shade of Palm Grove. Sport events included tug-o-war, a walking race, the very popular 'bun and treacle race' - which involved the eating of a series of buns, made by local Livingstone bakers Smith & James, covered in treacle and hung on strings - and 'tilting the bucket,' a popular challenge involving a wheelbarrow, spear, target and precariously suspended bucket of water (Shepherd, 2013). Clark was again present on the scene:

"The tilter rode in a wheel-barrow and was provided with an assagai which he had to get through a hole in a board under a bucket of water. If he missed the hole and hit the board, of course, the bucket swung round and he was drenched." (Clark, 1936)

Tilting the bucket

Erection of the Main Arch

Once the end posts and side spans were erected, in late 1904, construction of the main arch progressed quickly. In order to support the steelwork arms as they stretched out over the gorge a system of steel wire cables was used, anchored through tunnels cut into the rock on either side of the gorge. Two bore-holes were sunk back from the edge on each bank, 30 feet (9.1 m) deep and 30 feet apart, and joined underground by boring a connecting tunnel through the rock. Wire ropes suspending the weight of each half of the Bridge were passed down one hole, along the connecting passage, and out through the other hole, so that the weight was sustained by this solid mass of surrounding rock. To make assurance doubly sure, a weight of 500 tons of rails was piled also on the top of the rock. These cables, another of Imbault's ingenious innovations, supported the half arches as they reached out to each other across the gap. Adjusting the relative tensions allowed precise control and adjustment of the half-arches as they were erected. Hobson expands:

> *"The contractors' engineer* [Imbault]*... devised a system in which comparatively small wire-ropes, easily carried and handled, played the most prominent part. A high quality of steel was used, and each rope was 1 13/32 inch* [3.57 cm] *in diameter, spirally laid, 91 ply, and had a breaking stress of 130 tons. Each end of every rope was fitted with an ordinary screw-adjustment, proportionate to its size and strength. The total load to be borne being known, it was only a question of how many ropes would be required and how much of the solid rock in the adjoining ground behind the bridge it was necessary to lay hold of."* (Hobson, 1907)

Imbault's construction apparatus and cranes

Travelling along the cross girders of the two incomplete half-arches were two mechanical cranes, custom designed by Imbault for the purpose. The crane-arms, each commanding a radius of 30 feet (9.14 m), were able to revolve in an arc of nearly 180 degrees in order to lift and lower all of the steel sections into position. Capable of carrying 10 tons they were designed to be moved forward as each panel or bay of 25 feet (7.62 m) was completed.

Hobson describes the process of erecting the main arch:

Work progresses from both sides of the gorge

"To facilitate erection and secure accuracy in alignment, a turned steel pin was inserted at the point of intersection of each vertical and diagonal member with the top chord and arched rib... This system proved advantageous in every respect. Time in erection was saved and, once the pin was in its place, confidence in the accuracy of the work so far done was at once established. Reinforcement of the pin by rivets or service bolts was a matter that could be attended to when all the members constituting one panel were in place, and it was not necessary to wait for the insertion of all the rivets in one particular panel before proceeding...

"The first panels, being the largest and containing the most material, naturally occupied the longest time, 2 to 3 weeks; but this was gradually reduced until at the centre, eight posts and their fellow members were placed in position in 26 days, the work, of course, being done simultaneously from both sides of the river, so that each panel occupied 6 days in erection; and this rapidity was attained in spite of delay caused by the delivery of the material failing to keep pace with the progress of the erection... which constitutes fair testimony not only to the efficiency of the design, but also to the precision achieved in the workmanship." (Hobson, 1907)

Construction proceeded rapidly, section by section, with the two cantilever arms growing out toward each other across the chasm.

"It was estimated that when the two halves of the bridge were on the point of meeting in the centre, there would be a pull of 400 tons on each of the four corners, and as the bridge was built out towards the centre additional ropes were added to withstand the increased stress." (The Engineer, April 1905)

Hobson acknowledged the Cleveland Bridge Company, and specifically Imbault, for rising to the challenge of erecting the structure:

"The Cleveland Company... deserve credit for their skill in devising a simple, economical apparatus for the erection of the bridge. This is due to the ingenuity of their engineer, Mr G C Imbault, whose special knowledge, amongst his other qualifications, of the use and manipulation of wire ropes stood him in good stead in the present instance, and at the same time raised the reputation of this firm to the front rank." (Hobson, 1923)

A safety-net - to catch, as the contractors put it, 'boys and tools, should they inadvertently drop during construction' - was hung beneath the Bridge, stretched tight across the gorge and set as close up to the base of the arch as possible, about 90 metres above the water. It apparently made the workmen dizzy and even more nervous of the great height! Fortunately the net was never called into use other than to catch tools, of which there was a small collection when work finished.

The view from below

"To give confidence to the workmen, a huge net was slung under the points where building was in progress. Fortunately it had to catch nothing heavier than bolts and tools, and eventually it was removed, as the men complained that, instead of making them feel more secure, the sight of it caused nervousness." (Williams, 1909)

One author, who visited the Bridge at the end of 1905, recorded a heart-stopping moment:

"While the Bridge was being built, the cantilevers were held up by stout wire hawsers. One day the north cantilever suddenly slipped. Everyone dropped their tools and raced for the shore. They had about 60 yards [55 m] to run. The engineer stood with his arms folded and shouted, 'Don't run; if the bridge is going, it will go before you can reach the bank!' The tip of the cantilever stopped after falling about 10 feet [3 m], the hawsers having adjusted themselves." (Thornhill, 1915)

Connecting the Bridge

The building of the Bridge progressed rapidly and by the end of March 1905 the lower boom of the main arch was close to completion.

"Progress became more rapid as the cantilevers advanced, and the amount of steelwork in each panel - that is, section of bridge between two upright posts- diminished. The last eight panels at the centre of the arch (out of twenty-six in all) were put together in twenty-six days, and on April 1, 1905 - less than six months from the start - the great 3 foot [91.5 cm] square booms of the arc were joined. The rapidity of the work bears witness to the efficiency of the workmen and the designer, and to the precision with which the parts of the steelwork had been made." (Williams, 1909)

At that time of year the spray from the Falls is at its greatest intensity and it caused great discomfort to everyone employed on the works, particularly those on the southern approach.

"Although it had been the aim of the engineers to... [build the Bridge] in the dry months of the year 1904, and thus avoid the climatic period fraught with risk to the health of fresh blooded Europeans, it is interesting to note that, owing to various delays, the work was done in the following rainy season and that no serious harm ensued. The rains begin in October and end in May. The worst

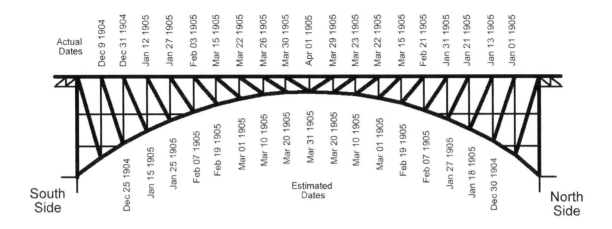

Actual Dates (top, left to right): Dec 9 1904, Dec 31 1904, Jan 12 1905, Jan 27 1905, Feb 03 1905, Mar 15 1905, Mar 22 1905, Mar 26 1905, Mar 30 1905, Apr 01 1905, Mar 29 1905, Mar 23 1905, Mar 22 1905, Mar 15 1905, Feb 21 1905, Jan 31 1905, Jan 21 1905, Jan 13 1905, Jan 01 1905

Estimated Dates (bottom, left to right): Dec 25 1904, Jan 15 1905, Jan 25 1905, Feb 07 1905, Feb 19 1905, Mar 01 1905, Mar 10 1905, Mar 20 1905, Mar 31 1905, Mar 20 1905, Mar 10 1905, Mar 01 1905, Feb 19 1905, Feb 07 1905, Jan 27 1905, Jan 18 1905, Dec 30 1904

South Side ... North Side

Construction progress against estimated completion dates for the Bridge

rainy months are March and April. In addition to rain the bridge is wetted by the spray from the Falls, which is, of course, influenced by the height of the columns of spray, which in the rainy season rise to 3,000 feet [914 m], and also by the direction of the wind. The spray is heaviest in the months of March, April, and May... The two centre panels of the arch were fixed about sunset on the 31st March, 4 months after the end posts had been erected, and it was found that the panels overlapped to the extent of about 1¼ inch [3.2 cm]. The steel truss had been exposed the whole of the day to the heat of the tropical sun and had elongated." (Hobson, 1907)

The engineers gathered early the following morning in great anticipation. Imbault's calculations had been so precise that he had allowed for the cooling effect of the spray on the expansion of the girders. Varian again described the scene:

"All were assembled at dawn. Connecting plates were in position, and on each side of the lower booms men stood by with drifts and service bolts ready to catch the rivet holes as they coincided and came into position. For some unaccountable reason on that morning and at that hour, the wind changed. The usual spray failed to fall on the bridge, with the consequence that the steelwork was dry and ready to absorb the heat, which might spoil the chance of a junction being effected that day."

Fortunately, the concerns of the workmen were unwarranted and the two great steel semi-arches were perfectly joined at 6 o'clock (local time) on the morning of the 1st April 1905.

"The sun rose, and started to warm one side of the steelwork, which

immediately began to expand, while the gap closed perceptibly from the expansion, the warm side faster than the cooler one. There was an anxious few minutes as we wondered whether the action of the winches on the steel cables would be in time to sway the whole body of the steelwork into the direct alignment before the fast-closing gap could forestall it. Then, slowly, with the action of expansion closing, and the winches swinging the joint laterally, they coincided to make a perfect butt joint. As soon as the rivet holes of the cover plate, some four feet [1.22 m] square, and those of the boom coincided, drifts were immediately driven and service bolts made the joint fast, very much to the relief of all concerned." (Varian, 1953)

Connecting the lower boom

There were then further anxious moments as everyone watched to see if the tension of the structure at the critical moment when the hinged bearings took the strain had been accurately calculated.

The Bulawayo Chronicle's special correspondent at the Falls, in a report dated Friday 1st April, recorded those present.

"The two halves of the Victoria Falls Bridge were successfully linked together at six o'clock this morning, in the presence of Sir Charles Metcalfe and Messrs W Tower (Resident Engineer), G C Imbault (Chief Construction Engineers), A L Lawley (Pauling and Co), F W Sykes (District Commissioner), T U Lapham (Controller of Posts and Telegraphs), F V Worthington (Secretary for Native Affairs) and other representatives of the Government and the Cleveland Bridge Company. The last pieces went into position without trouble." (Bulawayo Chronicle, April 1905)

The View from the Hotel

The Bulawayo Chronicle's correspondent, resident on the north bank, travelled over to the Falls Hotel the following day for news of the event.

"There I found Sir Charles Metcalfe, watching operations on the Bridge a mile away. From where we stood it could be seen that the arch supporting the road was complete , but that there was still a gap of several feet to be linked in. Sir Charles said it had been a very anxious time for them, but that their measurements had proved to be accurate...

"Mr Rhodes, he thought, would have been delighted with the Bridge. He would probably have made the Falls his permanent residence; he could picture him gazing there for hours, dreaming and pondering over that symbol of progress. He, Sir Charles, was thinking of cutting two medallions in the rock, one on each side of the Bridge, to Dr Livingstone and Mr Rhodes. He thought it was what Mr Rhodes would have liked.

"Turning to more practical matters, he informed me that he was considering a project to electrify the line from the Bridge to the new township so as to run a service of trolley cars. Questioned as to a few details, he thought an hourly service could be arranged and he did not see why it should interfere in the least with the regular traffic.

The Bridge connected

"He spoke most optimistically of the boating business he estimated would be done on the river, and referred in general terms to several schemes which were maturing for the better accommodation, entertainment and amusement of the number of visitors he expected would visit the Falls in the near future...

"He was glad to note that the mischievous rumours circulated some time ago about the health of the district were discredited and disproved. The locality, he continued, was as healthy and salubrious as any in South Africa, and he looked forward to the time when visitors would stay as many months as they now did days. The place only wanted advertising. He instanced an amusing experience of a lady who had never even heard of the Victoria Falls.

"There was nothing in the way of a ceremony, and very few visitors. Work was proceeding rapidly, and great rivalry existed between the gangs engaged on the two sections. Workmen had already crossed from one side to the other on the booms.

"Subsequently I visited the Bridge. It is crowded with workmen and machinery, and seen near by is of most imposing proportions. At present it is painted bright red, but when finished it will be repainted a light peach grey, a shade which will harmonise with the surroundings." (Bulawayo Chronicle, April 1905)

A Great British Enterprise

From his base at the Victoria Falls Hotel, Sir Charles Metcalfe conveyed the news of the connecting of the arch to the Chartered Company in London, who announced the news to the waiting world.

"The British South Africa Company on Saturday, received a cablegram from Sir Charles Metcalfe, their consulting engineer now on the Zambesi, announcing that the bottom booms of the Victoria Falls Railway Bridge were bolted up at seven o'clock on Saturday morning. The news conveyed in the telegram, when reduced to less technical language, implies that the two ends of the famous bridge over the Zambesi, each of which from the necessities of the case, has been projected gradually from either cliff across the gorge, have now been safely joined."

The Chartered Company similarly replied to Sir Charles by telegram:

"President and Directors of the British South Africa Company congratulate most heartily you and your staff and the contractors upon the linking up of the spans

of the Victoria Falls Bridge, marking another stage in the successful prosecution of a great British enterprise."

The Bulawayo Chronicle reported the great significance of the event:

"The junction this week of the two arms of the great steel arched Bridge which spans the Zambesi gorge... [is] evidence not only of British colonising enterprise, but of the skill and pluck of the British engineers, alike in design and construction. We have thus seen what was a generation ago an unexplored region subjected to the commercial and civilising influences of the railway engineer; and as the gorge spanned by the Bridge was one - perhaps the greatest - obstacle to that great scheme of Cecil Rhodes for opening up Africa by a railway from the Cape to Cairo, the close of the steel-work is an event of far reaching importance." (Bulawayo Chronicle, May 1905a)

In period news reports it was recorded that the official opening of the Bridge would be held in the first week of July.

"As we have already stated... arrangements have been made to open the new railway over the great Bridge in the first week of July, and the Duke of Abercorn will perform the opening ceremony. The members of the British Association who are to attend the meetings in South Africa in August will thus be able to cross the bridge by rail. It is an interesting fact that months ago the engineers fixed Monday last for the joining up of the bridge, or 48 hours later than the work was actually completed." (South Africa Magazine, April 1905)

In the event delays to the final construction phase would result in the official opening being delayed until the visit of the British Association in September 1905.

All Present and Correct

Powell recounts an obviously eventful evening of celebrations:

"It has been stated that when the two halves of the bridge were linked together, the men were given a holiday, and as most of them would have gravitated to the hotel to celebrate the occasion, they were told that the transporter would start from the south bank promptly at six o'clock [p.m.], to bring them over to their quarters. In the evening the time keeper reported that ten of the men failed to turn up, and were still at the Hotel. He was instructed to ascertain their names and hand them in next morning. At the starting time next morning they were all present and correct, on the north bank. After doing themselves well at the

Hotel, they were turned out at closing time. At eleven o'clock at night, in deep darkness, they climbed over the newly placed girder, 20 inches [50 cm] in width, over the centre of the gorge, and climbed out on the other side, and so to bed. It is difficult to legislate for the adventurous." (Powell, 1930)

Powell's account is supported by a letter published by Northern Rhodesia Journal in July 1963, from Mr William Trayner, resident of the Old Drift and editor of the Livingstone Pioneer and Advertiser. Mr Trayner had found himself celebrating with the Bridge workers at the Hotel that evening - and as a result of which claimed to have been the first member of the public, other than the Bridge builders themselves, to cross the completed archway.

"I was present on the morning of 1st April 1904 when the centre piece of the Bridge was dropped into place and had the honour of conveying the news to Livingstone, having kept a canoe at the Maramba overnight for that purpose... Records are easy if you happen to be on the right spot at the right time. On the afternoon of that 1st April I was back in the Cleveland Camp delivering a 'case' that had been ordered and was given an invitation to that night's 'bust' at the Falls Hotel...

"The 'bust' was equal to the occasion and went on into the small hours. We got an hour or two's sleep in the grass outside the rain forest and then on to the brig,' as those north countrymen called it. All were sober now and they turned to me saying: 'We are the brig' workers, we don't count, you're a Rhodesian, you go first and so have the record of being the first man over.' I went and walked upright across the centre girder as they commanded and was cheered when I got across." (Northern Rhodesia Journal, January 1963)

With the primary task of erecting the main arch of the Bridge complete, many of the Cleveland Bridge engineers took their leave to return home, with only a handful remaining to finish work on the top deck of the structure. Charlie Beech was replaced by Howard Longbottom as Bridge foreman, taking over the role for the rather daunting task of the final fixed-riveting of the whole structure.

Trayner's Rag

Mr William Trayner became, by chance rather than calculation, the publisher of the first official newspaper in North-Western Rhodesia. Mr Trayner was employed by 'Mopane' Clarke to operate the boat crossing, and as such undertook regular trips to the south bank, where he would hear news of the wider world from railway and Hotel staff. During 1905 Trayner started providing hand-written news updates for the Old Drift residents, with gossip and information from around the settlement and a scattering of news gathered from visiting travellers, leading to the rather informal evolution of an official newspaper.

"By popular request he prepared hand-written news-sheets which were passed from hand to hand or pasted up in one of the bars. These impromptu 'newspapers' had varying headings, examples being 'Trayner's Rag' or 'The Livingstone Liar.' No copies are known to survive." (Phillipson, 1990)

Demand for news from the 'home country' no doubt grew with the arrival of the construction engineers.

"It was a gradual growth without any intention on my part of starting a paper. I was given the job of running the Drift (the River Crossing). To those living in the camp on the north bank in utter isolation, the southern bank was the outside world and as I was over there and at the Falls many times a day, I was regarded as a source of news when I rolled up at the bar [on the north bank] *of an evening. In the very early days news was a bit scarce and had to be 'made-up' about crocs and the hippo we had seen or the lion spoor close to the drift."* (Northern Rhodesia Journal, July 1964)

These informal notes became typewritten with the donation of a typewriter, and more by accident than design the first 'official' newspaper was born.

"The Administration asked Trayner to register his paper and to issue it at regular intervals with a fixed title, so that it could be used for the publication of official Administration notices. The name Livingstone Pioneer and Advertiser was suggested and agreed upon and the paper appeared at regular weekly intervals, with interruptions due to the indisposition of the editor/proprietor, from 13th January to 29th September 1906." (Phillipson, 1990)

In March 1906 Leopold Moore (later Sir Leopold) founded the weekly Livingstone Mail in direct competition to the Pioneer. When Moore initially arrived on the north bank he took over the vacant role of chemist in the new town of Livingstone. Dr Findlay, the previous pharmacist, 'had wandered into the veld in a fit of malarial coma and been found dead some days later.'

Six months after Moore launched the Livingstone Mail, Trayner published the last issue of the Livingstone Pioneer and Advertiser. Moore produced the Livingstone Mail to high professional standards and the newspaper ran for over sixty years.

Within Reach of the World

By 1905 the Falls were being promoted as a global tourism attraction, one publication boldly declaring:

"The average man in the street has hardly yet realised that the Victoria Falls are within reach of anybody having a couple of months to spare... There are two routes to the Falls. One, the most direct and quickest, is via Cape Town and the Rhodesia Railways. The other is via Beira and the Mashonaland Railways. The first-class fares to Bulawayo are much the same by either, being a trifle over £40. The second route makes the railway journey shorter, and both methods of getting to Salisbury and Bulawayo have equal claims to recognition. The tourist can leave London on any Saturday, join the Union-Castle Company's mail steamer at Southampton, and reach Cape Town in a little over 16 days, and be in Bulawayo on the 21st day out from England. A train-de-luxe carrying first and second class passengers and the oversea mails leaves Cape Town every Wednesday, reaching Bulawayo on the following Saturday morning, the journey taking a little under three days. In addition to the train-de-luxe, there is an ordinary through service twice a week between Cape Town and Bulawayo."
(South Africa Handbook No.32, 1905)

The Union Castle Mail Steamship Company, official mail carrier from the United Kingdom to the Cape Colony in South Africa, was intrinsically linked with the early development of the Rhodesias. The Company sailed from Southampton every Saturday, taking 17 days to reach the Cape. From there it took three days by train to Bulawayo and a further 22 hours to reach the Falls. It was not uncommon for passengers to travel this great distance only to stay a few nights at the Falls Hotel and then start their return journey.

The Union Castle Line RMS Saxon

A 'Fait Accompli'

George Hutchinson, writing in early 1905, reflected on the growing developments at the Falls following a visit, in the company of Frank Rhodes, the previous year:

"It may be that with the advent of railways and hotels this element of romance will disappear, but at present it still survives. The Victoria Falls are now the meeting-place of civilisation and the desert, and this gives a certain charm to the everyday life there.

"At first sight it seems to be almost too 'civilised' - the new Hotel, the Canadian canoes, the crowds of camera-laden visitors, or the scene of bustle and activity at the railway station and the Bridge head, all appear singularly out of place; indeed the Victoria Falls have been described by one who knew them in the old days as 'a mass of water surrounded by tourists.' But in the rainy season it is very different, for the only inhabitants then are a few officials, and enterprising traders, content to endure the feverish climate of the Zambesi valley...

"It is of course inevitable that the great power known as 'Civilisation' should soon extend her realm beyond the Zambesi, and it is now clear that she will set her mark upon the Falls themselves, for already there is a Hotel, a railway station, cuttings and embankments, and watering-places in close proximity, and it has been necessary to surround the 'Rain Forest' with a wire fence. Within a year it is said that the passengers by the Cape to Cairo railway will cross by the new bridge, less than two hundred yards [183 m] distant from the Boiling Pot, with the spray beating on their faces, and the roar of the waters in their ears.

"It is the Bridge that is regarded as mainly responsible for all this, for when the present site was chosen it meant not only that the Falls should be accessible, but that all the accompaniments of civilisation should be deposited at their very edge. During the past year the choice of the site has been much criticised upon these grounds, but now that the Bridge is more or less a fait accompli further discussion is useless. It has, however, served to open the wider question of what is to be the future of the Falls.

"It is of course within the bounds of possibility that they should simply be 'exploited' as one of the commercial assets of the country; indeed, one argument used in favour of the bridge was that it would give to visitors in the future a view of the Falls which was previously unobtainable. And if this attitude is taken their fate is sealed." (Hutchinson, 1905)

Steelwork Completed

With the lower arch now connected work progressed to fix the upper chord in place and complete the steelwork structure. As the horizontal chord neared completion two hydraulic jacks were inserted into the small gaps between either arm of the arch, exerting between them a permanent pressure of 500 tons outwards, thus forcing the gap open and placing the entire Bridge under the required tension for the final sections to the fitted. The joints were quickly pinned and the jacks removed. Hobson described the technical details of the process:

> *"In order, therefore, to secure the proper distribution of stress in all members due to the complete structure, it was necessary to impart the correct stress to this member artificially. With this object, hydraulic jacks were inserted in recesses prepared in the top chord adjacent to the gap, and the ends of the top chord were forced asunder until the required stress was imparted, regard being had to the temperature at the moment. Packings were afterwards specially made to fill the gap exactly. Joint covers were then added, the rivet-holes at one end of each chord being drilled on the spot."* (Hobson, 1907)

Mr Chalmers, the Blondin operator, is believed to have had the honour of fitting the last pins and connecting the structure.

The upper deck of the Bridge was completed in June 1905, and a temporary track was immediately laid over the open steelwork suitable for light traffic, and alongside was laid a footway eight feet (2.44 m) in width made of loose timbers laid on the open steelwork, leaving the rest open to the gorge below. It was claimed that the first creature to cross the completed Bridge was a leopard.

The Financier (22nd July 1905) declared the connection of the Bridge *"one of the greatest engineering marvels of modern*

Connecting the upper boom

times and a most important link in the Cape to Cairo Railway."

Tiffin's Tale

In late 1950 the Bulawayo Chronicle printed the story of Mr Reid-Rowland, who was Chief Clerk of the Railway Company at the time of the Bridge construction, submitted in a letter from Mr J Tiffin.

"Just after the sleepers and rails had been laid on the bare top of the bridge, an old friend of mine, Mr Reid Rowland, who was chief clerk [of the Railway Company] at the head office, Bulawayo, came up to inspect the books of the Falls Hotel. The Hotel at that time was built of old corrugated iron, collected mainly from old dismantled engine sheds along the line, and was managed by a Mr Gavuzzi, an Italian, who was a good man at his job... I suggested a trip to Pauling's depot at the new Livingstone, which was just starting up: it was a sand belt in those days, where a post office and a District Commissioner's house had been erected. It was too risky to cross the Bridge as there was only planking at the end of the sleepers facing the Falls and no railings to prevent you from falling off the end of the sleepers, so I took him about two miles up the river, to where I had a rowing boat, and rowed him to the mouth of the Maramba River, where we landed and proceeded on foot for about three miles."

The two men explored the north bank, but were delayed on their return to the river. Reaching the Bridge in complete darkness they had a slight dilemma.

"I suggested that he should hold on to my coat and we should cross the planks at the end of the sleepers. Fortunately I have exceptional eyesight in the dark, and it was a very dark night indeed, when we started on that nightmare journey... We just shuffled along, Rowland hanging on to the back of my jacket, until, much to our relief, we came to the end of the bridge...

"Next morning I took Rowland to see the Bridge. Up to that time he had not had a sight of it. When we got there he stopped dead and turned pale and said, 'Do you mean to tell me that you brought me here over those planks?' I said, 'What of it? I got you safely across, didn't I?' I draw a veil on the language he used for the next ten minutes. However, he got over it and eventually looked upon the incident as a great adventure." (Bulawayo Chronicle, November 1950)

Mr Tiffin appears to have been involved in the construction of the Bridge, describing crossing the gorge via a *"wire rope attached to trees at both sides"* and *"with the Blondin... on top of a bundle of steel sleepers and on half a dozen railway rails picked up by the Blondin's long sling."*

First Train to Cross

The first engine to cross was the Jack Tar, crossing from the northern side where it had been shunting railway material transported over the gorge by the Blondin. In order to test the structure, Imbault had the two trucks fully loaded.

"Mr Imbault, the engineer in charge of the work, ordered the construction train to be loaded to its full capacity, and instructed the engine-driver to take the train over the Bridge at top speed. The driver hesitated, when Mr Imbault said, 'All right; get off the engine, and I'll do it.' The driver thereupon replied, 'No, sir! if you're game to do it I can do it' and getting up steam dashed over the bridge with his trainload of ballast, the whole structure swaying under the weight, whilst the engineer (Mr Imbault) excitedly shouted, 'Shake, you beauty... shake, you beauty,' meaning the Bridge, which he did not want to see too rigid." (Prahran Telegraph, July 1906)

Materials were now shunted over the Bridge overnight by the Jack Tar, two trucks at a time, starting in the evening as soon as the Bridge workers had finished work for the day. On one occasion when working trucks over the Bridge late one night its side rods killed a leopard crouching on the walkway beside the track. Perhaps injured or ill, or without space to run from this unfamiliar machine, the animal refused to flee and its skull was crushed by the advancing engine. It is thought that this was the same leopard which had previously claimed the title of first animal to cross the completed Bridge.

The Jack Tar working on the Bridge

Spreading the News

Sir Charles Metcalfe sent news of the connection of the Bridge to press outlets across the English speaking world, from London to Auckland. In May Sir Charles and Mr Hobson were interviewed by a correspondent of the London 'Daily News.'

"Among politicians, financiers, engineers, and travellers there was keen competition for the privilege of a few words with Sir Charles. I was so fortunate, however as to monopolise a little of his time. 'But,' he laughed, 'nothing in the way of a formal interview, if you please.'

"'You will say,' I pleaded, 'just one word about the famous Bridge?'

"'It has been 'built,' said Sir Charles, 'in record time, with record accuracy, and, I should think, at record cost...'

"'What do you think of the Falls?'

"'There is nothing like them in the world. You cannot describe them they must be seen.'

"'Does the Bridge mar the view?'

"'Not in the least. If you are in the Rain Forest, or looking at the Falls from their immediate vicinity, you are not conscious of the presence of the Bridge. Indeed, it is difficult to see the Falls and the Bridge at the same time...'

"From the engineer who has built the Bridge, I turned to Mr G. A Hobson, who designed it. 'Is it actually finished?' I asked him.

"'Practically, and to all appearance,' he replied, 'but 80,000 rivets have still to be put in.'

"'Was the site a difficult one?'

"'Difficult! It was an ideal site. What harder rock could you have than basalt? There was no element of chance or uncertainty about the building of that Bridge. There it is and nothing can harm it.'

"'An earthquake?'

"'Yes, perhaps an earthquake might, but nothing else, I fancy...'

"'And how long will it last?'

"'If proper care is taken it will last a century or so. If proper care is not taken, it won't...'

"'How many engineering records has the Bridge broken?'

"'I will tell you one,' laughed Mr Hobson, 'that it hasn't broken. An American journalist came to me and asked if it wasn't the largest Bridge in the world. Of course; it is very far from being that. One of the most interesting phases of the work was the initial one of getting the material across. For half the Bridge was built out from either side. I think you can speak of our cableway as a record one. A stout steel cable, 870 feet [265.2 m] long, was drawn across the ravine, being fixed to a steel tower on either side. A carriage, driven by electricity... carried across the sections of half the Bridge, as well as rolling stock, and all the material for fifty miles [80.5 km] of railway.'" (London Daily News, 1905)

Stamp of Approval

To celebrate the construction of the Bridge, the British South Africa Company issued a special set of postage stamps on 13th July 1905 showing the Falls, but strangely not the Bridge, or even the Bridge site. The image shows the Main Falls as viewed from the Rain Forest, and was based on one of Percy Clark's photographs. The release had been timed to coincide with the planned official opening of the Bridge, but the opening had by then already been delayed until September.

Accidents and Incidents

Contrary to many beliefs, especially among the local people, that many lost their lives during the construction of the Bridge, contemporary records from the Railway Company show that there were only two deaths directly attributed to the construction work, that of Mr Friel and an un-named African at the end of October 1904. Three other deaths also occurred, although not directly related to the construction, the first being that of Mr Samuel Alexander during the preparations for the rail cuttings, followed soon after by the death of the African labourer run over by a loaded trolley.

Powell describes the third fatality, involving a painter, again un-named, who fell

View from under the Bridge

from the Bridge. Although he survived the fall, he died three months later from his injuries.

"When the Bridge was nearing completion a large squad of men were painting the steel work. Each was suspended in a 'boatswain's chair' like sailors painting the side of a ship. Up above, the decking of the Bridge was being put down. A baulk of 12 inch by 12 inch [30.5 by 30.5 cm] timber was dislodged, fell through the bridge and knocked one of the painters, an Italian, out of his chair, to fall into a pool of mud near the foundations, 89 feet [27.1 m] below. Two Catholic Fathers were lunching with the chief engineer when the accident was reported by telephone. One gallant old padre raced down to the Bridge on the chief's horse, to give the last unction to a dying man. When he was lowered down in a bucket he found the man sitting up and complaining of 'a pain in the head.' The man was taken to hospital and was discharged a month later but died three months after the accident from the injury to his head." (Powell, 1930)

Hobson was keen to emphasise that no fatalities from fever or sickness occurred during the construction of the Bridge. It was also acknowledged, however, that *"many of the white men... suffered from malaria,"* and that *"some had even been invalided home"* (Rhodesia Railways Magazine, August 1955).

In May 1905 the Bulawayo Chronicle reported on the first session of the Livingstone High Court, and the case of an African labourer who had been injured in the construction.

"The High Court of North Western Rhodesia sat at Livingstone on Thursday the 18th for the first time. His Honour presided, assisted by Mr H Rangely, and Mr Hazell (Secretary for Native Affairs). The only case of any importance was a claim for damages against the Cleveland Bridge Company, proffered by one

Robate, who it may be remembered fell from the bridge down the side of the gorge, sustaining considerable injuries. The plaintiff was represented by Mr Lotts and the defendant Company by Mr D Welsh. The case lasted nearly all day and the Court found for the plaintiff, awarding £50 15s damages and costs." (Bulawayo Chronicle, May 1905b)

Inside Information

With each piece of steelwork being custom made to specific requirements it was essential that none were damaged during erection, as replacement would involve a lengthy delay whilst being specially re-manufactured and transported from England. Few sources record that towards the end of the construction a section of steelwork actually fell and was lost into the gorge and rapids below.

"The construction was happily unattended by accidents of a serious nature, though a few slight accidents to bodywork and the replacing from England of one piece of steelwork were recorded." (Girouard, 1906)

Wally Walters, an English trader and opportunistic gambler based at the Old Drift, was on the scene and was quick to see an advantage. Walters had apparently left Johannesburg in a hurry after being involved in a betting scam involving carrier pigeons, and after fortuitously finding a (presumably stolen) diamond hidden in a flower pot on his veranda, left Kimberley at similar speed. He soon after lost the diamond in a game a cards.

"Going northwards again Wallie arrived at the Victoria Falls Bridge site and he was present when the last girder fell into the river. No one thought that a replacement from Darlington could be obtained in time for the promised opening day. But Wallie had seen the wire go off from the telegraph office and he knew on what ship the replacement was expected. The old gambling fever arose and he began to lay bets that the opening would take place on 12th September 1905, as arranged. It did. Wallie stood to lose £2,000 but he made £500." (Brelsford, 1965)

A Shade of Grey

Once the steelwork construction of the Bridge had been completed, the whole structure was re-painted in protective undercoats of red lead and linseed oil, before a final three coats of specially selected silver-grey paint.

"This particular shade was chosen because a patch of rust in it will appear

conspicuous by contrast. It has the further advantage of absorbing little of the heat of the sun." (Hobson, 1907)

A hand-tinted B.S.A.C. Christmas card from 1905 shows the Bridge still in its original red undercoat.

Riveters Revolt

By July 1905 the main steelwork construction was complete, with only the riveting to be finished - a small matter of at least 50,000 individual rivets still remaining to be fitted. The whole framework had been temporarily connected with specially designed bolt-pins, which were then removed and replaced with permanent rivets. The riveting process proved troublesome, taking far longer than was anticipated, owning to the difficulty in procuring men for this specialist and demanding work. In early July the Bulawayo Chronicle reported that Imbault had been forced to travel to Kimberley in order to recruit men for the work.

> *"Mr G C Imbault, the engineer of the Bridge, has recently returned from Kimberley whither he had journeyed with the view of engaging more riveters. I understand that approximately 50,000 rivets have yet to be hammered in before the finishing touch can be made. The new coat of grey paint renders the structure as invisible as possible against the cloud of spray, and the undue obtrusion of the landscape which so many feared has been cleverly obviated. It will probably be well on in August before the Bridge will be quite completed and proclaimed open to regular traffic."* (Bulawayo Chronicle, July 1905a)

The rivets were heated in portable forges to red-hot temperatures and inserted into the plates; the headless end immediately rounded over with a pneumatic rivet gun.

> *"The riveting up of the Bridge proved to be a more formidable undertaking than had been anticipated. Several of the riveters we brought from England were unable to stand the climate, and we had to depend largely on the men in the country. We found that an average day's work in England and in Africa were two very different things. Although we had good hydraulic and pneumatic equipment, the rate of progress was rather slow."* (Powell, 1930)

The pneumatic riveting machines regularly fused the electrical power system, which also served the Falls Hotel and caused the Manager many headaches, especially with the less than efficient cold-room facilities. It was even suggested that the workers purposely fused the power at the end of each day in dissatisfaction!

Bridge Tales

The bush surrounding the Falls supported a wealth of wildlife, Prince recording an adventure that befell two of the riveters:

"They went a little way along the gorge and there found the remains of the reedbuck. They started to cut out the horns. Suddenly they heard a growl behind them. Turning, they saw a lioness with two cubs, who was evidently annoyed at this interference with her dinner. The two men did not stop to argue, but made a bee line for the gorge, down which they jumped - about as dangerous a proceeding, one would think, as facing the lion. Luckily they stopped sliding a good way down, and retuned very much bruised." (Prince, 1906)

Clark recalls an incident following the detention of a Bridge worker, his name and crime unrecorded, by the local police constabulary.

"Once they had to arrest a man who was working on the Bridge. They had only a pole and dagga hut to put him in, so they leg-ironed him for the night In the darkness he escaped, leg-irons and all. Next day the detachment under the corporal hunted for him all over the countryside, but without success. In the early hours of the morning that followed the corporal looked out of his window. On the fence six feet [1.8 m] away from him dangled the leg-irons. Whether the offender was too honest a man to take away Government property or merely gifted with an acute sense of humour I cannot guess, but he was never caught." (Clark, 1936)

In 1960 the writer L Green recorded the following details of an incredible tale.

"Yet men have fallen into that vortex at the foot of the Victoria Falls and have lived. While the bridge-builders were at work, Trooper Ramsay of the Northern Rhodesia Police one day paddled a canoe from Livingstone during the flood season. For seven miles [11 km] the merciless current swept him downstream until he came to the lip of the Falls. There man and canoe parted company and dropped four hundred feet [122 m] into the Boiling Pot. A policeman and several others watched the terrible scene, then rushed down to the edge of the swirling waters. One man made a line fast round his waist, ventured into the Boiling Pot and gripped Ramsay as the current bore him past. Both men emerged alive and unharmed, thus ending happily a true story of magnificent courage and luck." (Green, 1960)

The full story of this miraculous tale, entitled 'Over the Victoria Falls by Canoe' and written by Murray Stuart, was first published in The Wide World Magazine in 1929. Despite being presented as a true story (the magazine promoted the motto 'truth is stranger than fiction') it is certainly a fictional tale. Murray claimed the incident occurred on 10th November 1904 and was witnessed by a number of the Bridge workmen. Powell, writing in 1930, had perhaps heard this same story and recorded:

> "One hears weird stories of persons being washed over the Falls, and rescued, alive, from the waters below. The thing is impossible. As the waters emerge from the chasm, with the Devil's Cataract and the Main Falls on the left, and the Eastern Cataract on the right, they strike the cliffs on either side of the outlet, creating whirlpools 30 to 50 feet [9.15-15.25 m] across, some sucking down, others belching up, giving the appearance of a huge cauldron of boiling water. Hence the name, The Boiling Pot. Nothing but crocodiles and fishes could live in it. Below the bridge as the waters take the straight run to the first bend below the hotel, whirlpools are less but the river has the appearance of an angry sea and some strange action of the currents, objects in the water are sometimes thrown out onto a rocky ledge on the south side. During the construction of the bridge, a horse died, and it was decided to throw it into the gorge and to see what would happen. When the carcass struck water it was instantly sucked under and not seen again." (Powell, 1930)

As Powell played such a prominent role in the construction of the Bridge it seams impossible that he would not have known about this incident had it happened. No contemporary sources report the accident, and no other local references to a 'Trooper Ramsay' have been found by the author.

Chief Mukuni's Musings

Frank Worthington, who first arrived at the banks of the Zambezi with Major Robert Coryndon (the Chartered Company's Administrator of North-Western Rhodesia from 1900 to 1907) in 1897, was appointed District Commissioner for the Batoka District in April 1901 and promoted to Secretary for Native Affairs for North-Western Rhodesia in 1904. It fell to Worthington to inform Chief Mukuni of the proposed construction of the Bridge.

> "It fell to my lot to tell him of the Bridge which would stand astride the tumbling waters. He was interested, and gave his consent without reserve."

The Chief, however, expressed much doubt over the idea. When questioned on how the Bridge was to be built, Worthington confessed he was not sure, and invited the Chief to watch the construction as it progressed. He took him at his word, walking down to the Bridge site every day to observe the work from a rocky vantage point. Although impressed his doubts over the ambition of project remained:

"'Come and see the white man's Bridge fall into the tumbling waters,' was his daily invitation, and many came. 'I am sorry for these white men, for they work to no profit.'" (Worthington, 1922)

With wonder he watched the progress until the two sides were finally linked up.

"Now with great luck, they have got this thing across, the trouble will be when they try to put a train on it, which they evidently mean to do. What they should do to save it all would be to put a stick up from the bottom to hold it up, certainly it would have to be a long stick, but as they have got the bridge across, they should be able to do that as well, but it is not for me to tell them." (Varian, 1953)

However, the Chief's forebodings did not materialise and he stood alone on his rock vantage point as the first train rumbled across the Bridge. His response was that it must only be the finger of the white man's god that held the Bridge up. In his 1907 report to the Civil Institute of Engineers on the construction of the Bridge Hobson claimed that *"until the advent of the railway there were no natives living within 60 miles* [96.5 km] *of the falls owing to their superstitious dread of the locality"* (Hobson, 1907). This assertion would be repeated by many subsequent authors, despite there being well established settlements and communities on the north bank, with historical claims and cultural traditions incorporating the environment of the Falls. The impact of the Bridge on the cultural traditions of the local Leya people is, as a result, often overlooked.

The Falls, gorges and even the spray itself were all part of a sacred cultural landscape for the Leya. They associated the waters with powers of healing, using the natural swimming pools on the very lip of the Falls for cleansing rituals, whilst the ephemeral spray was home of ancestral spirits - the 'mists of the dead.' The Boiling Pot, over which the Bridge spanned, was a significant part of this culturally landscape, as McGregor records from interviews with the current Chief Mukuni in 2001:

"For Mukuni's Leya, the most meaningful northern aspect of the waterfall is known as 'Syuungwe mufu' or 'mist of the dead,' because it is associated with the memory of ancestors and played 'a central part in the life of the people.'

These 'mists of the dead' are now said to include three key places of particular significance.

"The first is at the foot of the Falls, and is called 'katolauseka' or 'make offerings cheerfully' and is now known as the boiling pot. This was a place of mystery, associated with the spirits of past communities. It is said that a light used to be seen there, or that one could hear the sound of drumming, of children playing, women stamping grain and cattle lowing. Offerings could be hurled into the boiling pot over the lip of the Falls from one of the islands perched on the edge."

"Another important ritual site was at the top of the waterfall and was known as 'Sambadwazi' or 'cleanse disease.' It was on the upper lip of the Falls by the eastern cataract where the water swung round and over the edge of the gorge, but in doing so created a pool where the water did not move swiftly, making it possible for people to immerse themselves. The diseased and afflicted jumped into this pool in a cleansing ritual in which they allowed their clothing to be washed away over the waterfall, carrying infection and ill health with it.

"The final site with special meaning was known as 'Chipusya,' and was the place where water was drawn for rainmaking and other rituals. The location was known only by some elders and the individual responsible for drawing the water, who did so alone and unobserved in the hours before daylight..."

"Old Leya people recall that ceremonies at the boiling pot ceased as the resort grew and people lost access to the waterfall: the light in the boiling pot was said to have gone out, and the sounds of past communities in the form of drumming, cattle lowing and children playing could no longer be heard... The building of the bridge over the river, for example, had defiled one of Mukuni's religious sites, as the supports for the bridge reached down into the sacred place of the boiling pot." (McGregor, 2003)

End of the Drift

It soon became apparent that the location of the Bridge and route of the railway would make the Old Drift crossing, and settlement, redundant - irrelevant of the health concerns over the site. After much consideration, including exploring the option of moving the whole settlement to the south bank, the Chartered Company's Administration narrowed the choice down to two possible sites on the north bank, both along the line of the railway - one that was 'close to the Falls and the river' (Imabult's Camp) and the other on the 'sand-belt some seven miles (11 km) north' (at Constitution Hill).

Without consultation with the settlers, Major Coryndon, the Company's Administrator, decided upon Constitution Hill, where the Government Station, Post Office and Court House had already been established, believing that the alternative of a town *"so close to the Falls would be bound to mar the natural beauty of the area"* (Phillipson,1990b).

The Old Drift community, led by Moore, did not agree with his choice. Writing at the end of the following year, Moore summarised the settlers arguments against the site chosen by Coryndon.

"Before Livingstone was inhabited, before even, it was surveyed, its political history began in the shape of a unanimous expression of popular dissatisfaction with the site selected... The inhabitants pointed out the distance separating the new site from the Falls; its inaccessibility to tourists and others; the distance from the water supply; and the absence of any industry or enterprise in the neighbourhood to justify its existence, in the event of its failing to become a resort for visitors. The danger of an opposition township springing up, in a more favourably situated position, on either the south or north bank, was urged, and subsequently the difficulty of constructing roads or of obtaining suitable foundations for brick building in the sandy soil." (Livingstone Mail, December 1906)

The Administration were unmoved and the new town was carefully planned. On 23rd February 1905, the Company auctioned 100 stands to the highest bidders. To avoid speculation purchasers had to agree to erect on their stands a building to the minimum value of £300 within twelve months.

Several months later, in May, members of the local community were still petitioning for an alternative site, complaining that the unpainted Bridge was a *"red monster,"* to reach which *"an ugly gash had been scoured across the countryside."* They also lobbied that the Falls Hotel should be completely demolished, arguing that all tourists should be accommodated and served from Livingstone - as had been intended when the railway, and Livingstone, had been originally planned (Rhodesia Railways Magazine, August 1955).

At the end of June 1905 the residents of the Old Drift were instructed to cease trading by 24th August. The threat of a one pound daily fine from January 1906 finally encouraged the last settlers to move, and by early 1906 the Old Drift was all but abandoned to the bush (Roberts, 2021c).

The Zambezi Express

By June 1905 three passenger trains a week were running to and from Bulawayo. Also featuring on the timetable was the Zambezi Express - a special weekly service from Kimberley to the Victoria Falls, which completed the final 450 kilometres from Bulawayo in under 18 hours, and fully equipped with bedding services and dining car. Passengers received an 'Annotated Time Table of the Zambezi Express on the Rhodesia Railways', which gave details of the times at the stops along the route in both directions, and interesting information and photographs on the places passed. A connecting train ran from Cape Town. Croxton recorded the following extract from the Cape Government Railways timetable of September 1906:

"A First Class Saloon for Victoria Falls leaves Cape Town on the 11.30 a.m. train on Tuesdays, and is attached to the Zambezi Express at Kimberley. It reaches Victoria Falls Station at 7.15 a.m. on Saturday. It is luxuriously appointed, and includes showerbath, etc. The distance from Cape Town is 1,642 miles [2,650 km], and the return fare £23 16s 8d. Terms at Victoria Falls Hotel, 21/-a day."

Of particular note was the dining-saloon, allowing passengers to dine to fine standards en route.

"In contrast to the hampers passengers had to carry on the first excursion service to the falls, those who enjoyed the comforts of the Zambesi Express could lunch in the dining-saloon... The menu consisted of: Tomato Soup; Boiled Kabaljoe with parsley sauce; Haricot Mutton; Roast Ribs of Beef; Assorted Vegetables; Cold York Ham and Roast Beef; Chicken and Tongue; Dressed Salad; Tapioca Pudding; Stewed Fruit; Cheese and Biscuits; and Black Coffee." (Croxton, 1982)

The Zambezi Express

The Zambezi Regatta

The first Zambezi Regatta was held on 12th June 1905 to celebrate the fiftieth anniversary year of Livingstone's first arrival at the Falls and the construction of the Bridge. The regatta was the highlight to three days of sporting events and celebrations aimed at promoting the accessibility of the Falls to the wider world.

The regatta was held on a mile and a half (2.4 km) straight stretch of water between Luanda Island (also known as Long Island) and the north bank. A camp site and temporary grandstand was set up at the finish line. Two of the Bridge engineers, Varian and Everard were involved in surveying the river above the Falls in preparation for the event. Varian also competed in one of the races, and gives a detailed account of events:

"During the construction of the first section of the line beyond the Falls, preparations were made for a celebration of the completion of the bridge. The programme consisted of a one-day regatta, a day's racing, and a day of athletic sports, for all of which courses had to be arranged. The celebration was a great success, especially the regatta. The course for this was a mile and-a-half [2.4 km] in length, on a straight reach of the river between Luanda Island and the left bank. While the Bridge works were in progress, Mr Everard, assistant-engineer on the Rhodesia Railways, and I were detailed to begin a preliminary survey for a power scheme of the Falls, the initial work of which took us along the left bank five miles [8 km] upstream to Secuti's Drift... With the experience thus gained, we were able to set out the regatta course, as well as a continuous path along the river's edge for the use of trainers of the various crews.

"A mile-and-a-half of railway [known as the Regatta Spur] was built from the Maramba depot to the river, to take the boats to the water, and carry spectators to the different sports-courses, which adjoined the finishing post of the regatta course. Part of the race-course was used for the sports meeting. A camp site was also prepared for the visiting crews." (Varian, 1953)

Major Coryndon imported a punt from England especially for the event. Umpire for the regatta was Lieutenant-Colonel Hugh Marshall Hole.

"There were many reminders of boating events and leisure back home. The Administrator at Livingstone [Coryndon] had punt imported from England, which had been launched on the Thames and which he used for the first time at the regatta." (Arrington-Sirois, 2017)

Sir Charles Metcalfe arranged the importation of four boats from Oxford especially for the event.

The Zambezi Challenge Cup

The main race was the Zambezi Challenge Cup 'Fours', with four-men crews from Cape Town, Port Elizabeth, and East London invited to compete. Teams from Johannesburg and Durban (as well as Bulawayo, Salisbury and Beira) had also been invited to participate but did not send crews.

The Reverend Alan Williams, Chaplin to South Africa and Vice President of the Alfred Rowing Club, travelled with the Cape Town crew, combined from the Alfred and Civil Service Rowing Clubs, and recorded their arrival at the Falls.

"We reached Victoria Falls at dawn on Whit-Monday, and from our carriage, which had been shunted during the night, and which was our 'home' for the time being, I saw a pink-tinged cloud rising above the treetops and heard the thunder of the Falls as the sun rose through the trees behind us. That day we all went over the unfinished bridge to the north side, on open trucks, a very foolish arrangement, for a bad jolt might have shot some of us through the open girders to the bottle-green torrent 400 feet [122 m] below.

"A grandstand had been erected at a point a mile or so above the Falls on the north side, where was gathered a motley strange crowd of whites and blacks - from the Commissioner, Sir William Milton, and his party, to Lewanika, Paramount Chief of Barotseland, and his followers. He was a fine tall figure in grey flannel suit and hat - with binoculars hung over his shoulder, and a hunting crop in his hand." (Northern Rhodesia Journal, July 1952)

The East London crew, Zambezi Challenge Cup winners

After a fine race East London, crewed by men from Leander Rowing Club and stroked by Mr Owen G Griffiths, came in winners with Cape Town a close second. Sir Charles Metcalfe presented the winning crew with the Challenge Cup and individual gold medals. Mr Griffiths, also carried off the win in the individual Diamond Challenge sculls.

The Rhodesia Challenge Cup

The Rhodesia Challenge Cup was presented by Mr Lawley for competition between the Rhodesian crews. North-Western Rhodesia fielded three teams of fours, from Livingstone, Kalomo (manned by Company Civil Servants) and Kafue (manned by a crew selected from Pauling's construction engineers - none of who had yet seen the Kafue River). The race was won by Kafue, with Livingstone second. During the race the boat of the Kalomo crew began to take on water and slowly sink. The crew and boat were rescued, and to the sombre tune of the 'Dead March' the boat was carried away.

Varian found himself part of the Kafue crew and describes the scene:

"The South African crews were naturally in a class of their own, so there were two major races, one for them, and one for the Rhodesians. Marsland and I, with Cumberpatch and Micklem as stroke in the Kafue boat, were all more or less lightweights, and won the Rhodesian race by a length. The Kalomo boat carried sixty-four stone with their cox, and included such giants as O'Sullivan of the Police, Skipper Swanston, and others of the same stamp. Of course, they hadn't a chance. After paddling up a mile-and-a-half on a hot afternoon, there was a delay at 2 o'clock owing to some fault in the steam-launch that carried the umpire, Mr Marshall Hole. By this time their boat, the Bleeding Heart, which had shown very little freeboard throughout, appeared to be definitely sinking. They managed to get home before it foundered, however, and carried the much-tried

The finishing line

craft up to the boathouse, to the strains of the Dead March." (Varian, 1953)

Kalomo based Company administrator Knowles Jordan records taking part in the scratch pairs.

"By a stroke of luck I became cox in a race for Scratch Pairs over half-mile course and we won easily. The three of us all came from different parts of South Africa and we each received a valuable silver cup." (Northern Rhodesia Journal, July 1951)

Also included in the regatta schedule were two 'native races,' with four and six man teams from Lealui, Sesheke and Livingstone competing in dug-out canoes.

"The race for Royal crews of native states was very exciting. The paddlers stood in native dugouts, some six a side and urged by the cries of natives on the banks urged their craft forward at a great pace. The crew of the Chief Litia of Sesheke was the winner. It was said that Lewanika told his crew that if it did not win he would put the lot on an island of the Zambesi on their return, and leave them there for the benefit of the crocodiles." (Northern Rhodesia Journal, July 1952)

In the event the crew of Chief Letia (Paramount Chief Lewanika's son) were victorious - it was not recorded what happened to Lewanika's loosing crew. In photographs Lewanika is seen proudly dressed in the expensive flannel suit, top hat and overcoat purchased during his visit to England. The local Leya people

One of the native crews head for the start-line

under Chief Mukuni and Chief Sekuti, who had traditionally controlled the river crossings, were notable for their absence from the event, having been eclipsed by the relationship formed between their Lozi overseers and the Chartered Company.

The View from the Grandstand

The Railway Company ran reduced fares on trains to attract travellers and the event was attended by an estimated seven hundred visitors, flooding the Falls, and the Hotel, with an unprecedented number of tourists. Varian, recorded:

"In those days the hotel at the Falls was a small galvanized affair, quite incapable of dealing with the situation, so the hundreds of visitors from all parts of South Africa were housed in trains on the nearby sidings. A disused engine-shed, brought up from Mafeking, was suitably decorated and transformed into a dining-room. It served as such for many years, until the present palatial building was erected." (Varian, 1953)

Visitors drank dry the stocks of beer and whisky and there were apparently ugly scenes in the 'outside bar' of the Falls Hotel when the last bottles were emptied. Percy Clark was less than impressed with the rush on local supplies:

"Crews came from all parts of Africa to compete, and there were close on a thousand visitors altogether. The capacity of the Hotel was good only for about a hundred of these, so the rest had to camp out. By the second day the hotel was cleared of beer and whisky, and food had almost run out. I was invited by a friend to dine there. The feast was worthy of the rude fellow's grace: 'Gawd! What a meal!' I wished I had invited my friend to my own place. The service

The regatta grandstands on the north bank of the river

was terrible, with a wait of twenty minutes between each of the courses. These were: soup - with the taste and appearance of weak Bovril; one bony cutlet and half a potato; biscuits and cheese with no butter. There wasn't a scrap of butter in the hotel, no joints, no poultry. For this magnificent (!) spread we were charged seven-and-six apiece. I'd sooner have bought a marriage licence. Along the regatta course were the usual 'joints' - poker tables, 'Under and Over, 'Crown and Anchor,' canteens, and the side-shows. The concessionaires, so to call them, must have raked in pots of money...

"I was besieged in my huts by Bulawayo friends who could not get accommodation in the hotel. They dossed down in rows and tiers in my huts, and all about them, and in the kitchen. Several had brought their own nosebags, and foodstuffs in bottle were plentiful, but my larder was sadly depleted. I had to feed them ultimately on bully beef and hard tack. But, as the saying is: 'A good time was enjoyed by all!'" (Clark, 1936)

The band of the Barotse Native Police were on hand to entertain guests.

"The Barotse Native Police Bugle Band discoursed music. It sounded strange to hear them play 'Come listen to this Band,' a very popular tune in England at that time." (Northern Rhodesia Journal, July 1952)

The regatta finished with an evening of festivities, with 80 guests attending a special dinner. Coryndon's speech was interrupted by the constant grunting of a bull hippo in the river nearby, loudly expressing its disapproval of their presence.

The Barotse Native Police on parade, Livingstone June 1905

"After dinner, visitors and Rhodesians gathered round a large camp fire exchanging experiences and many friendships were formed. The broad river gleaming in the moonlight, the rustling palms, the distant roar of the Falls, and the occasional splash of a hippo or big fish combined to make up an African picture to be remembered for many a year." (Northern Rhodesia Journal, July 1951)

During the course of the festivities it was decided to hold a cricket match, and on 23rd July a team comprised from Pauling's railway construction crew challenged local residents of the Old Drift to a game held 'on a very bumpy Maramba yard' (Shepherd, 2008).

The event received much promotion and coverage back in Britain, with the London Evening News describing the Zambezi as 'Our New Henley,' and a promotional booklet produced in 1905 by Union Castle encouraged travel to the Zambezi, 'the World's Riviera.'

The Company's annual report for the year recorded that *"thanks in a great measure to the organising ability of Sir Charles Metcalfe, Mr R T Coryndon, and Mr A L Lawley, the Regatta was a great success"* (British South Africa Company, 1906).

Hippo Hazards

Green recalls interviewing Mr Jack Rose (later Colonel Rose), one of the Cape rowers.

"It was a wild and exciting place in those days... Fever was a constant menace and there were few amenities but we enjoyed ourselves. There was lots to talk about - a bull hippo entered the marquee near the river where the boating club dinner was being held. We all cleared out pretty quick." (Green, 1968)

Hippopotamus have always been a hazard along the river, easily capable of capsizing a canoe and to be treated with utmost respect in the water or on the river bank. Sykes also wrote of the dangers of encountering hippopotamus on the river:

"Hippopotami may be seen occasionally amongst the islands above the Falls. They have been known to attack and capsize boats, and therefore should be approached with caution, or better still, avoided as much as possible." (Sykes, 1905)

He wrote from personal experience.

"In 1905 at the time of the regatta, Mr F W Sykes, a government official at Livingstone, escaped when the hippo overturned his boat near the lip of the Falls. Several natives were drowned. Gavuzzi the Hotel manager, was rowing about the same area with a crew of natives when a hippo tore a hole in the bottom of the boat. They all had to swim for their lives and all reached the shore safely. A journalist who was visiting the Falls at the time wrote; 'I have little sympathy with the idea of some visitors that these brutes should be allowed to multiply in the river at this place on the plea that they form picturesque adjuncts to the scenery. I should not only permit them to be shot off but I should put a reward on every hippo's head.'" (Green, 1968)

A Visit from Mr Hobson

A report in the Bulawayo Chronicle, dated 2nd July, detailed the visit to the Falls of Mr Hobson, the bridge's designer.

"Amongst the visitors this week have been Mr and Mrs Hobson and Miss Hobson. Mr Hobson is a member of the well known team of engineers, Sir Douglas Fox and partners. The principal object of his visit was to inspect the Victoria Falls Bridge, the construction of which during his stay he has thoroughly examined. He expressed unqualified satisfaction, and has cabled to his firm to this effect. Mr G C Imbault, the man on the spot, is to be congratulated upon bringing this great engineering work to its present stage, notwithstanding the many difficulties he has been called upon to face during its progress. For more than twelve months he has been continually superintending the work, which, under the most favourable conditions, must have been a severe tax on his ability and patience." (Bulawayo Chronicle, July 1905b)

View of the Victoria Falls Bridge and Gorges from the Hotel

Official Opening of the Bridge

The official opening ceremony for the Victoria Falls Bridge took place on 12th September 1905, officially opened by Professor (later Sir) George H Darwin, the second son of Charles Darwin and President of the British Association for the Advancement of Science (now the British Science Association).

The Association had originally been invited to the Victoria Falls in 1902, with the idea of holding their annual meeting at the Falls and plans to develop the Hotel to accommodate several hundred guests. In the event the main part of the tour and official meetings were held in South Africa, with the trip to the Falls as a special excursion. Professor Darwin later describing the honour of opening the Bridge as the 'crowning glory of the tour.'

Early Arrival

For the conveyance of the Association party and other special guests the Railway Company ran five special trains at half hour intervals from Bulawayo. The earlier trains arrived in time to enable guests to visit the Falls for sunrise. Mr James Stark Browne travelled with members of the Association on their tour of South Africa and published an account of their travels, recording his arrival at the Falls at 5 o'clock on the morning of the opening.

"The Hotel was situated a short distance off, and thither I bent my steps. From thence the ground, in the direction of the Falls,

The train advances

dropped somewhat, so that a very magnificent view could be obtained over the forest-covered country lying in that direction. Right in front, only a few hundred feet off, was the mighty gorge of the Zambesi, and further on, less than a mile away, I saw the new railway bridge across the river...

"We had no time to go to the Bridge before breakfast, which was ready for us at the hotel. Early as it was, the day was too hot for eating with any appetite; our chief desire seemed to be for drink. I do not think that either the food or the waiting could be called good; but the size of our party must have been a great tax upon the resources of an hotel, so many hundreds of miles from its nearest base of supply."

Following breakfast Browne walked down to the Bridge ahead of the arrival of the train bearing the opening party on the short run from the station.

"At the Bridge, we had half-an-hour to spare before the time of the opening ceremony. The structure was still in an uncompleted state, and in places, where the floor had not been quite boarded over, it was necessary to walk with care to avoid tumbling through... We could see the train in the distance approaching, the engine gaily decorated with flags and greenery. One of our officials was busily giving orders that all who had not violet tickets were to be told to go off the bridge; these violet tickets being the free ones given to the members of the 'official' party, while those of the 'unofficial' section who had paid for theirs had red ones. Most of the Rhodesian officers, however, declined to carry out these instructions, and we were left undisturbed. This attempt to turn us off the Bridge was a piece of official interference, which was greatly resented and caused much heartburning." (Browne, 1906)

Opening Ceremony

One of the newest 7th Class engines in the country at the time, decorated with two flags (that of the British South Africa Company and the Union Jack), palm leaves and floral dressings, pulled the six coaches which carried the guests for the opening ceremony and then halted on the Bridge for the passengers to alight. Mr Allan Martin Bowes is recorded as the driver. The party was met by Sir Charles Metcalfe and the Administrator, Major Robert Coryndon.

Sir Charles made the welcoming speech and invited Professor Darwin to declare the Victoria Falls Bridge officially open. To conduct the opening ceremony Sir Charles presented Professor Darwin with a special hand-held staff of highly polished Zambezi wood in which was set an engraved representation of the Bridge

Preparing to open the Bridge

and a gold plate with inscription, made by Bulawayo jeweller W H Blackler. The staff was designed with a metal loop at the head, and used by Professor Darwin to fuse the connection and officially open the Bridge.

"Then, touching a button with a staff the cord stretching across the roadway was fused and the first train steamed across. The staff which Prof. Darwin used was an exquisite piece of workmanship, made of Zambesi wood and beautifully polished. On the apex of the staff is a disk cunningly engraved, showing a view of the Falls with the Bridge across. The disk is encircled with an enamelled wreath. On the front of the staff is a gold plate upon which is engraved:

"'Presented to Prof. Darwin, in commemoration of his opening of the Victoria Falls Bridge over the Zambesi River during the visit of the British Association, September 12th, 1905.'" (Scientific American Supplement, Nov 1905)

The following day the Bulawayo Chronicle recorded the details of Professor Darwin's speech:

"He said it was a most fortunate coincidence that this great enterprise had been brought to a stage at which it was proper to declare the bridge open during the visit of the members of the British Association to South Africa. Thanks to the generosity and care of the [Cape] *Government Railways, they had just performed an astonishing journey of 1,700 miles [2,736 km] in luxury and comfort. (Cheers.)*

"One could not but feel that it was almost an impertinence that they should have been able to come, in electrically lighted sleeping cars, with restaurant

saloons, to a place which the heroic explorers had spent many months in fruitless endeavours to reach. This was a thing which impressed itself on the imagination. Another thing which impressed them as Englishmen was that they were still under the Union Jack. (Loud cheers.)

"But two days ago they stood by the tomb of Cecil John Rhodes in the Matopas, and, amid that scene of wild beauty, all felt that the grave of the man who had thought in continents was fitly chosen. The great enterprise of the Cape to Cairo Railway, of which this bridge is a part, was due to his inception. It seemed nothing short of a fairy tale to stand on this bridge over the Zambesi. It was due to the influence of steam that this great enterprise had become possible, and he couldn't refrain from quoting the remarkable forecast, written by his great grandfather, Erasmus Darwin, in 1785:

*"'Soon shall thy arm unconquered steam, afar
Urge the slow barge and draw the flying car.'*

"How little could the writer of these lines have foreseen that his great grandson should have the honour of declaring a railway bridge open in the heart of equatorial Africa. (Cheers.) Professor Darwin concluded by declaring the Bridge open, touching a button which fused a cord stretched across." (Bulawayo Chronicle, September 1905a)

Many eminent scientists, professors and engineers were present among the members of the Association party, including Sir Benjamin Baker, Sir Colin Scott-

Professor Darwin declares the Bridge formerly open to traffic

Moncrieff, Lord Ross, Sir William Crookes, Sir William Henry Preece, Admiral Sir William James Lloyd Wharton (who died in Cape Town on the return journey) and Sir Richard Jebb (who died soon after returning to England) to name a few. Also among the distinguished guests was a Mrs Agnes Livingstone Bruce, wife of Colonel Alexander Low Bruce and the eldest daughter of Dr David Livingstone.

There was, apparently, much speculation between them as to the exact height of the Bridge above the water. Sir Oliver Lodge, the British physicist, stepped forward with a plan.

"They told him that the height of the Bridge above the water was 310 feet [94.5 m], and he said he would test this by dropping a stone and measuring the time of its fall by his stop watch. A little crowd gathered round him on the middle of the bridge. He had his watch in his right hand and a stone in the left.

"'Now,' cried Sir Oliver. He pressed the starter of the watch, dropped the watch into the water and stood staring at the stone. A moment later, without a blush of any exclamation, he turned to the crowd and said: 'There you are - exactly 310 feet! [94.5 m]'" (Rhodesia Herald, March 1957)

With the opening ceremony complete the train slowly drew forward amid cheers. The main group of guests alighted on the northern bank where they could explore the Palm Grove or visit Livingstone Island. The remainder of the guests visited the Rain Forest, under the guidance of Mr Allen, and then back to the Hotel for lunch, by which time the train returned with the first group and collected the second group for the trip to the north bank.

Opening train on Bridge

Mr E Knowles Jordan, in the employment of the Administration at Kalomo, was one of those present on the Bridge and described a hair-raising moment.

"In 1905 the Victoria Falls Bridge was officially opened, and I made one of a party to cross to Northern Rhodesia in the first passenger train. Four or five of us stood on a carriage platform looking at the scenery. As the heavy Pullman cars moved slowly along, a railwayman standing on one of the girders watching the progress of the train suddenly slipped and for a moment it looked as if he would be precipitated into the torrent far below. Fortunately, however, he managed to grip the girder and slowly drew himself into a position of safety." (Northern Rhodesia Journal, July 1951)

Guests were given voucher tickets for the train, tours and meals, issued together with a special commemorative programme.

Evening Entertainment

In the evening the Victoria Falls Hotel served dinner for nearly two hundred guests, after which trips to see the Falls by moonlight were offered. Sir Charles read a telegram from the President and Directors of the Chartered Company, congratulating him on the opening of the Bridge.

"Very fitting that foremost representatives of science should be associated with inauguration of modern engineering. Regret the founder of country is not alive to witness realization of part of his great ideal."

Entertainment was provided by the local Barotse Native Police Band:

"Music was supplied during the evening by the Barotse police band, dressed in Khaki uniforms with red turbans, not one of whom knows a note of music, and are taught by having the tunes whistled to them." (Bulawayo Chronicle, September 1905b)

Mr Browne concluded *"I thought they played with a great deal of spirit, only occasionally with too much noise."* (Browne, 1906)

Only Professor Darwin and the most distinguished guests had rooms at the Hotel, with many guests being accommodated on the train carriages. The high number of visitors caused service and supply problems for the Hotel, with one member recording: *"Had to dine late owing to the fearful crush. Food vile, so dined on bread and marmalade"* (Balfour, 1905).

Impact and Influence

The visit of the British Association stimulated much scientific interest in the Victoria Falls, and resulted the publication of many scientific papers on the region. At the Association's invitation the geologist George W Lamplugh spent July and August 1905 surveying the geology of the Victoria Falls gorges, presenting his report during their tour. Lamplugh's research supported the work of Molyneux, published in the same year, who was the first to show evidence that the Victoria Falls and Batoka Gorge were the result of slow and gradual erosion.

"It is difficult for anyone standing on the brink of the Chasm, after having seen the placid flow of the Zambesi above the Falls, to believe that the fissure into which the river is so suddenly precipitated has been formed gradually by the action of the river itself, and not by some great convulsion during which the very crust of the earth was rent... Hence it is not surprising to find that the explanation given by David Livingstone half a century ago, that the majestic Zambesi has here been intercepted by a rent due to some earth movement in the solid rocks, has been adopted without question in all the later descriptions of this wonderful spectacle." (Lamplugh, 1905)

Maid of the Mist

During the preparations for the Bridge, Mr Townsend collected the bulbs of an interesting flowering iris he found growing under the spray of the Falls. He sent them to Sir Francis Fox in England, who in turn sent specimens to Sir William Turner Thiselton-Dyer, Director of the Royal Botanical Gardens at Kew:

"It is a Gladiolus of a type which is rather widely spread in Tropical Africa - and comes, apparently, very close to one named Gladiolus primulinus. But from a horticultural point of view it seems to me quite unique, and a brilliant discovery. It ought to be the starting-point of a new race of garden Gladiolus."

The flower was notable for its pure yellow colour and being so shaped to shield the inside of the flower from never-ending spray.

"These flowers, which we had named 'Maid of the Mist,' were exhibited at the Royal Horticultural Society's Show on August 23rd, 1904, and attracted much attention... We sent seeds and corms to our friends not only in England, but in Canada, United States, France, Belgium, and Holland, who also hybridised it. The result is that the blooms are to be seen in most gardens." (Fox, 1924)

Global Significance

The opening of the Bridge was celebrated with typical imperial 'triumphalism' and fanfare, with Sir Charles again ensuring word of the opening reached far and wide. The Globe (13th September 1905) celebrated this *"interesting event in the heart of Central Africa,"* important because the Bridge could *"claim the distinction of being the highest in the world, has been erected in the heart of the Dark Continent and furthermore, represents the forging of another link... in the great scheme proposed and started by Cecil John Rhodes."*

For the British travel agent Thomas Cook and Sons, official passenger agent for the Cape Government and Rhodesia Railways, the opening was *"an event second only in importance to the completion of the* [Cape to Cairo] *line itself."* Their magazine, the Travellers Gazette (October & November 1905), described *"the memorable scene"* of the special trains carrying Professor Darwin *"through trackless, uninhabited tropical bush to the renowned Falls"* (McGregor, 2003).

Vital Statistics

The total weight of the complete steelwork structure (including side spans) as originally built was calculated as 1,644 tons.

Span of south approach	87 ½ Feet	26.67 Metres
Span of main arch	500	152.4
Span of north approach	62 ½	19.05
Depth of main arch at bearings	105	32
Depth of main arch at centre	15	4.57
Rise of main arch at crown	90	27.43
Height of rail level above water (wet season)	355	108.20
Height of rail level above water (dry season)	411	125.27
Distance of Bridge in direct line from Hotel	4,850	1,478.2

The Rhodesia Railways General Manager's Bulletin, No 34, November 1922 gives details of the stresses and strains the original structure was design to withstand, including; a train on each of the two lines, consisting of two engines and weighing 1.75 tons per lineal foot, followed by heavy trucks weighing 1.33 tons per lineal foot, temperature stresses caused by a variation of 60 degrees Fahrenheit above or below the mean and wind stresses due to a wind pressure of 30 lb per square foot (30.5 square cm) on the train and Bridge, or 45 lb per square foot on the Bridge alone.

For Sale

In early October the following announcement of the sale of construction assets by the Bridge Company appeared in the pages of the Bulawayo Chronicle.

"Completion of Victoria Falls Bridge. For Sale at a Bargain.

"One Iron Building, steel frame, 40 ft. x 20 ft. [12 x 6 m].
Two Iron Buildings, steel frame, 12 ft. x 9 ft. [3.6 x 2.7 m].
One Iron Office, steel frame, three rooms - 9 ft. x 12 ft. [2.7 x 3.6 m], 9 ft. x 12 ft. [2.7 x 3.6 m] and 6 ft. x 15 ft. [1.8 x 4.5 m].
Two Steel Cranes, each fitted with two 10-ton jibs, can be worked by hand or electricity; complete with motors, rope, blocks, etc.
Numerous Small Tools for rivetting, fitting etc.
Wire Ropes.

"All details on application to Cleveland Bridge Co, Victoria Falls, N.W. Rhodesia." (Bulawayo Chronicle, October 1905)

Back to Nature

The Bridge contract stipulated that after construction was complete all traces of the construction sites and camps were to be removed. The site of Tower's camp was cleared and the huts burnt by Imbault. Percy Clark tried, but failed, to take up residence at the site, and the camp was quickly reclaimed by nature. However the decommissioning of the construction camp buildings still provided an opportunity for Mr Clark:

"Among amusing memories... is an incident connected with the building of one of my huts. The operations were being supervised by a trooper, who acted as my clerk of the works in his spare time. One day, in company with this trooper, I was coming away from one of my frequent visits to the police camp when I spotted, outside the corporal's hut, a very nice window-frame. It was just want I wanted for the new building, and my clerk of the works agreed with me. In due course the hut was finished and the corporal was asked over to inspect it and have a 'sundowner.' While putting back his drink he suddenly spotted the window. It was draped with curtains, but he recognized it.

"'Well, I'm damned!' said he. 'So it was you, was it, you blighter, that pinched my window!'

"'How the devil did you recognize it?' I asked.

"'How the devil shouldn't I recognize it?' he replied. 'I had a hell of a job pinching it myself in the first place!'

"The window had come from a dismantled hut belonging to the Cleveland Bridge Company." (Clark, 1936)

On the north bank, the area immediately before the approach of the Bridge was left as a large open area, with a magnificent view down to the Boiling Pot and across the Knife Edge. The location would later become known as 'scandal alley' - Livingstone residents would gather there on Sunday afternoons for picnics and to revel in the week's gossip.

Imbault Departs

In mid-November it was reported that Imbault had completed his work at the Bridge site and had departed for the south.

"Mr Imbault left for the South on Friday on the completion of the Bridge. He is to be heartily congratulated on the success of his work. All evidence of the construction, such as native huts, &c, will be burnt down and the place thoroughly cleared, so that beyond the Bridge itself no trace will remain of the great work that has been carried out there." (Bulawayo Chronicle, 18th November 1905)

Mr Longbottom's medal

Finishing Off

With the main work of the contract completed the Cleveland Bridge Company wound down their presence at the site. Howard Longbottom was credited as being the only one of the leading workmen to be involved for the entire length of the contract, from the start to the finish, his last day of work on site recorded as 10th November 1905. In recognition of his role, 'under exceptional and trying conditions,' Sir Charles Metcalfe later awarded him a gold medal, specially made by Bulawayo jeweller W H Blackler, featuring a view of the Bridge and the words 'Victoria Falls Bridge, Erected 1904-5' on the face and 'To Commemorate a Great Work, H Longbottom, from Sir Charles Metcalfe' on the reverse. Longbottom would later work again for the Cleveland Bridge Company, and Imbault, on the construction of the Blue Nile Road and Railway Bridge in Sudan, erected between 1907-9 (Longbottom, 2018).

Deck Details

During 1906 work continued finishing the permanent deck of the Bridge. Hobson describes some of the problems encountered:

> *"With the exception of the railway-tracks... the deck was formed of carefully selected pine timber, 3 inches [7.6 cm] thick, laid in 9-inch [22.9 cm] planks with air-spaces ½ inch [1.3 cm] wide. To preserve it from the rain and spray the timber had been thoroughly creosoted; while to shield it from the heat of the sun and from the danger of fire liable to be caused by burning cinders from passing engines, it had been covered with a thick coat of Stockholm tar and strewn with sand and fine gravel. The result had been disappointing. The fierce heat of the sun and the extreme dryness of the atmosphere in the winter months had distilled the creosote and the tar and thereby released the sandy covering, which had been gradually wafted away. Rigid injunctions against raking out ashes on or near the bridge were now therefore issued to engine-drivers and a watchman was stationed to inspect the deck after the passing of each train."* (Hobson, 1907)

Two Lines

The temporary construction deck of the Bridge bore only a single track railway although the final deck carried two as designed. The Bridge had not originally been designed to take a permanent road, nor was it seen as desirable, from the Railway Company's point of view, to provide a roadway, which would have added considerably to the initial construction cost.

The double tracks were planned to be used alternatively, traffic being switched approximately every six months to ease any possible strain on the Bridge. When it was decided to change from one track to the other it was merely a matter of swinging the single approach tracks on either side of the Bridge into line. This was confirmed by Mr W L Bonny, an engineer with the Railway Company, in an article in the Rhodesia Railways Magazine, who recorded use of the two tracks alternated in this manner up until 1929 when the deck of the Bridge was reconstructed. *"But don't let anyone ever tell you that there were ever two trains on the bridge at the same time,"* emphasised Mr Bonny (Rhodesia Railways Magazine, October, 1963).

View of goods train on Bridge showing two sets of track

Views on the Bridge

We now look upon the Victoria Falls Bridge as an integral part of the landscape of the Victoria Falls area, but its construction, so close to the Falls themselves caused much controversy and objection at the time. An unnamed writer for Scientific American magazine, in an article published in July 1905, expanded:

"Before the scheme was put in hand, there were not a few complaints in the public press, declaring that the erection of a bridge at the Falls would mar the beauty of the surroundings. To ascertain the general feeling of the visitors on the site chosen, a book was kept at the engineers' camp, and a very large majority of the opinions are favourable to it, many visitors being converted from hostility to approval on seeing the facts of the case - in fact, one guest goes so far as to say the following: 'The Falls in their present position cannot possibly detract from the beauty of the Bridge.'" (Scientific American Magazine, July 1905)

Hobson defended the decision to build the Bridge in its current position and strongly dismissed the objections of those who protested against its location:

"It was the lot of engineers occasionally to be charged with perpetrating acts of vandalism, and the engineers in the present instance had not escaped the attacks of those highly aesthetic people who asserted that utilitarian works of man should not be permitted to exist in the presence of scenery famous for its natural beauty. It was sometimes possible to sympathize with these views, but, on the other hand, even a railway bridge need not necessarily spoil; it might even add a charm to a beautiful spot, and a line of metals might give considerable interest to a grand scene without the least detriment." (Hobson, 1907)

"The opinions of those - happily they are very few in number - who protested against the location of a railway bridge near this unique spot, are worthy of all respect, because they are based upon an intimate knowledge of the place, and a love for its beauty that is to them above every other consideration. I think, however, that until they saw the bridge which is now built, they failed to understand what sort of structure was to be erected. Dreams of unsightly towers shooting up into the air, or nightmare visions of Charing Cross bridge straddling in horrid lines across the gorge and projecting black cylindrical legs into the depths below, probably afflicted them. All such notions, however, have now been dissipated: no one objects to the bridge... indeed, it has been the object of many flattering observations. So that there only remains in the minds of a few individuals, for whom I entertain the greatest regard, the lofty view that no handiwork of man should be placed in such close proximity to the grandest work of Nature. But this is quite a matter of taste." (Hobson, 1923)

Ignoring widespread objections to the location of the Bridge, Rhodes' wishes had prevailed. Hobson visited the Falls during the latter stages of construction in mid-1905 and recorded meeting Colonel Frank Rhodes, one of the prime objectors to the site, with both men staying at the Victoria Falls Hotel:

"When at Victoria Falls last July (1905), I had many talks with one of the chief malcontents, the late Colonel Frank Rhodes, whose untimely end I cannot but deplore, for a more charming personality I never met. Looking at the Bridge from our breakfast table, in his cheery way he said: 'Well, I have done all I could to prevent the bridge being built there; but there it is, and nothing is now left for me to do but pray daily for an earthquake.' But he confessed that he liked the thing itself very well." (Hobson, 1923)

Colonel Frank Rhodes contracted malaria whilst at the Falls, dying from blackwater fever after returning to the Cape in late September, aged 54. His prayers however, were nearly answered a few years later when in 1910 an earthquake shook the town of Livingstone, sending a shower of rocks into the gorge. Before sending a fully loaded train across the Bridge a pilot engine conducted a test journey, but thankfully the Bridge was unaffected.

The Victoria Falls Bridge has been cited for its elegance of design and to the way it relates to its natural setting as well as its practical functionality. Sir Alexander Kennedy, President of the Institute of Civil Engineers (1906-1907), is recorded as saying:

"The lines of the structure, themselves quite beautiful, brought out at once the vastness of the gorge itself, which without the structure could not be realized. Before the bridge was built the gorge was something very beautiful but quite indefinite, but directly that beautiful arch was put up it gave an entirely new interest to the landscape." (Hobson, 1907)

Hobson adds that Sir Alexander *"did not think anybody who had seen the Victoria Falls Bridge would ever find fault with the engineers who designed it."*

The Bridge has been described as a 'poem in steel,' Lord Curzon writing in The Times in 1909 of 'the filigree span of the railway bridge - an ornament rather than a desecration to the scene.' According to the American Society of Civil Engineering the Bridge 'embodies the best abilities of the engineer to enhance the beauty of nature rather than detract from it.' Views, however, are still divided. In one recently published coffee-table book on the Falls, the authors reflected:

'A poem in steel'

"Once construction is complete, it is much more difficult to remove it than if it were simply disallowed in the first place. In time it becomes an accepted part of the landscape, and eventually an object of historical curiosity. Few now would wish to see the Victoria Falls Bridge removed, but it is, in truth, a hideous monument to Victorian vanity." (Teede and Teede, 1994)

At the time the Bridge was claimed as the highest railway bridge in the world, being approximately between 355-411 feet (108.2-125.3 m) above the water, depending on the season and river levels. The title was soon relinquished to the Fades Viaduct, in Puy de Dôme, France, the central span of which is 434 feet (132.2 m) above the Sioule River, built in 1909. Several higher bridges have since held the record. In September 2016 Chinese authorities announced the connecting of the Beipanjiang bridge, in mountainous south-western China. The 1,341-metre span soaring a new record of 1,854 feet (565 m) above the river opened to road traffic in December 2016.

Part of the Attraction

The Bridge soon became an instantly identifiable icon and recognised symbol of the Falls, as well as an important part of the visitor experience, allowing tourists to explore both sides of the Falls with ease and opening up a new view of the Falls, from the Bridge itself. Passenger trains crossing the Bridge would pause to allow travellers the opportunity to admire the Falls, and no doubt reflect on the vision of Cecil Rhodes in daring to imagine his railway crossing 'where the trains, as they pass will catch the spray from the falling Zambezi.'

Sykes, author of the first official guidebook to the Victoria Falls, published by the British South Africa Company in 1905, records:

"The view from the centre of the Bridge affords the visitor the best possible idea of the height of the Falls, and in that sense the most impressive." (Sykes, 1905)

Clark, writing in his Guide to the Victoria Falls published a few years later recorded:

"Standing on the Bridge (which is the highest in the world), a magnificent view of the Gorge and Boiling Pot, and of the 'Rainbow Fall,' may be had, and the visitor will doubtless tarry awhile to drink in the beauties of the scene. Proceeding on the journey across the Bridge, and at the extreme or north end, and ascending a flight of steps, a magnificent panorama is presented to the view." (Clark, c.1911)

Tickets Please!

John Walter ('Jack') Soper was employed by the Railway Company as the Bridge watchman and toll-master, arriving to take up duties in December 1905. Soper's main task was to guard against the risk of fire on the wooden deck of the Bridge, walking after each passing train to ensure any coal embers dropped by the engine were extinguished.

A small toll-house was built close to the southern approach, from which tickets for foot-passengers, at one shilling each way, were issued.

"A certain Mr Jack Soper was the guard for a number of years, circa 1906, and he had perfected a 'tube' to hold the printed 'toll' tickets supplied by the railway's chief accountant. It worked surprisingly well, but the fun started when Mr Soper went on leave.

"Mr Breach, who was station master at the time, persuaded an unattached local resident to cover Mr Soper's duties. All went well until a trainload of excursionists arrived and naturally wished to walk over the bridge. They achieved their objective, but it was what went on behind the scenes that led to all the fuss.

Soper's south-bank toll hut overlooking the Bridge

"When Mr Breach saw the relief guard that evening to find out how the trippers fared, the latter explained that all had gone well, but that he had had great difficulty in issuing so many tickets as he could not get them out of the tube except by using a pin. He said he thought the whole idea of the 'tube' was stupid.

Early Bridge ticket

"To Mr Breach's horror he found that the tickets had been issued out of sequence, from the top of the tube (with a pin) instead of being drawn out at the bottom in the usual way. And, of course, they were somewhat mutilated. The relief guard had simply not thought of anything so simple. The whole affair meant a special letter of explanation to the chief accountant and 'much binding' ensued."

Soper's role ensured he met almost every visitor to the Falls in those early days as nearly all visitors crossed the Bridge to view the Falls from both banks.

"Mr Soper had his living quarters close to the Toll House and one of the attractions for visitors was a young cheetah which was kept in a cage. Thousands of photographs must have been taken of this animal as a souvenir of 'Darkest Africa' at the time. More than one of them found their way into popular overseas magazines." (Rhodesia Railways Magazine, August 1967)

The toll levied on pedestrians crossing the Bridge was cancelled in March 1914 (Rhodesia Railways Magazine, September 1957).

Crossing the Kafue

After Kalomo, which had been reached by mid-1905, the next target for the railway were the zinc and lead mines at Broken Hill (Kabwe). The contract was again awarded to Pauling, who committed to build the 281 miles (452.2 km) of track from Kalomo to Broken Hill in 277 working days. A major hurdle was the bridging of the Kafue River, one of seven bridges on the line and again designed by George Hobson of Sir Douglas Fox and Partners. The wide floodplains of the river were reached in mid-February 1906.

"Designed by G A Hobson and destined to have 13 spans of 100 ft. [30.5 m] each, it was to be at that time the longest bridge in Africa. Accordingly it posed a formidable challenge to Arthur Lawley, but he rose magnificently to the occasion. His massive pontoon, 95 ft. [28.9 m] long, 45 ft. [13.7 m] wide and 5 ft. [1.5 m] deep, could carry either a locomotive or two trucks. Spans were slid one at a time on to the pontoon, and hauled out into the stream to be floated into position. Once in the right place, they were raised by hydraulic jacks to their resting place on top of the piers. All 13 spans were put into place within eight days." (White, 1973)

Photographs show at least two engines being floated across the Kafue by means of Lawley's pontoon during this period, a 4th Class 4-6-0, No.75, hired by Pauling from the Cape Government Railways, and a 7th Class 4-8-0, both of which must have crossed over the partially completed Victoria Falls Bridge before travelling north.

The total length of the Kafue Bridge was 1,365 feet (416 m). The 100 miles (161 km) of line from the Kafue to Broken Hill, were built entirely with materials ferried across the Kafue River on a steel pontoon. By the time the bridge was completed the line had already reached its destination, the railway construction gangs again showing off their skills as they reached the end of the work:

"Some of the plate-laying gangs had been with Paulings' on the work for many years, in some cases even from the start of the line from Vryburg in South Africa. As a final exhibition of their skill, the last half-mile into Broken Hill was laid with materials off-loaded from the plate-laying train behind, carried forward by hand, and laid with such rapidity that the train passed over the newly-made track without a pause, or even a slackening of the turning of its wheels... The last dash was recorded in a cinematograph picture. Cinema photography was then in its very early infancy, and the Pathé cine man who braved the wilds was, as far as I know, the first to come to Rhodesia. He had a very energetic morning, busily dodging from one antheap to the next (and there were many antheaps in that country) in his attempts to keep abreast of it all." (Varian, 1953)

On 20th June 1906 the first official train reached Broken Hill.

"A V.I.P. train arrived there on the 20th June, 1906, to celebrate, the guests having been given the doubtful honour of filling the first truck to carry minerals away from the mine." (White, 1973)

It had been expected that mine production would call for a train a day, but the

A 7th class 4-8-0 being ferried over the Kafue

service was quickly cut to only two trains a week, and soon after only one.

> *"The line to Broken Hill (now Kabwe) was officially handed over and opened for traffic on 1st September 1906. The quality of mineral ore at Broken Hill proved poor, and the service cut from two to one a week. Unfortunately, after moving 13,428 tons of ore from Broken Hill, this traffic suddenly ceased in May 1907 owing to difficulties in the treatment and separation of the lead and zinc ores at the refinery in Wales. So the expected daily train did not materialise and the service was cut to one train a week."* (Croxton, 1973)

Varian, who after a brief period assisting with the bridge engineers had become District Engineer for the Railway Company on the line north, later wrote:

> *"The Cape to Cairo Railway came to an end in the middle of a burnt-out vlei, without even a buffer-stop at the rail terminus. Beside it stood a solitary telegraph pole, and in this atmosphere of desolation, it languished for several years."* (Varian, 1953)

Maramba No.1

In mid-1905 Pauling received delivery of a second shunting engine, also manufactured by Manning, Wardle & Company. The small engine, works number 1656, was initially stationed at Pauling's Maramba Depot and named 'Maramba No.1.' The locomotive varied in a number of differences to the Jack Tar, some perhaps specifically requested by George Pauling himself.

> *"A close comparison of photographs of the two locomotives reveals a number of differences in their design, the chief of which are that the 'Maramba' has*

evenly spaced wheels; much more protection in the cab for the driver; a higher, thinner chimney; two steps instead of one, no vacuum brake, and the usual safety valve on the boiler top instead of 'Jack Tar's' tapered brass valve. Other minor differences are also visible. The only known 'vital statistics' of 'Maramba' are that the cylinders were of 12 in. [30.5 cm] *diameter and 18 in.* [46 cm] *stroke compared with 'Jack's' cylinders of 11½ in.* [29 cm] *by 19 in.* [48 cm] *stroke."*
(Rhodesia Railways Magazine, July 1967)

The Maramba engine was used on the construction of the line north to Broken Hill and the subsequent extension to Elizabethville (now Lubumbashi) in the Belgian Congo (now the Democratic Republic of Congo). The retired engine is displayed outside Lubumbashi Station.

One Year On

A year after the official opening of the Bridge, and with the Bridge now handed over to the Railway Company for management and operation, Mr Townsend wrote to Mr Charles Corner, the Resident Engineer at Bulawayo, regarding a few minor unfinished aspects of the construction.

"When the construction of the Victoria Falls Bridge was completed, there were a few pins and two of the side panels of the bridge missing, and these had to be forwarded from England. I have now received advice... that these articles have been shipped... I shall be obliged if you will take delivery of the articles and do what is necessary. I have advised the Station Master, Victoria Falls, to hand the goods over to your representative when they arrive." (Rhodesia Railways correspondence, September 1906)

At the Falls, Mr James Buchan, the District Engineer, was responsible for the receipt of the parts and overseeing their installation.

Rust and Repairs

In January 1907 Sir Douglas Fox and Partners requested a six month inspection and review of the Bridge, drawing particular attention to the examination of the steel paintwork and deck timbers, which it had been suggested should be covered with a 'cement solution' for protection. Care was also expressed to check the concrete foundations of the Bridge:

"Will you take an opportunity of examining the main bearings and see whether the whole of the concrete is sound and free from cracks. If there should be

Goods train crossing Bridge

any cracks, they should be carefully grouted up with cement and it would be a good thing if the whole of the concrete was covered with tar, so as to make it impervious to moisture. This should however be done in the dry weather." (Sir Douglas Fox and Partners, January 1907)

The subsequent inspection revealed that during the course of the rains, rust had indeed started to attack the structure. In February Sir Douglas Fox and Partners advised:

"We are duly in receipt of your letter of the 19th January, and note that since your visit of July last, when the Bridge showed no signs of rust or peeling, that there are now signs of rust in a few places and that in your opinion the Bridge will now require repainting as quickly as possible... We are inclined to think that the peeling and rust referred to will not be general, but will occur in spots, as is generally the case with new steelwork, in consequence of the first coat of paint having been applied to surfaces of steel which have not been thoroughly cleaned or from which the mill-scale has not been perfectly removed. Patches of paint on these spots must inevitably peel off. It is very important, before applying the new coat, to thoroughly clean off all rust and dirt by means of scrapers and wire brushes. The whole of the rust should be carefully and thoroughly removed and the bared steel well covered with three coats of red lead paint, and after this has properly dried and set, the final coat of silver-grey can be applied." (Sir Douglas Fox and Partners, February 1907)

The following month the company arranged to send from England over 2 tons of red lead paint, 150 gallons (682 litres) of linseed oil, 2 tons of final silver-grey paint, four dozen paint brushes and three dozen wire brushes for the work on the Bridge (Sir Douglas Fox and Partners, March 1907).

Harnessing the Falls

With the paint only just dry on the steelwork of their great engineering achievement of spanning the Zambezi gorge, the Chartered Company turned their attention to promoting the next grand scheme in their plans - harnessing the power of the Victoria Falls themselves.

The British South Africa Company had originally sold the contract to develop the hydro-electric potential of the Zambezi in the vicinity of the Victoria Falls in 1901 as a key part of the industrial development of the region. On 24th July 1901 the African Concessions Syndicate Limited obtained a seventy-five year concession from the Company to harness the water power of the Zambezi at the Victoria Falls for the development of electrical power to supply mining and other industries.

In October 1903, Sir Charles Metcalfe and Mr I F Jones (manager of the Chartered Company) visited the United States to investigate the system by which the power of Niagara Falls was harnessed. Sir Charles was interviewed in the New York Times in regard to the Victoria Falls power scheme.

> "It is to develop the iron and coal industry that we intend to utilize the 9,000,000 horse power [6711.2 MW] which the Victoria Falls possess. Within seventy miles [112 km] there exists probably one of the greatest coalfields in the world, and experts are now examining large iron deposits in the same vicinity. We expect to find at Niagara most useful hints for the establishment of a similar plant in Rhodesia." (New York Times, October 1903)

Visions quickly spread of the industrial growth that would follow:

> "It was confidently assumed that urban and industrial developments would be on the scale of Niagara City and Buffalo, which had grown up on the basis of power generated from the Niagara Falls... The South Africa Handbook of 1903 noted that thanks to the proximity of coal, minerals and water power, the site possessed 'all the factors for the creation of a great manufacturing centre. A new Chicago, let us call it Cecilton, will spring up near the banks of the Zambezi.'... [In contrast] Niagara's precedent was invoked again in debates over conservation, this time offering a negative example. Lord Curzon was not alone in feeling that the Victoria Falls were more sublime than Niagara on the

grounds of the 'lack of signs of civilization,' and it was widely believed that new industrial prosperity in Niagara had spoilt its aesthetic appeal." (McGregor, 2009)

At the time of the construction of the Falls Bridge, Varian, and another engineer, Everard, were detailed to conduct a survey of the Victoria Falls, above and below the Falls, to access the feasibility of a hydro-electric power generation scheme. Along with others of the same period, such as Molyneux and Lamplugh, they were the first to conduct scientific geological surveys of the area. In 1906 further details emerged on the potential of the scheme, aimed primarily at potential investors in South Africa.

"Engineers propose to put the Zambesi River, at points near the Victoria Falls, at work generating power, that is to be forced into many parts of South Africa - indeed, to points, it is hoped, many hundreds of miles away. American and Continental electrical experts are in accord in favour of the scheme, and all agree as to its feasibility, practicability, and ultimate value. Professor Forbes, who was so intimately connected with the work at Niagara was the first to point out the possibilities of the Zambesi, and to him, more than any other man, will South Africa owe its gratitude should the efforts now being made result in anything like the success anticipated...

"Luckily on the Zambesi, as on the Niagara, dams and canals are not required. The fall is perpendicular and abrupt, or nearly so. The Zambesi has possibilities, it is believed, readily available, reaching as high as 500,000 horse-power [373 MW]. At present the Rand, which the projectors of the present scheme hope to supply with power, uses 150,000 [112 MW]. There is an available head at the Victoria Falls of 330 ft. [100.5 m]. By cutting a canal fifteen to twenty miles [24-32 km] in length, which can be easily done, a head of 1,000 ft. [300.5 m] will be obtainable, which would mean the possible development of 1,000,000 horse-power [746 MW]. The construction of such a canal would cost comparatively little, and the beauty of the falls would not be marred." (New Zealand Herald, May 1906)

Despite the positive spin placed on the scheme by the Syndicate, doubts were also expressed as to the feasibility of transmitting the generated electric power the great distance required to reach the South African gold mines.

"At the comparatively low voltage to which the alternating current system is limited in long distance transmission, a South African expert says, the enterprise would be killed by the capital cost of the large and expensive *transmission cable required to carry the power by the best route to the Rand, which would involve the traversing of a distance of at least 700 miles [1,126.5 km].* " (New Zealand Herald, May 1906)

Victoria Falls Power Company

The concession to develop the power of the Falls which had been granted to the Africa Concessions Syndicate was ceded in late 1906 to the Victoria Falls Power Company Ltd. (renamed the Victoria Falls and Transvaal Power Company Ltd. in 1909). By this agreement the Company was allowed to make use of the entire water power of the Zambezi in the vicinity of the Victoria Falls for the purpose of developing and transmitting electrical power.

At the beginning of December 1906 it was reported that the Transvaal Government had rejected the Victoria Falls power scheme, fearing that importing hydro-electric power from outside the territory would upset the local coal mining industry. Despite the apparent lack of interest in the in the scheme in South Africa, the new Victoria Fall Power Company's share issue in London and Berlin was fully subscribed in the same month.

Industrial Visions

The prospects of harnessing the power of the Zambezi quickly led to predictions of widespread industrial growth. The 1907 Christmas Issue of the Livingstone Mail contained an interesting fictional piece entitled 'A Peep into the Future' and imagined the Falls and Livingstone fifty years into the future. Moore had perhaps been inspired by an article written by L S Verner in The World's Work of September 1907, forecasting a southern Africa in 1957 where the hydro-electric power of the Falls had been harnessed to industrialise the region.

"At Victoria Falls there will be another Manchester... Victoria Falls will light Bulawayo and the Upper Zambesi Valley." (New Zealand Herald, October 1907)

In his article Moore lets his imagination run wild with dreams of unrestrained economic growth and tourism development, with little appreciation or awareness of the need to conserve and protect the natural aspects of the Falls.

"Livingstone covers an area of some 30 square miles [48.3 square km]; the banks of the river, both above and below the Falls are crowded with hotels and blocks of flats of various periods of construction and styles of architecture - the oldest and ugliest being in this immediate vicinity on the South bank. On either

side, for ten miles [16 km] above the Falls, there are excellent terraced roads, the South side is almost covered with hotels, interspersed with palatial private residences, many of which have of late fallen into the hands of enterprising caterers; the islands in mid-stream, of which there are a great numbers, have been converted to like uses, though some of the larger are utilised as pleasure grounds and are nightly crowded with holiday makers attracted thither by illuminations, music and entertainments. In the day time the river is almost covered, from bank to bank, with craft of every conceivable description, from the pre-historic rowing boat and motor launch to the more familiar surface-skimming aerostatic vessels...

"The South bank is the fashionable side; here are to be seen the travellers and tourists from America, Europe, Australia and the East, promenading of driving on the esplanades, or shopping among the curio booths and kiosques which line certain portions of the upper drive... Bridges of fantastic pattern span the huge canon from Livingstone and Cataract Islands to the Rain Forest, and hydraulic lifts descend every few minutes through the rock to the edge of the boiling tumult of waters below. The Eastern end of the Falls - which has been dry since '25, and after the tragedy following the phenomenal rain-fall in '33 has been protected by the Imbault barrage - has been made into a popular bathing resort, a magnificent flight of steps having been cut from the top of the bank to the level of the back-wash below; there are, of course, lifts as well.

"The gorge below the Falls is lined with mills, factories and workshops of mammoth proportions. Metal-working, textiles, cellulose and beverages seem to be the chief industries and manufactures. Some four million hands are regularly employed and their dwellings and institutions cover an are which stretched from the North bank to the Old Town, seven miles [11.2 km] away." (Livingstone Mail, December 1907)

Livingstone residents and investors in the power scheme would, however, have to wait over thirty years before development of the Victoria Falls hydro-electric scheme became a reality. Fifty years later the extensive industrial development of the Falls envisaged by Moore was fortunately still an unrealised dream.

Epic Adventures...

On 21st September 1908 the first motor vehicle visited Livingstone and received special permission to cross the Bridge, with a receipt for the 20 shilling toll noting on the bottom 'First motor car to cross Zambezi Bridge.' It was driven by Lieutenant Paul Graetz on his expedition from Dar es Salaam to Swakopmond, the first

Graetz in Livingstone before crossing the Bridge

motorised transit of the continent from east to west coast, completed between 1907-09.

...and Fabulous Beasts

In 1911-12 Graetz crossed Africa again, in a journey completed in two stages using motor-boats for significant sections, first travelling from the east coast up the Zambezi and then Shire River to Lake Nyasa (now Lake Malawi) and transporting overland before reaching Lake Bangweulu (part of the upper Congo basin located in north western Zambia), and later traversing the Congo River. Whilst in the region of Lake Bangweulu Graetz recorded reports from local people of a unknown reptile, *"a degenerate saurian which one might well confuse with the crocodile, were it not that its skin has no scales and its toes are armed with claws"* (Graetz, 1912).

Graetz's written account of this monstrous lizard, together with some rather inconsistent and incredible accounts from subsequent travellers, appear to have originated from local African belief (common throughout the region) in a mythical river spirit-serpent, here known as *Mokèlé-mbèmbé,* merging with European imagination to create a twentieth century legend of the 'Congo Brontosaurus.'

To Be or Not to Be?

The ongoing existence of the Victoria Falls Hotel was a source of frustration for Major Coryndon, the Administrator of North-Western Rhodesia. He supported the concerns of Livingstone residents and did his best to have the Hotel removed from its site, deploring the positioning of the buildings within sight of the Falls. The Livingstone Mail finally concluded early in 1907:

"[The Administrator] *announced that he had failed in his endeavours to have...* [the Hotel] *abolished. It had originally been erected as temporary accommodation for engineers, etc. employed on the Bridge and Railway construction, and for visitors to the Falls, and was to be pulled down as soon as a new township* [of Livingstone] *was laid out; He could hold out no hope of this being done, however."* (Livingstone Mail, January 1907)

Livingstone became the capital of North-Western Rhodesia at the end of the same year, bringing at least some life to the struggling township. The town remained the capital after the formation of Northern Rhodesia in 1911 (following the amalgamation of the territories of North-Eastern and North-Western Rhodesia) up until 1935 when the administration was moved to Lusaka, the current capital.

Landslide Washes Line Away

Originally the railway line ran round in front of the Falls Hotel, trains arriving at the Railway Station before turning on a special extension of track and then looping back round in front of the Hotel before passing on down to cross over the Bridge. In early 1909, a torrential rainstorm, during which seven inches of rain fell in five hours, eroded the sandy soils and created a substantial landslide, resulting in a section of the line in front of the Hotel becoming unstable. The line was soon after re-laid with trains passing straight through the Station, on a new section of track curving down to the Bridge.

On to the Congo

Rich copper deposits had been discovered to the north, including at Bwana M'kubwa (near Ndola), 200 kilometres north of Broken Hill, and also in the Katanga Province of the Belgian Congo (now the Democratic Republic of the Congo) and plans were made for one more extension of the railway. Pauling was again awarded the contract and in May 1909 construction work started to the Congo border and beyond to Elizabethville, some 300 miles (483 km) from Broken Hill.

On 11th December 1909 the railway crossing of the Congo frontier was celebrated by a gathering of British and Belgian notables, at which point the final rail lengths on the border were connected with specially made copper fishplates, placed by Mr (later Sir) Lawrence Aubrey Wallace, Administrator of North-Western Rhodesia (1909-1911), and Col. Wangermée, Lieutenant Governor of Katanga. The great push of railway construction northwards had all but come to an end.

"The track was laid to the Congo border by 1909 and by 1910 passengers could travel from Cape Town to Elizabethville, over 2,300 miles (3,680 km) across Africa, and nearly half way to Khartoum. By the time of the outbreak of the First World War, 2,000 route miles (3,200 km) of track had been completed in less than 20 years in Southern and Northern Rhodesia." (Hyder Consulting, 2007)

The Weekender

From 1910 a local passenger train service ran from Livingstone to Victoria Falls on Saturdays, known popularly as 'The Weekender,' transporting Livingstone socialites over the Bridge for Saturday night dances at the Hotel. The train comprised a Nasmyth Wilson locomotive, hauling one composite first and second class coach.

"The train was colloquially known as The Weekender and the Saturday night dances at the Falls Hotel brought good patronage from the young people, especially as the railway detached one or two carriages at Victoria Falls station into which in the small hours the tired dancers would retire for a few hours rest before the carriages were coupled up to the northbound train back to Livingstone.

"For a time in 1916 the steam train was replaced by the first Rhodesian railcar. This 'rail motor coach,' as it was officially described, was propelled by a 70 hp petrol engine; it was 24 ft. [7.3 m] in length and seated twenty passengers with a little space at one end for light packages. Built by the Drewry Car Company in England it did not remain in service for a very long." (Croxton, 1982)

This petrol-driven railcar operated for between Livingstone and the Victoria Falls,

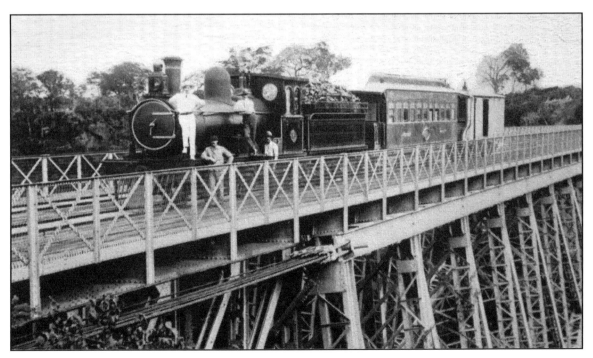

The Weekender pauses on the Bridge

The railcar on the Bridge, with north bank watch-tower in top right corner of image

operated between 1916-1922, and at weekends took passengers across to the Falls at the modest price of sixpence return.

Rail Connections

Special connecting train services were the life-blood of early tourism to the Falls, bringing cruise liner passengers to ports from the Cape in the south to Beira on the east coast, often in groups of hundreds at a time. First class return trips from the Cape to the Falls took thirteen days, including three nights at the Falls Hotel. To gain a sense of perspective on the size of the Falls, travellers were informed that eleven Union Castle mail steamers placed end to end would just reach across their length.

One such visitor was Mrs Getcliffe, of Cheshire, England, who travelled on a special train service from Johannesburg to the Falls and wrote of her travels in the 'Macclesfield Courier & Herald' in 1910. The train carried 100 passengers, 20 staff, two dining cars, a food supply wagon and five tons of ice.

> *"There were three passengers in each compartment, the remaining berth being used for our luggage. The seats were very comfortable, being fitted with springs, and at night they were turned into beds with pillows, sheets, etc. Each compartment had a lavatory basin and a looking glass so that passengers could either dress in their compartments or, if they so preferred, in the bathrooms."*

Mrs Getcliffe and her companion stayed at the Falls Hotel and recorded they were *"not charmed with the accommodation or the service, but when we felt inclined to complain we reflected that all the food had to be brought from Cape Town or Beira, and that there are no shops nearer than Bulawayo, which is a 20 hours journey by rail."*

Mrs Getcliffe appears similarly unimpressed by having to pay Mr Soper a shilling for crossing the Bridge:

"There is a railway bridge across the Zambesi guarded by a man in the employ of the railway company. He lives in a hut at one end of the bridge and allows foot passengers to cross on payment of one shilling. As no visitors come in the summer we asked him how he spent the time. He told us he went up country shooting game, large and small." (Rhodesia Railways Magazine, March 1962)

A 1911 South African Railway pamphlet promoting the Falls described them as *"the most beautiful gem of the earth's scenery"* (Green, 1968).

Soper's Curios

In 1911 Jack Soper established Soper's Curios next to Clark's Huts, and set about giving Clark some healthy competition in the growing souvenir trade. Clark meanwhile had diversified into offering rickshaw rides and river cruises, businesses which he would later sell to the Hotel.

Soper, together with another resident, is recorded as being the first to descend the face of the Falls down into the gorge. Soper described the first part of the descent, from Livingstone Island, and made with the aid of ropes, as 'precipitous,' but the lower part as moderately easy climbing. During the descent Soper obtained some unique photographic views which he used on his own series of postcards. But it was not altogether a pleasure trip, and it was recorded that they had no desire to repeat the achievement (Varian, 1953). Soper became an expert crocodile hunter, and was known amongst locals as the 'Crocodile King' for his skills and abilities in catching these dangerous predators, establishing a captive crocodile pool as an attraction next to his store.

"His recreation was killing crocodiles, due to one of them taking his dog, and his favourite point of vantage was above the Silent Pool from which point he shot many hundreds of them... [He also] made crocodile traps which he placed in the Maramba River, again catching and killing many hundreds of these reptiles. There was, however, no demand for crocodile skins at that time so Mr Soper sometimes exported them live. His workshop, where he manufactured curios from local products, was something out of the Ark. Low-roofed, with no electricity, he had natives lying on their backs on tables pedalling cycle wheels to apply power for the lathes!" (Rhodesia Railways Magazine, July 1958)

The author Lawrence Green recalls hearing a story from Jack Soper:

"He told me about two Livingstone residents named Mackenzie and MacLaren who were riding over the Victoria Falls Bridge on a motorcycle when they encountered a fully-grown crocodile. They stopped a car, borrowed a coil of rope, tied the jaws securely and loaded the crocodile into the back of the car. The crocodile lashed the men with its tail and they were glad when Soper relieved them of the struggling brute." (Green, 1968)

Soper's Curios traded for over 100 years, having changed hands after Soper's death in 1953 and relocating from its original site in 1975 to a new site behind the Post Office. This shop closed its doors in May 2016 before relocating to its current location within the adjoining Elephant's Walk Shopping and Artists Village complex.

The Hotel Rebuilt

By 1912 plans were well advanced for the complete redevelopment of the Hotel. Having secured the future of the Hotel on the site, the Railway Company now planned to erect permanent brick buildings. Preliminary drawings were supplied by Sir Charles Metcalfe, but the final designs, dated April 1912, were executed in Bulawayo by the Railway Company's chief architect Frank Scott (Creewel, 2004).

The new buildings were constructed from 1914, with the work delayed by the impacts of the First World War. Furnishing and fitting of the buildings further delayed the opening of the new Hotel building until mid-1917, at an approximate construction cost of £40,000. The old Hotel buildings remained on the site and were used as overflow accommodation for many years.

The cool and spacious single-storey building, consisting of a central wing and two flanking side wings, housed twenty-four bedrooms and two private suites, overlooking the stunning view of the gorges, Bridge and rising spray of the Falls. Guests could relax in the Lounge, find time for quiet reflection in the Writing Room, or socialise in the Drawing and Music Room, Smoking Room or small private bar.

The spacious new Dining Room was designed with echoes of features from the original railway shed which had served as the Hotel's first dining room, an example being the high oval windows, also a feature of the Lounge. Another short wing housed the Hotel's kitchens.

The Hotel laundry was steam operated from the customised boiler of a Kitson-Meyers railway engine, decommissioned in 1912 after service at Wankie Colliery, and which remained on site and operational for over eighty years.

The new Victoria Falls Hotel

The Hotel was significantly expanded during the latter half of the 1920s, with the addition of new wings and second floors, growing and expanding into the grand Hotel we know today. The Hotel underwent a significant refurbishment during the 1990s which restored many of the original architectural features of the buildings and recaptured its historical ambience (Roberts, 2021a).

A Vital Link

During the period of the First World War (1914-8) the Falls Bridge was a strategically important transport link for the movement of British South Africa Police and Rhodesian troops - and a potential target for German saboteurs, with German South West Africa (now Namibia) only 80 kilometres away. To prevent attack the Bridge was defended with a military guard, consisting of two officers, ten European rank and file from the British South Africa Police and fifty armed native police from Southern and Northern Rhodesia, supported with two mounted Maxim recoil-operated machine guns.

> *"As soon as war was declared the combined detachment of both British South Africa Police and Northern Rhodesian Police under Major A E Capell D.S.C, B.S.A.P, at the Victoria Falls Bridge was instructed to guard the railway Bridge and to patrol both banks of the Zambezi River above the Bridge. Blockhouses were erected and an electric light plant supplied at the bridge, and an observation post consisting of one officer and twenty-five men was placed at Kazungula, on the Zambezi River, fifty miles [80.5 km] west of Victoria Falls."*
> (Brelsford, 1954)

A reinforced concrete watchtower commanded a view of the Bridge and a rail-mounted mobile searchlight shunted back and forth along the Bridge, until finally it was decided to position it off the Bridge, from where it could light up the entire structure.

"The second track was used on several occasions to site the searchlight correctly and... was no easy task. The searchlight was mounted on a bogie truck which was moved from one position to another both on and off the bridge before the authorities were satisfied. Finally it was parked on the south bank, in the vicinity of the Rain Forest, and from this point it was able to command not only the approaches but almost the entire bridge itself even down to the foundations." (Rhodesia Railways Magazine, May 1964)

I Spy...

During research for the first edition of this book, I was contacted by Geraldine Morris, who told me the story of her father, Mr Sydney Burton, who had come to Rhodesia from South Africa in 1911 to join the postal service. He had been postmaster in various parts of the country and in 1914 was sent to Victoria Falls as the postmaster there to replace a Mr Jan Lotz who had 'disappeared.' Mr Burton recorded in his unpublished memoirs:

"I had previously worked with Lotz, a most likeable fellow, in the Bulawayo office. After checking the office records (in Victoria Falls) to the best of my ability, I reported a small discrepancy in the office cash. Incidentally, the

Watchtower and searchlight (to left of image) overlook the Bridge

sergeant in charge of police at Victoria Falls at that time was a charming fellow who had previously received his blue for hockey at Oxford. This sergeant, Sgt. 'Podge' Burton (no relation) informed me that a warrant for Lotz's arrest had been issued before my arrival at the Falls and, as a result of investigations, the postmasters' coat together with a German revolver, with a spent cartridge had been found half way across the bridge. From these clues, it was surmised that Lotz had shot himself and his body had fallen the 412 feet [125.5 m] into the Zambezi River below. Lotz was an enthusiastic photographer and, although he was German, had been recruited to the Rhodesian Postal service from the Orange Free State of South Africa. He was an excellent Morse telegraph operator and had managed to wrangle a transfer to the Falls after Bulawayo.

"As it ultimately transpired, he was a German spy! Among his belongings were intricate photos of the Victoria Falls Bridge. This incident occurred just a few weeks before the outbreak of the First World War and an interesting fact is that, some years later, early in 1918, when I was serving in the War in East Africa, during a transfer of European prisoners at Luklede Mission, who should greet me but a big, though thin, grizzly bearded fellow, who was none other than my old friend, Jan Lotz in a dilapidated German officers' uniform! I tried to locate him later but was told he had been sent to a prisoner of war camp in Bombay."
(Morris, 2011)

Mounted police patrol the Bridge

O'Sullevan's War

Upstream of the Falls British and German interests came into direct contact through the Caprivi Strip, ceded by the British in 1890 and connecting German controlled South West Africa with the Zambezi. In 1909 the Germans established an administrative base at Schuckmannsburg (renamed Luhonono in 2013), opposite Old Sesheke. With the outbreak of war in Europe this isolated outpost suddenly became of significant strategic importance to both sides.

"In September, 1914, it was decided that the occupation of Schuckmannsburg, the German post in the Caprivi Zipfel opposite Sesheke on the Zambesi River, would allay considerable apprehension amongst the native tribes in the British territory, and would safeguard the trade routes on the river. Schuckmannsburg was occupied without resistance on the 21st September by Major Capell, who had moved his joint Southern and Northern Rhodesian detachment from Victoria Falls to Sesheke for this purpose. The German resident and his European police subordinate were made prisoners of war and a Commissioner for the Bechunaland Police Force put in charge of the station." (Brelsford, 1954)

Irishman Captain J J O'Sullevan, now seconded to the Northern Rhodesia Police, led a mobile reinforcement column in the occupation, recording:

"The largest, most vindictive, and venomous mosquitoes I have seen ... in the wet season it is a swamp and unhealthy; in the dry weather the heat is terrific, whilst the sand is deep and uncomfortable to walk in." (Paice 2007)

In late July the following year Captain O'Sullevan distinguished himself in leading the defence of Saisi (on the north-eastern border of Northern Rhodesia) against a German force of 1,500 men. Vastly outnumbered, O'Sullevan and approximately 400 men withstood eight days under continuous siege, refusing German pressure to surrender. O'Sullevan was promoted to Major and awarded the Distinguished Service Order for his leadership.

After several engagements along the border of Northern Rhodesia with German East Africa (now Burundi, Rwanda and mainland Tanzania) O'Sullevan was wounded and invalided back to Britain in October 1915. In April 1916 he was appointed Commanding Officer of the 19th (Labour) Battalion of the Cheshire Regiment, which he led to the western front in France. In July 1916 he assumed command of the 11th (Service) Battalion of the Sherwood Foresters (23rd Division), taking part in the severe fighting on the Somme, until he was again invalided,

British entrenchments, south east Africa.

wounded and gassed, in August 1916.

Lieutenant Colonel O'Sullevan was appointed Commandant of the Ballykinlar Command Depot, County Down (Ireland), in April 1917. After the end of the War and establishment of the independent Irish Free State he moved to Killarney, County Kerry, where he served as Resident Magistrate, retiring in 1922 to breed horses. His son, Peter (later Sir), born in 1918, would go on to become a famous horse racing commentator for British television and radio, becoming known nationwide as 'the voice of horse racing.'

A Tale of Two Boats

The Bridge and railway from the Cape played a strategically important role in the balance of power north of the Zambezi, illustrated in an audacious British plan to challenge German control of Lake Tanganyika. Adjoining German East Africa, German dominance of the lake was broken in a series of engagements known as the Battle for Lake Tanganyika.

At the start of the war Germany had two large warships on the lake, the 60-ton 'Hedwig von Wissman,' and the 45-ton 'Kingani.' The sinking of the British African Lakes Corporation's steamer, the 'Cecil Rhodes' in November 1914 gave them unchallenged control of the lake and ability to launch incursions into the Belgian Congo and Rhodesias.

In April 1915, John R Lee, a big game hunter and veteran of the Second Boer War, arrived in London with an ambitious plan for the British Admiralty. Lee brought news that the Germans were assembling a third ship, the 1,200 ton 'Graf von Götzen,' which had been constructed in Germany, disassembled and packed into 5,000 crates and transported by ship to Dar-es-Salaam and then by rail to the lake. Lee proposed the transportation of two small and highly mobile motor launches, armed with mounted guns, from Britain to the Cape by sea, then from the Cape to Elizabethville by rail (crossing the Victoria Falls Bridge in the process) and then hauling them overland the final distance to the shores of Lake Tanganyika.

Admiral of the Fleet, Sir Henry Jackson, approved the plan with the words *"It is both the duty and the tradition of the Royal Navy to engage the enemy wherever there is water to float a ship."* Lee was appointed second in command of the expedition, under the command of the only available officer, Lieutenant-Commander Geoffrey Basil Spicer-Simson. Lt-Cdr Spicer-Simson was a rather colourful character, literally, his upper body covered in tattoos. Spicer-Simson assembled a 27 man team to travel with the two selected motorboats, initially built for the Greek Air Force, which he creatively suggested be named 'Cat' and 'Dog,' names promptly rejected by the Admiralty. His alternatives, 'Mimi' and 'Toutou,' meaning 'Miaow' and 'Bow-wow' in French, were somehow accepted.

The boats were launched and tested on the Thames in early June 1915, and by mid-month started their epic journey, transported by steamship to the Cape together with Spicer-Simson and his unit of men, and then on from the Cape by rail the 3,700 kilometres to Elizabethville, where they arrived in late July 1915. Three months later the boats had been transported 240 kilometres through the Belgian Congo and over the Mitumba Mountains with terrain varying in altitude from 2,000 to 6,000 feet (600-1,828 m) above sea level. Responsible for overseeing the transportation of men and machines through the virgin bush, carving out roads and constructing over 150 temporary bridges along route, was ex-Cleveland Bridge engineer Arthur Davison. The boats were then assembled and sailed the final 640 kilometres down the Lualaba River to the shores of Lake Tanganyika.

And Then There Were Three...

It was late December, however, before HMS 'Mimi' and 'Toutou' were finally launched on the lake, each armed with a fore-mounted 3-pounder Hotchkiss gun and aft-mounted Maxim gun. With the element of surprise still on their side, the 'Kingani,' with her 6-pound artillery gun, was quickly captured and relaunched under the British flag - renamed by Spicer-Simson as HMS 'Fifi.' She was the first enemy warship to be captured by the British during the war.

It was some time before the Germans came looking for the 'Kingani.' The 'Hedwig,' armed with a 12-pounder gun, was engaged in February 1916, and following a prolonged cat and mouse chase lasting several hours was finally critically hit by HMS 'Mimi' with their last available ammunition shell. The Germans abandoned ship, scuttling her in the process. Spicer-Simpson was by now promoted to Commander, but reluctant to take on the much larger and more heavily armed 'Götzen,' which soon came out in search of the missing 'Hedwig,' with his small flotilla of boats. On seeing the superior enemy ship Spicer-Simpson apparently went back to bed, forbidding his men from attacking. Instead he went off for several months on a mission to find himself a bigger boat.

Meanwhile the British had provided the Belgians with four Short floatplanes to attack the 'Götzen' whilst moored in harbour, and after several unsuccessful bombing runs the Germans withdrew in late July 1916, scuttling the ship in the process. Only later was it discovered that her guns were wooden dummies - having been removed by Lieutenant Colonel von Lettow-Vorbeck for use by his mobile artillery units in his overland campaign against the British.

The exploits on Lake Tanganyika caught the public imagination, and inspired C S Forester as the basis for his book 'The African Queen,' later made into the film of the same name, directed by John Huston and starring Humphrey Bogart and Katharine Hepburn.

Following reports of his erratic behaviour Spicer-Simson was not given another command. He become known for his unconventional habit of wearing a skirt, which combined with his tattoos earned him a rather eccentric reputation. The 'Götzen' was later raised by the British, when it was found that little work was needed to be done to repair the ship. She returned to service on 16th May 1927 under the name 'Liemba,' and still sails Lake Tanganyika as a passenger and cargo ferry.

HMS Mimi, with Spicer-Simson (standing)

The Lion of Africa

The main threat to British territories in southern Africa came from a small German unit under the command of Lieutenant Colonel Paul von Lettow-Vorbeck, known as the German 'Lion of Africa.' Stationed in German East Africa (now Burundi, Rwanda and mainland Tanzania), he ignored defensive orders from Berlin and the colony's governor, embarking instead on a determined offensive guerrilla operation to disrupt and attack British activities.

General Paul von Lettow-Vorbeck

Von Lettow-Vorbeck avoided direct engagements with British forces, instead directing his men to engage in raids into British East Africa (now Kenya), the British Protectorate of Uganda, Northern Rhodesia and Nyasaland (now Malawi), targeting forts, railways and communications. It was only on the 14th November 1918, three days after the official surrender of German forces, that von Lettow-Vorbeck was informed of the armistice and agreed to a cease-fire at the spot now marked by the Von Lettow-Vorbeck Memorial in present-day Zambia. Essentially undefeated in the field, the now General von Lettow-Vorbeck was the only German commander to successfully penetrate British overseas territory during the War.

Dinosaur Hunt!

The opening up of the remote regions of the Congo to European travellers resulted in further incredible stories of fabulous creatures from the depths of the vast jungle swamps. Engineer turned settler Arthur Davison recalled the beginnings of one such story when interviewed by the writer Fuller some years later:

"Arthur Davison had a fund of stories which could not have been explored adequately had I been able to stay a fortnight at Ngosa farm. He talked of Imbault, the French engineer in charge of the work on the Falls Bridge; of William C Collier, who, in discovering the Roan Antelope Copper Mine, went far to set in motion the huge industry of the modern Copperbelt; of Norton Griffiths, a railway contractor nick-named 'Dynamite Jack' for his part in blowing up Romanian oil wells in the First Great War; ...and of a score of others whose names I could not even note with sufficient speed. But the tale which most

took my fancy, perhaps on account of its very absurdity, was the story of 'Brontosaurus Dave,' an old-timer with an imagination and a sense of humour which was apt to take him into dangerous places. Dave was a prospector. At one period in his career he did much work in the Congo. It happened that one day while in that country he met a party of missionaries, some of whom lent a somewhat too credulous ear to the stories told by this new acquaintance. Now unfortunately, one of the clergymen considered that he possessed journalistic abilities and was on the watch for stories which might be suitable for submission to certain prominent newspapers with which he claimed to have contacts.

"Perceiving that this listener at least had a liking for the marvellous, Dave obliged with a lively description of a meeting with a brontosaurus, a species of prehistoric beast normally supposed to have been extinct for uncounted years. Dave was a first-class story-teller and, doubtless, he added many a little touch of verisimilitude to lend conviction to his narrative. And the missionary-journalist listened, marvelled, asked questions, and, in due course, wrote, with the result that the story appeared in certain British and American publications.

"Soon thereafter, Dave was sought by journalist who eagerly demanded further details of his apocryphal adventure. And, culminating absurdity, eventually an American expedition arrived in the Congo with the avowed intention of visiting the brontosauri in the natural haunts." (Fuller, 1954)

In late 1919 Captain L Stevens set out from London on a one-man (and his dog) expedition to hunt down the beast and generating world-wide newspaper coverage, and some ridicule, in his search for the 'Congo Brontosaurus.' Despite the excited media hype the reports were *"regarded in London with mingled amusement and scepticism"* (New Zealand Herald, December 1919).

Trolley Transport

Always on the lookout for a new business opportunity, Percy Clark claims to have been the first to see the potential of a local rail transport system to take tourists from the Hotel to the Falls, and also to the boat landing stage, from where he operated his river safaris.

"I now got another idea of making money, and I took a trip home on the strength of it. My notion was to run a trolley-line down to the bridge and the landing-stage. I was very kindly received by the B.S.A.C. office in London... but after exhibiting details of my scheme I was told that the whole thing was in the province of the railway company... Then years went by, however, before the

trolley-line came into being. I have always believed that I got the idea first, and believing that I think I ought to have shared the profit." (Clark, 1936)

The local rail trolley system was finally developed in 1920 by the Railway Company, at a cost of £4,000.

"The trolley system had three sections, not physically connected. From the hotel, a double track ran one mile northward to 'Trolley Junction,' where passengers changed to two single track lines leading to the various points of interest. One line (the longest) ran eastward beside the Rain Forest to the Victoria Falls Bridge, and was later paralleled by a road; the other ran northward to the Landing Stage and Boat House... From the terminus of this line, three-quarters of a mile upstream from the Falls, tourists could join launch or canoe trips to the islands in the river. Photographs show two types of vehicle, a four-seat trolley with cross seats pushed by two Africans, and a knifeboard eight-seat trolley pushed by three or four. Each trolley had a roof and canvas awning, and a screw handbrake applied from either end." (Price, 1966)

Telephone boxes were installed at each terminus and junction so that a trolley could be summoned when required. The fare was one shilling each way. The trolleys were available during the hours of daylight only, although special arrangements could be made with the Hotel Manager for night-time trips to see the lunar rainbow.

The Victoria Falls Hotel rail-trolley service

Following development of a local road network the trolley service was discontinued in 1957, replaced by the Hotel with a road minibus service. During their life the trolleys were used by an estimated two million guests in 'thirty-seven years of romantic yet reliable service.' Under the shade of the mango trees in the Hotel courtyard stands a reminder of days past, with one of the original trolleys used to transport guests to the Falls preserved and displayed, and offering a shady seat for quiet contemplation and reflection on bygone days.

End of Charter

In the early 1920s the Chartered Company and British Government began negotiations over the future of the Rhodesias following the end of the period of the Company's Royal Charter. Many expected that Southern Rhodesia would become part of the Union of South Africa, and detailed proposals were drawn up in Johannesburg (even including the drafting of postage stamps showing the Victoria Falls). Southern Rhodesia was granted self-governing status on 1st October 1923. Northern Rhodesia became a British Protectorate in on 1st October 1924, setting the two countries on very different paths to eventual independence.

Reconstruction of the Upper Deck

Urgently required upgrades were carried out to the Bridge in 1929, strengthening the structure to allow for heavier train loads and the addition of a road and pedestrian footway, removing one of the two sets of rails. The whole of the original deck of the Bridge down to the underside of the cross girders was replaced with a stronger, wider and higher deck. The works were detailed in the Rhodesia Railways Bulletin of November 1929:

"During the past 25 years the weights of engines and rolling stock have steadily increased, so that the present loads of trains are far higher than were dreamed of when the Bridge was built. It was therefore decided to strengthen the Bridge to enable it to carry trains with 20-ton axle loads, thus leaving a considerable margin for future increases in the weights of engines and rolling stock.

"At the time of the building of the original Bridge, road traffic was negligible, and it was therefore considered not necessary to provide a bridge to carry road vehicles. This has now been changed by the tremendous progress made in the development of motor vehicles. In designing, therefore, the alterations now being made to the Bridge, provision was made for the inclusion of a motor road, and this road over the Falls Bridge will form an important link in the Great North

Road... To obtain a road wide enough to take two streams of traffic and to allow pedestrians ample footway free from danger, it has been necessary to increase the width of the deck by about 13 feet [4 m], the added width being obtained by an overhang on either side of the Bridge." (Rhodesia Railways Bulletin, November 1929)

The new deck improved the overall strength of the original structure whilst also raising the level of the deck and rails, addressing two shortcomings of the original design and construction. At the time of the presentation of his report on the Bridge to the Institute of Civil Engineers, London, in 1907, Mr R J G Read observed:

"The cross girders carrying the floor were placed along the top chord, at and between the intersections of the bracings. This brought a secondary stress upon the top member which was said to be provided for; but it seemed that the intermediate cross girder might have been omitted, and the cross girders rested on the intersection of the bracing. The girders would have had to be a little deeper, and that would have raised the roadway higher." (Hobson, 1907)

The flaw in the original design appears to have been the major motivation for the upgrade:

"The old deck consisted of cross girders 12 ft. 6 in. [3.8 m] apart, which had the disadvantage of placing a load midway between the panel points of the Bridge, thus introducing a bending load on the top chord of the arch. The new deck will do away with this, the cross girders being spaced on the main span 25 feet [7.62 m] apart and coinciding with each panel point. This needs a much deeper type of girder for the rail bearers, and the new cross girder is therefore raising the rail level 4 ft. 7 in. [1.4 m]."

The contract for the replacement deck was drawn up in December 1928, the work again being awarded to the Cleveland Bridge Company. The contract timetable committed to the erection of a 25 foot (7.62 m) bay of the new deck each week. Rail traffic over the Bridge continued throughout the reconstruction, with the rails raised to their new position under a temporary supporting structure.

"Before the erection of the new steelwork could be commenced, the track over the bridge had to be raised on temporary structures to the new level and also moved to a new alignment at as near the centre of the Bridge as possible. The new design of the Bridge deck permits one line of railway track only." (Rhodesia Railways Bulletin, November 1929)

The contractors were allowed only 14 hours, one day a week, during which they could hold up traffic. In the event traffic was only delayed between 8 to 10 hours each period. The total cost of the contract was just over £32,870. The work commenced on 23rd July 1929 and the last section was placed into position on 4th December, with only minor stoppages of the heavy railway traffic passing over the Bridge.

"The contractor's plant consists of a Smith's 7-ton locomotive steam crane, and a large steam boiler which supplies steam for the running of a steam-driven air compressor. This compressed air is used for working the pneumatic riveting hammers and a drill. Steam is also provided to run an electric generator, which supplies current for working two electric drills and, in case of need, supplies electric light. They also have an oxy-actylene plant for burning through certain parts of the existing deck to facilitate removal. As a stand-by they have a portable air compressor driven by an internal combustion engine." (Rhodesia Railways Bulletin, November 1929)

Additional works to the structure of the Bridge included strengthening of the two bottom chord members of the bridge at both ends of each arch by the addition of side plates to the existing members; strengthening of the bottom cross bracing of the bridge by addition of transverse lateral struts; replacement of bolts on some

The new deck of the Bridge

Positioning the new deck sections of the Bridge

of the existing connections of the principle members of the main span; and the cleaning and adjustment of bearings at the ends of the approach spans.

The contract also detailed that all new steelwork was to be painted with red lead and pure boiled linseed oil paint on both meeting surfaces of any steel plates or sections before they were to be installed and riveted. Afterwards the new steelwork was to be cleaned, scraped and painted again with a coat of red lead and linseed oil before the final two coats, *"the first of Dampney's Graphite and the second of Dampney's Miraculum of light grey colour or other approved paints."*

Excavating the new road approaches to the Bridge took some time, as blasting was not allowed so close to the Bridge and all the work had to be carried out by hand.

"The road approaches to the motor crossing are now being cut [March 1930]. As no blasting is permitted within half a mile of the bridge, and the rock is basalt, the work will take some time, but it is anticipated that the bridge will be open to road traffic at the end of March next." (Powell, 1930)

First to Cross

The road across the Bridge was opened in 1931 and the first member of the public to cross in a private vehicle was Ms Marina King who, with a friend, was travelling to Cairo in a Morris Cowley. She records in her autobiography 'Sunset to Evening Star,' that she was, however, disappointed to have been beaten to the honour of being the first across the new road by a Mr C K Thompson, a railway engineer who was closely associated with the work. He had crossed in a motor vehicle less than an hour earlier.

On the Road

During the period 1925 to 1928, a dirt road had been constructed between Bulawayo and Victoria Falls, providing access to the area for the growing number of regional tourists travelling by motor-car, and by 1931 a Motor Service Station had been developed close to the Falls Hotel, offering running repairs and spare parts.

Edward Herbert ('Ted') Spencer was initially posted to the Falls after joining the British South Africa Police in April 1923. He soon saw the potential of a motor garage and car hire business, 'Spencer's Garage and Service Station,' to service the growing numbers of vehicles arriving at the Falls.

Driving over the new Bridge roadway

Flight of Angels

In the late 1920s a further transport innovation gave guests to the Victoria Falls Hotel a new and breath-taking way to experience the Falls, from the air - the 'Flight of Angels.' The short-lived Rhodesian Aviation Company was established with the aim of tapping the tourism potential of the Falls, with their first aircraft, an Avro Avian, operating commercial 'flips' over the Falls from 13th June 1929.

> *"The company was formally registered on 17th April, 1929, but owing to a serious delay in the delivery of the 'Bluebird', the commencement of flying operations had perforce to be postponed... a second-hand Avro Avian aircraft was purchased... and was immediately flown up to Livingstone, where it was put to work operating 'flips' over the Victoria Falls."* (McAdams, 1969)

The Bluebird, when it arrived, proved very popular for flights over the Falls, the side-by-side seating making conversation between pilot and passenger easy.

Spencer's Airways

In July 1935 Spencer purchased a second-hand de Havilland Puss Moth aircraft, ZS-ACB (re-registered as VP-YBC), and employed the services of a recently qualified young pilot Jack McAdam, to offer game viewing and charter flights. Operating under the name of Spencer's Garage and Air Service (later simply Spencer's Airways) flights were serviced from the Victoria Falls Aerodrome, which Spencer himself cleared out of the bush. In early 1936 Spencer acquired a DH.83 Fox Moth biplane (VP-YBD), in which he trained and soon also qualified as a pilot. Spencer is recorded practising aerobatics and amazing his ground-bound African spectators - so much so that 'Spensaar!' became a commonly adopted local exclamation of amazement (Whitehead, 2014).

Flights were not without the occasional problem. McAdam recorded in early 1937 the propeller came off the single-engined Fox Moth mid-flight over the Falls, and a hasty forced landing was made in the bush, incredibly without serious damage to pilot or plane (Stirling and House, 2014).

Spencer's Puss Moth VP-YBC above the Falls

Access All Areas

An article in the Rhodesia Railways Bulletin of July 1937 detailed further additions to the Bridge completed in that same year:

"For many years it was felt that facilities for inspection and painting of the Falls Bridge were inadequate, especially after the new deck with its roadway, railway track and footpath was added in 1929... The present scheme combines the purpose of utility and good appearance.

"On each side of the bridge there are two gangways running from shore to shore, with a system of intercommunicating ladders. Top gangways are placed against the top booms of the bridge, under the deck, where the heavy shadows from the roadway and footway make them inconspicuous and in fact invisible from any great distance. The handrails of these top gangways are capably of carrying travelling cradles for use in inspecting and painting the outer faces of the main arch girders.

"The lower gangways follow the curve of the arch and here the handrails have

Under the deck of the Bridge

been designed to be used also as compressed air mains. It is necessary only to couple a compressor to either handrail for compressed air to be available at any part of the Bridge to operate pneumatic tools for any necessary work.

"Cradles have also been arranged to work from the outer hand rails of the roadway and public footway, while steel ladders give access to main bearings and other important points." (Rhodesia Railways Bulletin, July 1937)

Despite the light-weight construction of the gangways, with open mesh floors, they added over sixty tons of material to the Bridge, bringing the total weight of the Bridge steelwork to 1,868 tons.

In 1937/8 some forty-two men (two Europeans and 40 Africans) were employed for six months repainting the Bridge:

"Owing to the heavy spray from the Victoria Falls the steelwork of the Bridge is almost constantly wet for nearly six months in each year, and painting can be done only during the remaining six months when the steel work is comparatively dry. This involves the application of over 1,200 gallons [~5,455 litres] of paint. On many of the large bridges in other countries it is possible to keep a small gang almost constantly employed, and the work of painting and maintenance is thus rendered easier." (Rhodesia Railways Bulletin, July 1937)

View of the Falls from the new deck

Power from the Falls

Located in the bend of the third and forth gorges, known as the Silent Pool, construction of the Victoria Falls hydro-electric Power Station was finally started in mid-1935 by the Victoria Falls and Transvaal Power Company. The station was opened in 1938 by Sir Hubert Young, Governor of Northern Rhodesia (1935-8).

"His Excellency Sir Hubert Young, the then Governor of Northern Rhodesia, cut the first sod of the canal from the north bank of the river on the 6th May 1935... [and] set the first turbine in motion on the 16th March 1938. The building was erected on solid foundations 13 feet [3.9 m] *above the then highest known level of the Zambezi River at this point."* (Woods, 1960)

The initial scope of the scheme was to supply electricity to the neighbouring town of Livingstone, with power transmitted by underground cable, as well as serving the Falls Hotel and Railway Reserve on the south bank.

The Power Station

"At the request of the Government great care was taken to avoid spoiling the beauty of the Falls. The water inlet is some distance above the Falls and an underground pipe-line leads to the top of a gorge some distance below them. An overhead power cable was necessary in one place [to cross the gorge and serve the Hotel]*, but it was put as far from the Falls as possible and it will not be seen by tourists. Even in the dry season the quantity of water taken by the Power Station is negligible in comparison with the total flow over the Falls."* (Parsons, 1938)

In 1949 the then Northern Rhodesian Government acquired all interests in the Power Company for the sum of £104,000. The original capacity of 8 Megawatts (MW) was expanded in 1969 with the addition of six generators of 10 MW each (installed underground) and again in 1972 with an additional four units, increasing the total maximum capacity to 108 MW. The expansions and subsequent plant developments have significantly increased the infrastructure impacts both above and below the Falls, as well as increasing the volume of water diverted from the Eastern Cataract of the Falls.

Suspected Sabotage

In the build up to the Second World War suspicions arose over a young German man, Hans Rhuys, who had settled in Livingstone. Rhuys had gained employment with Leopold Moore, married and fathered a son, yet still piqued the interest of Mr Norman Brody, then Chief of the Criminal Investigation Department at Livingstone. In September 1939, two days before the outbreak of war it was discovered that Rhuys was planning an imminent departure, for one only, into Angola. Brody, without any solid evidence, gambled and arrested Rhuys, and ordered a search of his flat, discovering a German cipher and, after infinite trouble, a diary conveying the activities of espionage and sabotage to which he had been committed.

"A thorough examination was then made of the Bridge and, sure enough, engineers discovered that a hole had been drilled into one of the main supports - a hole large enough to have held sufficient gelignite to weaken the whole structure and render it unsafe for use. For a while the C.I.D. tried to solve whether this malicious interference was, in fact, the work of Hans, or whether it was the product of some previous agent, whose activity it was to 'cap' during the next day or so by 'planting' the explosive, firing it and bolting for the border. But the truth about Rhuys's case may always remain concealed, for, shortly afterwards, the central figure of the drama died, and of his own will." (Rhodesia Railways Magazine, December 1953)

On the outbreak of the War, the Bridge was again placed under military guard during which time it was constantly patrolled. It is recorded that whilst on duty one Rhodesian guard fell to his death.

Side-view of the Bridge

Wings of War

During the period of the Second World War (1939-45) the Falls were visited by many Allied soldiers and airmen receiving their basic training in the country. A major Flying Training School operated outside Bulawayo for trainee airmen from across the British Commonwealth. A total of 8,500 British Royal Air Force (R.A.F.) crew were trained in Southern Rhodesia over the period of the war, and training continued into the fifties. One such young pilot recalled his visit to the Falls:

"Our party was booked into the excellent Hotel and we were escorted to our rooms. We had lots of robust fun during our stay and were impressed to see that the... Bridge across the deep gorge had numerous long ropes (or chains?) dangling from it. We were impressed because these ropes had been fitted to stop R.A.F. pilots from looping the loop around the bridge!" (Conroy, 2003)

The story is unlikely, not only for the improbability of performing loop-the-loops around the Bridge, but also that the area for 120 kilometres from the Falls was restricted airspace during the period of the war.

It has long been local rumour that Ted Spencer was the first to attempt the daring stunt, flying his Puss Moth under the Bridge in July 1938, although fellow pilot McAdam is on record as discounting the story. There is, however, a photograph of Spencer flying incredibly low over the Devil's Cataract. Later writers credited Livingstone based pilot Noel McGill as the first to have achieved the feat (Meadows, 2000).

View from the air, with train crossing and wing of plane in bottom right of image

Livingstone Joins the Jet-set

In 1950 Livingstone Airport was developed on a new site approximately three miles (4.8 km) to the north-west of the town, with a fully modernised control tower and tarmac runway.

It was proudly reported that the spray from the Falls could be seen from the control tower. The opening ceremony for the new £1.5 million facility was performed by Lord Pakenham, Northern Rhodesia Minister of Civil Aviation, on 12th August 1950. Lord Pakenham himself chose to arrive by the Solent flying boat service (Stirling and House, 2014).

> *"The inaugural flying display which followed caused immense interest; many of the spectators had never seen a jet aircraft, so it can be imagined that a fine exhibition of formation aerobatics by four South Africa Air Force Vampire pilots... caused something of a sensation."* (Flight Magazine, August 1950)

The airport served as the main international gateway for the region, including guests of the Falls Hotel, until the opening of Salisbury Airport in 1956 and the subsequent development of the Victoria Falls Airport in 1967.

In the same year as the new Livingstone airport opened Mr H D Bridge was appointed Northern Rhodesia's first Tourist Officer as the country attempted to capitalise on its new aviation advantage. Based in Livingstone Mr Bridge's brief was to promote the country's tourism attractions at home and abroad.

Growth of Commercial Air Travel

On 2nd May 1952 the 'Yoke Peter' (G-ALYP), a de Havilland Comet Mark 1, took off from London Heathrow to Johannesburg carrying 36 passengers on the world's first commercial passenger jet flight, proudly operated by B.O.A.C. and heralding the new age of the jet airliner. The flight

DH Comet 'Yoke Peter' at Livingstone Airport, 1952

stopped for refuelling at Rome (Italy), Beirut (Lebanon), Khartoum (Sudan), Entebbe (Uganda) and Livingstone before arriving in Johannesburg, a distance of 6,700 miles (10,782 km) in 18 hours 40 minutes flying time - and a total journey time of 23 hours 20 minutes. A single fare cost £175 and a return £315.

The subsequent growth of long-haul commercial air travel opened up direct, and faster, travel to the Falls, further boosting tourism. International carriers serving Livingstone soon included B.O.A.C, Air France and South Africa Airways. For a period all passengers disembarked at Livingstone Airport to stay overnight at the Falls Hotel before either continuing their flight to South Africa or travelling by land to many of the National Parks and other destinations within the region.

The development of national and regional aviation routes, including those of Central African Airways (formed in 1946) during the 1950s, marked a significant development in tourist travel, breaking nearly fifty years of railway dominance. Despite this, the railway-owned and managed Falls Hotel continued to flourish during this period.

Rhodes Centenary Exhibition

The 1953 Rhodes Centenary Exhibition in Bulawayo was a significant event and boost for tourism to Rhodesia. The Railway Company promoted its primary role in the development of the country with a large exhibition pavilion.

Included in the railway exhibits was Cecil Rhodes' personal coach and the restored Jack Tar (both now housed at the Bulawayo Railway Museum), as well as a scale model of the Victoria Falls Bridge, complete with moving model train making the crossing with the Falls in the background and sound effects.

Scale model of Bridge with moving train

"Thirty thousand people have passed through the Rhodesia Railways Pavilion at the Rhodes Centenary Exhibition in considerable less than a month. They have, almost without exception, classed it as among the most spectacular and interesting on view." (Rhodesia Railways Magazine, July 1953)

Falls in Flood

In 1957 and 1958, during the construction of the Kariba Dam, the Zambezi experienced unprecedented seasonal floods. In March 1957 the rising waters flooded part of the Power Station in the Gorge.

"In 1957... the river rose higher than ever known before and reached, on the surge, a height of about 11 feet [3.3 m] above the level of the floor of the Power Station. All the windows by that time had been bricked in and practically all the main doorway was bricked in and reinforced with sandbags. No one knew how long the building could withstand the tremendous buffeting of the high waves of the Zambezi in spate and the Power Station staff with pumps going night and day cleared the building of water as it seeped in through many places in the walls. Access was gained by a temporary bridge of two steel pipes which swayed and swung as the mighty surges of water swept around the building like gigantic rollers on the sea shore.

"Profiting by the experience gained during this drama of man against nature, protective measures were taken and a reinforced concrete wall set in 2-3 feet [60-90 cm] of solid rock now surrounds the building to a height of 20 feet [6 m] above the floor level inside. An access bridge on concrete pillars now leads to an emergency doorway and the main entrance has been fitted with watertight doors... Again the Zambezi turned to fury in February and March 1958 and rose to an unprecedented high level, surging up to 15 feet [4.5 m] above the level of the floor inside the building with occasional waves splashing over the roof on the down-stream side. The Power Station staff were, however, the victors once again and marked yet another score against the Zambezi on the painted post at the side of the main entrance marking the highest levels reached by the turbulent water... It is estimated that with the heavy concrete protection now

The flood waters surround the Power Station

completed the building can withstand a river level of up to 10 inches [25 cm] *more than the 1958 record flood."* (Woods, 1960)

Above the Falls on the northern bank of the Zambezi a stone monument erected by the National Monuments Commission marks the highest recorded level of the Zambezi in March 1958.

The Kariba hydro-electric dam was constructed between 1955 and 1959 at a cost of $135 million, creating the largest man-made lake (by volume) in the world - holding an estimated capacity of 180.6 cubic kilometres of water - a title it still holds to this day. The formation of the lake displaced an estimated 57,000 Tonga people from their cultural homelands along both sides of the river valley.

A Whispering Giant

In 1959 engineers undertook work to control rail movement and reduce vibration as trains passed over the Bridge. Apparently the vibrations were so bad that a rumbling noise would be made as trains crossed - so loud that it could easily be heard above the roar of the Falls and even on the Hotel veranda nearly a mile away, the Bridge becoming known as the 'Whispering Giant.'

"This is now a thing of the past for the rails over the Bridge have been welded into 120 ft. [36.6 m] *length and are supported by rubber pads on the running*

Tourists enjoying the view from the Bridge

timbers. This, and other maintenance work such as stiffening the hand rails, has virtually eliminated the noise, so that now all that can be heard is the 'click' of wheels as the pass over the rail joints." (Rhodesia Railways Magazine, March 1959)

Two Europeans and thirty Africans were employed on the periodical maintenance works which included a complete re-painting of the Bridge, which had last been repainted in 1948-9. The work took a total of 18 months, spread over three years, interruptions occurring when there was heavy spray from the Falls, particularly during the record Zambezi floods of 1957 and 1958.

Federation Folly

The short-lived Federation of Rhodesia and Nyasaland, also known as Central African Federation, was formed in 1953, comprising self-governing Southern Rhodesia, and the British protectorates of Northern Rhodesia and Nyasaland.

Growing African nationalism and general dissent, particularly in Nyasaland, persuaded Britain to agree to the dissolution of the Federation only ten years later. The 'break-up' negotiations, known as the Central Africa Conference, were hosted at the Victoria Falls Hotel over several days in July 1963. The Federation was officially dissolved on 3rd December 1963. After the break-up Nyasaland became independent Malawi on 6th July 1964, and Northern Rhodesia independent Zambia on 24th October 1964.

Southern Rhodesia, however, was to follow a longer, and more difficult path to democratic independence. In reaction to rising calls for majority rule, the white minority Rhodesia government, led by Ian Smith, made its Unilateral Declaration of Independence (U.D.I.) on 11th November 1965. Smith made the Declaration after days of tense negotiations with British Prime Minister Harold Wilson, who was only prepared to permit independence on the basis of giving the black majority population a fair share of power. The British Government, the Commonwealth, and the United Nations condemned the declaration as illegal, leaving Rhodesia unrecognised by the international community.

The Zambian customs and immigration post was built on the old 'scandal alley' site soon after Smith's Unilateral Declaration of Independence. On 30th June 1967 the unified railway system was split between newly independent Zambia and Rhodesia. Subsequent tensions between Zambia and white minority-led Rhodesia would once again make the Bridge the focus of much military activity.

Diamond Jubilee

During the period of the Bridge's Diamond Jubilee the whole steelwork structure underwent an extensive repainting programme. Sixty years after first being placed in situ and painted, the entire Bridge was stripped of its protective paint down to the bare steelwork, before being thoroughly inspected and then repainted.

"This is the first time since the Bridge was built that the steelwork has been stripped 'naked' of paint. Some sections were covered with up to thirteen coats which have inter-acted against each other allowing air pockets to form and corrosion to set in." (Rhodesia Railways Magazine, April 1965)

Work started in June 1963 and took over three years, not being completed until 1967. Painting was not the only work undertaken, with the whole Bridge undergoing a thorough and detailed examination.

Work in hand

"Work started on this gigantic task early in June when the first scaffolding was lowered to provide a platform for the special gang, two dozen strong, that is engaged on the 'cleaning up' process. They are using special pneumatic chipping hammers and pneumatic rotary wire brushes. When the work is in full swing over 630 labourers will be employed on the operation." (Rhodesia Railways Magazine, August 1963)

The old paint was chipped off and the steel exposed by using high-speed pneumatic chipping hammers and rotary brushes. Once the steelwork had been completely 'stripped' the bare steel was heated by means of gas flame torches to burn off any paint residue. Finally a new protective undercoat was applied. Repainting was carried out by 600 labourers and required an estimated 17,275 litres of paint, applied in three different coats.

"The first coat that is being applied is red lead and red oxide in the proportion of 70 to 30 and it is estimated that 1,800 gallons [8,183 litres] will be needed before the task is completed. The red lead is followed by a coat of micaceous iron oxide and then finished with a coat on non-bitumastic aluminium with an anti-fouling compound. A dried protective overall covering of five-thousands-of-an-inch is achieved. The second and third coats each require an estimated 1,000 gallons [4,546 litres] of paint making a total for the finished job of 3,800 gallons [17,275 litres]." (Rhodesia Railways Magazine, April 1965)

It was hoped that this treatment will last for about 60 years until the 'double Diamond Jubilee' of the Bridge in September 2025, although the Bridge was still to be given a new coat of aluminium paint every six years.

Providing the only rail link between Rhodesia and Zambia, the Bridge had carried many millions of tons of goods and thousands of passengers over the Zambezi. News reports emphasised that 'every lump of Rhodesian coal destined for Zambia's copper mines, and practically every ton of Zambian export copper,' had been carried across the Bridge over the last sixty years.

The reconstruction of the main Bulawayo to Victoria Falls strip road as a fully-tarred highway began in 1963 and took several years. The new road largely followed

Catching the spray from the falling Zambezi

the route of the old road, although re-aligned to a more direct line in places. The freedom of movement offered by the expanding road network attracted increasing overland travellers from regional markets, in particular South Africa, on self-drive safaris.

Victoria Falls Casino

The Victoria Falls Casino

Growing tourism levels eventually saw the construction of the Victoria Falls Casino, later known as the Makasa Sun Hotel, in 1966 on the site immediately next to the Victoria Falls Hotel.

"The modern, luxurious Casino Hotel was opened in 1966. It is air-conditioned throughout and has a bank, hairdressing salons, jewellery and other shops for the convenience of its patrons, besides a la carte restaurants serving breakfast 24 hours a day." (Rhodesian National Tourism Board, 1967)

Victoria Falls Airport Opens

The Victoria Falls Airport was opened in 1967, prior to which the Victoria Falls had been served by Livingstone Airport. With Zambian independence in 1965 the resulting customs and immigration formalities had become an inconvenience to travellers staying at the Falls Hotel. The new airport was built at some distance, 20 kilometres, from the Victoria Falls and the growing tourism town.

Despite all the new developments at the Falls, a late 1960s tourism information leaflet, produced by the Rhodesian National Tourism Board, still proudly presented the Falls as untouched by man and modern development.

"Today the Falls are almost exactly as Livingstone first saw then, unspoilt in all their grandeur. Nothing has been allowed to mar the natural beauty of the surrounding; even the disfiguring precaution of guard rails has not been permitted. As Livingstone stood, lost in wonder, so do many thousands of visitors each year." (Harris, 1969)

Seventies Struggles

Following the declaration of independence life in white-ruled Rhodesia initially carried on much as before, despite being unrecognised on the international stage and the imposition of trading sanctions. But with the ruling white elite representing less than ten percent of the national population the call for a popular representative government was steadily gaining momentum. In an effort to establish international recognition Rhodesia broke its last ties to Britain and declared itself a republic on 2nd March 1970, yet still found itself in international limbo. Political relationships between independent Zambia and white-controlled Rhodesia deteriorated and the Bridge was frequently closed to goods and passenger services. In 1969 the passenger service over the Bridge was indefinitely suspended, with Rhodesian trains terminating at the Falls.

Two main exiled independence groups rose to prominence in the struggle against Ian Smith's government. The Zimbabwe African National Liberation Army (Z.A.N.L.A.), the armed wing of the Zimbabwe African National Union (Z.A.N.U.) led by Robert Mugabe, operated largely from Mozambique and supported by the Mashona tribes in the eastern and central areas of the country. The Zimbabwe People's Revolutionary Army (Z.I.P.R.A.), the armed wing of the Zimbabwe African People's Union (Z.A.P.U.) led by Joshua Nkomo, was active in the north and west, using bases in Zambia and Botswana, and supported mainly by the Ndebele in the western half of the country.

The early 1970s saw an escalation in the struggle, with independence fighters based in Zambia launching strategic incursions and attacks against communication and infrastructure targets on the southern side of the river. On the night of the 16th January 1970 the Police Camp and Sprayview Hotel were attacked and shots were also fired at the Victoria Falls Airport buildings. During the subsequent operation to capture the insurgents the

Ian Smith at the Falls

railway line south of Victoria Falls was blown up. Land mine incidents and train derailments followed over the subsequent months as the conflict intensified. The following year, on 3rd August 1971, a train was derailed on the line to the Falls.

Eventually, on 9th January 1973, Smith announced the closure of border posts with Zambia, including Victoria Falls, until he received satisfactory assurances from the Zambian Government that it would no longer permit terrorists to operate and launch attacks against Rhodesia from within its territory. In response Zambia closed their side of the border with Rhodesia on 1st February 1973. The border remained tense, with the Falls Bridge again closely watched from observation bunkers on either side of the gorge.

Despite the official closure of the border, freight was still transported over the Falls Bridge. A Rhodesian engine would reverse a string of coal or grain trucks out on to the middle of the Bridge, and a Zambian engine would back-up onto the Bridge and pull them into Zambia, and vice-versa, several times a day.

On 15th May 1973 a tragic incident occurred resulting in the death of two Canadian tourists. Whilst exploring the gorges below the Power Station with friends, Marjan

Iduna Drijber and Christine Louise Sinclair (both 19) were both shot and killed by rifle fire from the north bank (Terpstra, 2008). Tourism collapsed on both sides of the river, with national tourism arrivals to Rhodesia decreasing to 250,000 in 1975.

Bridge Over Troubled Water

On 25th August 1975 the Bridge was the site of unsuccessful peace talks, known as the 1975 Constitutional Conference. The talks, lasting nine and a half hours, took place aboard a South African Railways coach from the 'White Train,' used in the 1947 British Royal Family Tour of southern Africa, positioned across the middle of the Bridge.

Supervised by South African Prime Minister John Vorster, the tense negotiations included Rhodesian Prime Minister Ian Smith, Zambian President Kenneth Kaunda, and representatives of the African National Council, led by Bishop Abel Muzorewa. The Rhodesian delegation sat on their side of the coach

Peace talks on the Bridge

whilst nationalist representatives sat on the Zambian side. One account records the staff were apparently rather too liberal with the bar service and two members became intoxicated and disruptive, helping talks to continue throughout the day. The talks failed to reconcile the representatives divergent viewpoints and the independence war gained intensity.

Lines of Attack

On 6th October 1976 independence fighters targeted the railway bridge over the Matetsi River, 30 miles (48 km) south of the Victoria Falls, with a mine detonating as a freight train passed over the bridge. The damage to the bridge temporarily cut the railway to the Victoria Falls and beyond, but after only five days repairs had been affected and the line reopened. A few months later, in early December, it was reported that the bridge had been targeted for a second time (New York Times, December 1979).

Insurgents directly targeted tourism in the town the evening of Saturday 30th October 1976 with an armed attack on the Peter's Motel in which one person died.

> *"African guerillas armed with grenades and automatic weapons attacked a motel at Victoria Falls late last night, killing one person and wounding two others, a spokesman for the Peter's Motel said today... Between 20 and 30 guests were staying at the motel at the time of the raid, the spokesman said. Victoria Falls, just across the border from Zambia, is a favourite holiday resort for Rhodesians... Rhodesian security forces have organised a search for the commandos."* (The Canberra Times, November 1976)

On 12th December 1976 a passenger train travelling south of Victoria Falls detonated a landmine. The locomotive and four passenger coaches were lifted from the track but did not overturn and no serious injuries were sustained. The passenger service to the Falls was subsequently suspended until after the war.

Falls under guard

Hotels Hit

By 1977 hotels and campsites were closing in the face of security concerns, including the Rainbow Hotel, mothballed until more favourable tourism conditions returned. Upstream of the Falls the Zambezi Camp was closed and access to the town controlled as increased security surrounded the tourism resort. In the early 1970s annual tourist arrivals to the country had reached 360,000. By 1979 there were only 79,000 recorded - the lowest total since 1963.

"Tourism was badly affected by the war and the country's hotels survived only because of support from Government in the form of subsidies and subsidised travel by local and international visitors. To help the battered tourism sector, the national airline and hotel groups introduced the Super Six scheme, in which guests went on air and road packages for up to six nights at significantly discounted prices. The scheme met with reasonable success and the number of visitors to hotels, including the Victoria Falls Hotel, was remarkable given the overall situation in the country." (Creewel, 2004)

On 2nd November 1977 the exclusive Elephant Hills Country Club, opened in 1974, was destroyed in a fire caused by a SAM 7 heat-seeking missile launched from Zambia. Apparently fired at a Rhodesia United Air Carriers light tourist aircraft which was circulating above the Falls, it missed its target and by chance landed on the thatched roof of the Hotel. The explosion was reportedly heard as far away as the Falls Airport. Luckily there were no casualties, but the hotel was completely gutted by the fire. The passengers from the light aircraft, piloted by Eddie Marucchi, apparently took it all in their stride. One, Mr Lief Bjorseth, was recorded as saying: *"It's not every day you get shot at - I got something extra for my money"* (Teede and Teede, 1994).

Elephant Hills burns

A few weeks later, on 19th December 1977 several people were wounded when the town and Falls Hotel came under mortar attack, with one off target shell narrowly missing the laundry outbuilding and causing minor damage. On Christmas Eve the town came under attack again, although without casualties.

Minefield Menace

In order to try and prevent insurgents entering the country along its vast borders with neighbouring Zambia and Mozambique, Rhodesian Security Forces resorted to the establishment of a protective 'cordon sanitaire,' consisting of a 25m wide strip of land, bordered with barbed wire fences on either side and containing three rows of anti-personnel land mines, running along extensive sections of its borders. At the Victoria Falls the whole town was enclosed within a surrounding 'cordon sanitaire,' which then ran downstream 220 kilometres along the gorges to Mlibizi, and containing one of the highest densities of mines in the world, with over 788,000 mines identified during clearance operations (I.C.B.L, 2009).

The minefields would continue to pose a serious threat to people and wildlife for decades after the war. It would take until 2015 before the vast majority of these minefields would be cleared (Victoria Falls Bits and Blogs, June 2015).

By 1979 the estimated number of insurgents operating inside Rhodesia totalled at least 12,500 and it was evident that insurgents were entering the country at a faster rate than the Rhodesian security forces could hope to contain or counteract.

Ready to Blow

In the latter stages of the decade Joshua Nkomo's Z.I.P.R.A. forces, with Russian backing, were actively planning and preparing fighters in Zambia with the intent of launching a major invasion across the Zambezi. Soviet Union President Nikolai Podgorny had even visited Livingstone and the Falls in March 1977, looking across to Rhodesia and *"the border between freedom and slavery that divides today's Africa"* (New York Times, March 1977).

> *"Back in Salisbury there was increasing alarm when a capture brought first-hand news of a Soviet-orchestrated invasion plan that would see conventional forces attack Rhodesia from bases in Zambia in a three-pronged offensive through Kariba, Chrundu and the Victoria Falls... Once in the country, with support of forces already in situ, the Soviet-backed army would take over the airports at Wankie, Kariba and Victoria Falls, then move on Salisbury and claim military victory. To oversee the plan the Soviets appointed Vladimir Buchihev, a hard man from the K.G.B, along with twelve advisers, to help Nkomo and his lieutenants get the job done."* (Wessels, 2015)

To prevent independence forces crossing the Falls Bridge the road surface was removed and in late 1978 and the Bridge set with explosives, ready to blow a critical section should it be necessary (Burrett and Murray, 2013).

One of the key individuals involved in the operation recently recalled:

"The job was a great one for any army engineer. Basically it was to take out the road component of the bridge but leave the bridge standing, just a case of knowing where to put the charges you would think but not so easy... First off to the railways, where we were given samples of all the steel that made up the framework of the bridge... Now as any engineer will tell you when cutting steel it has to be in a particular fashion and there is a formula to work out how much explosive you will require... So now we had the steel and the formula and went to the range to make sure it worked. Well it didn't!!! That steel had hardened over the years or it was just great steel when it was made, but it was not going to make our job easy! We added a third more explosive and tried again and this time with more success...

"The guys from S-Troop were magnificent decked out overalls and looking as if they were painting the bridge and in the meantime taking the charges out and gluing them on and connecting them up with cordtex. (Looks a bit like that yellow plastic washing line but is an explosive in its own right.) The irritation came the next day when checking with binoculars I saw two baboons sitting on the frame of the bridge eating the cordtex!!" (Anon, 2011)

The Victoria Falls Bridge with road surface removed

Zambia Isolated

In April 1979 Rhodesian forces bombed the Kazungula ferry, Zambia's only link with Botswana, and a vital transport connection for freight imports. The subsequent cutting Zambia's rail route to the east coast, with the destruction of bridges on the Tazara Railway in October 1979, left land-locked Zambia entirely dependent on the Victoria Falls Bridge as the last transport route into the country.

In early November Rhodesia announced that it was blocking crucial maize supplies into Zambia as a result of continuing incursions by independence fighters. Zambia, already suffering a national maize shortfall, now faced the spectre of widespread food shortages before the end of the year. Prior to the announcement three train loads of South African maize were being imported across the Victoria Falls Bridge into Zambia every day (The Canberra Times, November 1979).

Road to Peace

After the failure of a national power-sharing agreement, negotiated with moderate independence groups in 1978 but unrecognised by the two main exiled liberation groups, the British government invited all parties to peace talks in London. After fourteen weeks of talks, and with Rhodesia and Zambia on the brink of full scale war, the Lancaster House Agreement was finally signed on 21st December 1979.

International economic sanctions were lifted in late 1979 and the country reverted to temporary British rule until elections could be held. Lord Soames was appointed by the British government as Governor-Designate, arriving in Salisbury on 12th December. On 21st December 1979 a cease-fire was finally announced. The Falls Bridge reopened to rail traffic and in the last week of December 1979 a team of workmen restored the road surface.

Opposite sides meet on the Bridge,
December 1979

New Beginnings

The Zimbabwe flag proudly flies at the Hotel

National elections were held in February 1980, with the Zimbabwe African National Union-Patriotic Front, led by Robert Mugabe, receiving 63 percent of the vote. On 18th April 1980 interim British rule ended with divided Rhodesia becoming independent Zimbabwe, the country's capital being renamed from Salisbury to Harare.

Rail passenger services to the Victoria Falls resumed from 6th July 1980, although passenger services over the Bridge remain suspended to this day. Rhodesia Railways became the renamed National Railways of Zimbabwe in May 1980.

At the time there were concerns over the continuing increase in heavy freight traffic over the Bridge, and it was proposed by some that a new bridge should be built to take traffic away from the town and Victoria Falls environs. The Bridge, it was suggested, could be retained for pedestrian traffic and as a sightseeing foot-bridge for tourists (Bulawayo Chronicle, March 1980).

After the liquidation of Rhodesia Railways and the formation of the National Railways of Zimbabwe in May 1980, the remaining non-railway joint assets of Rhodesia Railways, which included the Victoria Falls Bridge and the Falls Hotel, were transferred to the ownership of the Emerged Railways Properties (E.R.P.), an interstate company under the shared ownership of the Governments of Zambia and Zimbabwe and eventually formed in 1997. The E.R.P. contracts the ongoing maintenance of the Bridge to the National Railways of Zimbabwe.

The Bridge was declared an International Civil Engineering Landmark in 1995.

Africa's Adrenalin Capital

During the late 1980s and early 1990s Victoria Falls saw the development of thrill-seeking adventure activities, earning the town a new identity as the 'adrenalin capital of Africa.' In addition to the traditional tourism activities - game drives, river cruises and flights over the Falls - new activities, such as white-water rafting and bungee jumping attracted a younger generation of travellers to the Falls.

White-water rafting on the rapids below the Falls was pioneered by an American company Sobek with the first expedition to traverse the rapids of the river below the Falls to Lake Kariba in October 1981, using inflatable rafts. Commercial rafting started soon after.

The fact that they had no specialist inflatable rafts did not stop the first Zimbabwean group to raft the rapids a couple of years later, who notably completed the trip in home-made rafts comprised of the tractor wheel inner tubes and bamboo frames. Professional Zimbabwe based companies followed, with Shearwater Adventures the first to run commercial rafting trips from the southern bank in 1985.

The narrow zigzagging Batoka Gorge offers some of the best quality white-water rafting in the world, with nearly half of the rapids classified as Grade 5 - the highest commercially runnable grading (Grade 6 is 'unrunnable'). The stretch of the river that runs downstream of the Falls is claimed to have the highest concentration of grade five rapids anywhere in the world, making the Zambezi the best white-water rafting experience money can buy - in the world. From 1996 to 1999 it was estimated that 50,000 tourists annually rafted the rapids below the Falls. Raft guides adopted the mythical river spirit-serpent of the Kariba Gorge, *Nyami-nyami*, as their totem, publicised after the construction of the Kariba Dam.

White-water thrills and spills

3, 2, 1, Bungee!

The Victoria Falls Bridge Bungee, the first commercial jump in Africa, was started by Kiwi Extreme in 1992. With a free-fall of 111 metres and the dramatic background of the Falls, it is one of the most scenic and spectacular jumps in the world. Establishment of the activity on the Bridge initially raised some complaints, as well as some consternation, among locals.

"'How much do they pay you to do that?' asked an elderly Zambian incredulously, as he put down his groceries to stare at the extraordinary spectacle. When told that they actually paid for the privilege of thus risking their skins, he went off shaking his head. White men were a strange breed, as everyone knew, but this was too much!" (Teede and Teede, 1994)

Chief Mukuni gets ready to jump

Notable jumpers included Chief Mukuni Siloka III, who appeared on the Bridge in full ceremonial regalia and accompanied by many locals, who were all in festive mood. After a brief hesitation he toppled into the void, to the accompaniment of wild cheers from the onlookers.

The activity, now operated by the Zambezi Adrenaline Company (part of the Shearwater portfolio of companies), has expanded to include a hair-raising 80m Bridge swing and 300m zip line. To date over 225,000 people have committed themselves to the thrill of jumping off the Bridge. In June 2011 Mr Kevin Banks became the oldest man to jump off the Bridge, undertaking a bungee swing. Mr Banks, 85 years young, had spent his professional life working on ropes and ladders on ships, perhaps accounting for his confidence.

The Bridge bungee became worldwide news when a freak accident occurred on New Year Eve 2011. During 22-year-old Australian Erin Langworthy's jump the bungee cord snapped just short of its maximum extension and she dropped head-first into the Zambezi River. Miraculously she survived with just minor injuries

(Victoria Falls Bits and Blogs, January 2012). Video footage of the accident was shown on global news channels and reached several million views on You Tube within days. The Bungee now has some of the most rigorous and regular safety tests in the industry - and a new rope.

The End of Steam?

During the 1980s the Zimbabwe rail system was electrified, with modern electric engines replacing the old steam-powered engines across the country. Subsequent decades of declining investment in infrastructure and rolling stock has resulted in the slow but steady deterioration of the national rail network and service. Towards the end of the 1990s there was a revival in tourist travel by special train, with first-class luxury train services such as the Rovos Rail 'Pride of Africa' making regular visits to the Victoria Falls, travelling from the Cape on through Zambia and Tanzania to Dar es Salaam.

Bridge Centenary

Approaching its one hundredth anniversary, the Bridge was closed to heavy traffic for over a year to allow for emergency work. A report, published in January 2005 by the National Railways of Zimbabwe, highlighted 'excessive vibrations being felt whenever a heavy truck transverses the bridge.' During the restrictions trains crossed at less than walking pace and haulage vehicles were limited to a load of 36 tons.

A classic view of the Bridge looking downstream

With the support of World Bank funding, the E.R.P. contracted Ramboll, a Danish firm of engineering consultants, to carry out extensive structural integrity studies and strength assessments to determine the condition, and remaining life-span, of the Bridge. They found the Bridge to be generally of sound condition - a reflection of the rigorous design, high quality steelwork and construction - and that the load carrying capacity of the Bridge, previously assessed as 46 tons, was in fact higher than thought. The consultants concluded that with a scheduled program of maintenance work identified over the short, medium and long terms, the life-span of the Victoria Falls Bridge could well be extended by a further 100 years (Ramboll, 2016).

After repairs costing $1.7 million the Bridge re-opened to heavy traffic in June 2006, sustaining loads of up to 56 tons. A programme of ongoing maintenance and repairs was scheduled and funding sought for longer term works, including $1.9 million required to replace the deck of the Bridge.

Royal Livingstone Express

In November 2007 Zambia welcomed the launch of the Royal Livingstone Express, a period-style steam train experience operated by Bushtracks Africa using a restored engine and refurbished carriages, furnished to luxurious standards. Hauled by the 10th Class Princess of Mulobezi, built by the North British Locomotive Company in 1922-4, the train regularly departs from the outskirts of Livingstone and runs down to the Bridge, treating passengers to sun-downers before retreating to the Palm Grove siding where a five course dinner is served. An extended route is also operated along the Mulobezi line,

Steam and Spray

where the engine originally hauled timber for Zambezi Sawmills. The engine was saved from the scrapyard in the 1970s by David Shepherd, the English wildlife artist, conservationist and steam enthusiast, and had previously operated on the Zimbabwean side of the Falls for many years.

Batoka Gorge Hydro-Electric Scheme

In December 2012 Zambezi River Authority (Z.R.A.), an interstate company representing the governments of Zambia and Zimbabwe, formed to manage the construction and operation of the Kariba Dam, invited expressions of interest from prospective civil engineering companies for the construction and operation of Batoka Gorge Hydro-Electric Scheme, 54 kilometres downstream from the Falls.

The potential for hydro-electric power generation in the Batoka Gorge was originally identified in a report by Sir Alexander Gibb & Partners in 1972, along with other potential sites on the Zambezi, including the Devil's and Mupata Gorges (upstream and downstream respectfully of the Kariba Dam). In 1981 a second report revised the location of the proposed dam site due to a mapping error. Technical, legal and environmental feasibility studies were carried out in 1993, and a revised Environmental Impact Assessment undertaken in 1998. Zambia pulled out of the project in favour of developing less expensive national schemes, before unsuccessful attempts were made to relaunch the project in 2007.

Early in 2012 the governments of Zambia and Zimbabwe agreed the settlement of outstanding debts relating to the construction of the Kariba Dam and break-up of the Federation, clearing one of the last major obstacles to the advancement of the scheme. In December 2013 the Z.R.A. secured $6 million from the World Bank for the updating of feasibility studies relating to the project.

The current proposal is to supply two 800 MW power stations, on either side of the river, and it is planned to build a 181 metre tall dam wall of the gravity-arch type design at an estimated construction cost of $4 billion.

The proposed scheme would flood the gorges and rapids below the Falls, changing their unique nature and affecting the habitat of its rare and vulnerable wildlife. The gorge is particularly valuable breeding habitat for many important bird species, including the endangered Taita falcon (*Falco fasciinucha*), Verreaux's eagle (*Aquila verreauxii*) and rock pratincole (*Glareola nuchalis*). The flooding of the rapids will also negatively affect tourism, drowning many of the rapids and severely limiting commercial white-water rafting (Roberts, 2021b).

Centre of Attention

Since the official opening of the Victoria Falls Bridge in 1905, the Bridge has become an integral feature of the landscape surrounding the Victoria Falls. Today the Victoria Falls Bridge is the second most famous landmark of the region, after the Falls themselves, and an essential part of a visit to the Falls.

In 2010 an expanded bungee reception facility, including a restaurant and bar with viewing deck overlooking the Bridge, was opened on the northern bank. The visitor centre includes a small interpretive museum displaying information on the history of the Bridge, free to visitors, and the starting point for the entertaining and informative guided historical tours. Participants are taken on a fascinating trip back in time to the construction of the Bridge, including the opportunity to explore the gangways under the Bridge. The bungee jump is as popular as ever, together with several other associated high-wire activities.

Following stakeholder consultations in November 2010, the E.R.P. was granted authority by the Governments of Zambia and Zimbabwe to introduce a toll on heavy vehicles crossing the Bridge to raise funds towards maintenance and refurbishment. The toll was implemented for larger vehicles from January 2018 (Victoria Falls Bits and Blogs, December 2017).

In August 2013, in celebration of the joint-hosting of the United Nations World Tourism Organisation (U.N.W.T.O.) General Assembly by Zambia and Zimbabwe, Telecel announced that it was spending $100,000 on sponsoring the illumination the Victoria Falls Bridge for the next 15 years.

The Bridge illuminated

The Bridge is painted once every 6-8 years and an examination of the steelwork and its structural integrity is carried out at least once a year. The latest repainting being completed early in 2016. Towards the end of the works, one of the team of six painters, Mr Tafi Shava, suffered serious injury when he tragically slipped and fell whilst painting the bridge railings at the beginning of February 2016. His fall was broken by the steelwork below, saving him from a life-threatening fall into the gorge below, but breaking his back (Victoria Falls Bits and Blogs, February 2016).

Recapturing the Romance of Steam

Although there are still no regular rail passenger services over the Bridge, special historic steam train excursions are now offered from both sides of the Falls. In March 2016 Bushtracks Africa launched the Bushtracks Express, operating from the Victoria Falls Station on the south bank and running down to the Bridge for sundowners and then out to Jafuta Sidings for a five course dinner service in wild bush surroundings. The train is hauled by an original 14A Class engine, Number 512, built in 1952 by Beyer Peacock in England and which saw operation on the national network from 24th November 1952 to 1994, and is comprised of restored luxury period carriages. In addition, several luxury tourist safari trains make the journey from South Africa to Victoria Falls and Livingstone.

Victoria Falls Airport Expands

A new chapter in travel and transport to the Victoria Falls began in April 2013 with the commencement of significant $150 million redevelopment and expansion of the Victoria Falls International Airport, partially opened at the end of 2015 and officially opened by President Robert Mugabe on 18th November 2016. Works included the construction of an extended four kilometre runway and associated taxiways, the construction of new terminal buildings with air-traffic control tower and supporting emergency services.

The new airport runway, expanded from a length of 2,200 metres to 4,000 metres and doubled in width to 60 metres, and will allow international travellers to fly directly to Victoria Falls, accommodating the Boeing 747 and new generation of wide-bodied aircraft. The new terminal building has been designed to handle 1.2 million international travellers (compared to the previous capacity of 400,000) and 500,000 domestic passengers per annum.

The expansion of the Victoria Falls Airport initiated a flurry of activity from the tourism sector, becoming known as the 'game changer' for its impact. The increased handling capacity of the airport has resulted in predictions of an additional 80,000 tourism arrivals a year. Concerns have been expressed, however, on the associated impact of increased tourism numbers, with pressure to develop new accommodation and concerns over the visitor carrying capacity of the Rainforest during peak-season (Roberts, 2021b).

Bridges and Borders

The Victoria Falls Bridge remains an essential transport and trade link connecting Zambia and Zimbabwe, the busy road, rail and foot crossing accessed through two border control posts on either bank. Recent upgrades to border facilities on both sides have, however, increased light pollution impacts, negatively affecting the nocturnal viewing of the lunar rainbow on both sides of the river.

Tourists and residents on either side of the Falls have to go through tedious border formalities, with associated visa restrictions and vehicle charges, to visit the other side of the river. The year-long trial of a tourism 'Univisa' in 2015, allowing unrestricted visitor travel on both sides of the river, was welcomed as a success by tourists and industry. After a lapsed period following the trial the Univisa was finally re-introduced in late 2016 (Victoria Falls Bits and Blogs, July 2016).

Despite the development out an out-of-town truck stop with driver facilities where paperwork is pre-prepared and vehicles wait until cleared to cross the weight-restricted Bridge, haulage vehicles still frequently tailback alongside the Rainforest entrance and block the road back up into town, with vehicles sometimes waiting days to cross. Tourism operators have protested against the negative impacts in accessing the Rainforest and Bridge for tourism activities, whilst local environmental groups highlighted pollution concerns from vehicles and direct local impacts from delayed drivers on the natural areas surrounding the road (Victoria Falls Bits and Blogs, February 2019).

In June 2019 it was proposed that the Bridge should ban all heavy vehicles and be restricted to local and tourist travel, with the suggestion that the Batoka Gorge Hydro-Electric Scheme should be expanded to provide a road crossing some forty kilometres downstream of the Falls (Victoria Falls Bits and Blogs, June 2019a).

Plans to develop a 'One Stop' border crossing at the Falls, combining both exit and entry border control procedures at a single location in either direction of travel, and thus reduce infrastructure at the site, have been in progress since 2017 (Victoria Falls Bits and Blogs, October 2017). In early 2019 it was announced that the project had been delayed by lack of designated development space for the necessary facilities (Victoria Falls Bits and Blogs, January 2019b).

Kazungula Bridge

The development of the Kazungula Bridge, a road and rail bridge linking Botswana and Zambia, 75 kilometres upstream of the Falls, and replacing the existing ferry service, will hopefully divert some of the high volume of freight and other heavy goods vehicles crossing the Victoria Falls Bridge.

The 923 metre bridge is being constructed at the confluence of Zambezi and Chobe rivers, the meeting point of four countries - Botswana, Namibia, Zambia and Zimbabwe. The creation of a short section of boundary of about 150 metres between Zambia and Botswana was apparently agreed during various meetings between the four states during the planning for the Bridge. The agreement separates a previously claimed 'quadripoint' (where four countries meet) into two 'tripoints,' separating Namibia and Zimbabwe.

The cost of the $260 million bridge is financed through loans from the Japan International Cooperation Agency and the African Development Bank (AfDB) as well as contributions from both the Zambian and Botswana governments.

Construction officially began in October 2014 but has been significantly delayed by rising costs and financial shortages. In 2018 Zimbabwe and Namibia joined the project as financial investors to help progress construction of the project. The new bridge was officially opened in May 2021, with an estimated total development cost of $290 million (Victoria Falls Bits and Blogs, August 2015).

The Kazungula Bridge under construction

Zimbabwe had proposed a rival project, building a new bridge over the Zambezi at the site of the Old Drift (and the site originally rejected by Hobson). The associated road infrastructure would have bisected the Zambezi and Mosi-oa-Tunya National Parks on either side of the river.

The bridge includes a central 2,170 metre single-track of rails, and a new 367 kilometre railway is also proposed, connecting the Botswana rail network via Kazungula to Livingstone (Victoria Falls Bits and Blogs, June 2019b).

Into The Future

With the 115th anniversary year of the completion and opening of the Victoria Falls Bridge due in 2020 the Bridge continues to be an iconic symbol of the Victoria Falls, a landmark engineering achievement, tourist attraction and vital transport link between Zambia and Zimbabwe.

In the years to come the Bridge will again have to be stripped bare of all its paint, inspected and repainted, as previously performed in 1965. In time the whole of the top deck will have to be again reconstructed to cope with increasing road and rail traffic requirements. It is estimated that the replacement of the railway deck could cost close to $800,000, that of the footway deck $300,000 and the roadway $800,000. But with appropriate maintenance and investment the Bridge should have a secure future, continuing to span the decades as well as the gorge high over the Zambezi.

The Bridge today

In September 2018 a Chinese infrastructure construction company, the China Communications Construction Company, even went as far as drawing up proposals for the construction of a new state-of-the-art bridge at the Victoria Falls. The company put forward three hypothetical designs for a new bridge; named the 'Wing Bridge,' the 'Flying Bird Bridge' and the 'Rainbow Bridge' (Victoria Falls Bits and Blogs, September 2018).

Whatever its long term future, that the Bridge has survived over a hundred years of road and rail traffic is testimony to all involved in its design, construction and maintenance, from the steelworks of northern England to the banks of the Zambezi, the Bridge remains an outstanding tribute to the vision and achievement of all involved.

Acknowledgements

The path of research for this book has taken many years over several editions and involved the input of many people along the way. Thanks go to all of them, but special mention must be made to some.

Firstly I would like to thank the Victoria Falls Bridge Company, operators of the historical Bridge tours, who supported the research and publication of the first edition of this book. I would also like to thank Geoff Cooke for his assistance in the early stages of the research. Special thanks also go to Gordon Murray, Curator of the Bulawayo Railway Museum, for allowing access to their archive and for his assistance in locating reference material, and Dr Friday Mufuzi, Keeper of History at the Livingstone Museum, for his time and help. I would also like to thank Alex Mutape, of the National Railways Zimbabwe (Bulawayo) and members of the Emerged Railways Properties for their support and assistance.

A special acknowledgement must also go to descendants of those involved in the building of the Bridge or other aspects of this story, including; Clive Longbottom with information on his grandfather Howard Longbottom (and photograph on page 149); John Reid-Rowland for sharing his grandfather's personal memoirs; Doug Leen for information and images from his grandfather, Edwin Verner; and Laurel Douglass in Hawaii for information on the Alexander family. I am also grateful to Marta Micheletti of the Museo dell'emigrante, Roasio, Italy for information on Giacomo D'Alberto from documents donated to the museum by his family.

Thanks also go to members of the online community, notably Eddy Norris and his blog 'Our Rhodesia Heritage' (www.rhodesianheritage.blogspot.co.uk), who shared appeals for information on the Bridge, and also Douglas Rolls for assisting with an especially elusive reference source. It was as a result of these requests that I was contacted, among others, by Geraldine Morris with the story of her father, Sydney Burton, who came to Victoria Falls as Post Master in 1914 and unwittingly uncovered the activities of a German spy. To my knowledge this information has never been published before, and I thank Geraldine for allowing me to quote from her father's memoirs.

Among the many members of the Victoria Falls and Livingstone communities who have helped me with this work I must especially thank Peter Jones, Tony Barnett and Robert Koch for their local knowledge and assistance. Finally my biggest thanks must go to my parents and brother for their respective, and significant, roles in supporting the development of the first edition of this book.

Members of the British Association disembark for the opening ceremony

The images used in this publication have come from many diverse sources. In most cases it has been difficult to identify the original source locations of historical images, but I would like to acknowledge the National Archives, Harare (Zimbabwe) and National Archives, Lusaka (Zambia), where many of these photographs are undoubtedly held, as well as the archives of the Bulawayo Railway Museum (Zimbabwe) and Livingstone Museum (Zambia).

Thanks go to Heiko Wolf for the preparation of digital archive images for the first edition, many of which are again used here. I would also like to thank Howard Bradbury, Tony Barnett and the Victoria Falls Bungee Company for the use of additional images. Special thanks go to Dr Anthony Klein for the image used on page 206 and information on the restoration of the bridge roadway in 1979. The images on pages 24 and 25 are from Shepherd, 2008, and page 104 from Shepherd, 2013, and used with thanks (both booklets are a treasure trove of archive images). The photographs on pages 207, 213 and 217 are by the author. I must also acknowledge the Institute of Civil Engineers, source of the technical drawings by G A Hobson on pages 40 and 41, and the work of F H Varian for the graphic on page 36.

Thanks also go to Travellers Guest House (www.travellerszim.net) for hosting me during many visits to Bulawayo, and likewise others too many to mention in Victoria Falls and Livingstone, for their hospitality and friendship over many visits over many years.

References

Two primary archive libraries for references are indicated; the archives of the Bulawayo Railway Museum (Zimbabwe), identified as 'BRMA' in the reference list, and the archive collection of the Livingstone Museum (Zambia), labelled 'LMA.' Website links are correct as of October 2021.

Agate, W. (1912) Diary of a tour in South Africa. Holness, London.

Arrington-Sirois, A. L. (2017) Victoria Falls and Colonial Imagination in British Southern Africa: Turning Water into Gold. Palgrave Macmillan.

Anon (2011). Personal communication with the author, August 2011.

Balfour, H. (1905) Diaries of Henry Balfour (1863-1939) South Africa 1905 [Online source: www.prm.ox.ac.uk/manuscripts/balfourdiaries1905.html]

Beet. G. (1923) The Story of the Ox Wagon - The Story of a Famous Engineering Feat. [In Weinthal, L. (1923) Vol.I]

Bendigo Advertiser (September 1904) A Trip to the Victoria Falls. 3rd September. [Online source: https://trove.nla.gov.au/newspaper/article/100523321]

Black & White Magazine (1906) The Leading Personalities in the Rand-Zambesi Power Scheme. 15th December, p.779.

Brelsford, W. V. (1954) Story of the Northern Rhodesian Regiment. The Government Printer, Lusaka.

Brelsford, W. V. (1965) Generation of Men - the European Pioneers of Northern Rhodesia. Stuart Manning for the Northern Rhodesia Society.

Browne, J. S. (1906) Through South Africa with The British Association for the Advancement of Science. Spiers, London.

British South Africa Company (1905) Annual Report.

British South Africa Company (1906) Annual Report.

British South Africa Company (1907) Rhodesia, A Book for Tourists and Sportsmen.

Bulawayo Chronicle (September 1903a) A Chat with Imbault. 12th September.

Bulawayo Chronicle (September 1903b) The Victoria Falls. 12th September.

Bulawayo Chronicle (October, 1903) The Victoria Falls - Alleged Vandalism. 10th October.

Bulawayo Chronicle (February 1904a) Zambesi Notes. 13th February.

Bulawayo Chronicle (February 1904b) A Plucky Rescue. 27th February.

Bulawayo Chronicle (June 1904) Victoria Falls Hotel. 4th June.

Bulawayo Chronicle (July 1904a) Victoria Falls Hotel notice. 9th July.

Bulawayo Chronicle (July 1904b) Blondin Conveyor Crosses. 30th July.

Bulawayo Chronicle (September 1904a) Advert, 3rd September.

Bulawayo Chronicle (September 1904b) The Royal Visit to Victoria Falls. 24th September.

Bulawayo Chronicle (September 1904c) Sensation at the Falls. 24th September.

Bulawayo Chronicle (October 1904) Victoria Falls Notes. 29th October.

Bulawayo Chronicle (November 1904) Serious Accident at Victoria Falls. 5th November.

Bulawayo Chronicle (December 1904a) The Recent Fatalities at Victoria Falls. 3rd December.

Bulawayo Chronicle (December 1904b) Victoria Falls Notes. 10th December.

Bulawayo Chronicle (April 1905) Victoria Falls Bridge, Final Piece in Position, and Livingstone Notes. 8th April.

Bulawayo Chronicle (May 1905a) Zambesi Bridge. 3rd May.

Bulawayo Chronicle (May 1905b) Livingstone High Court. 27th May.

Bulawayo Chronicle (July 1905a) Livingstone Notes. 1st July.

Bulawayo Chronicle (July 1905b), Livingstone Notes. 15th July.

Bulawayo Chronicle (September 1905a) British Association at the Victoria Falls: Opening of The Bridge. 13th September.

Bulawayo Chronicle (September 1905b) British Association at the Victoria Falls: Dinner and Speeches. 14th September.

Bulawayo Chronicle (October 1905) Advert. 7th October.

Bulawayo Chronicle (November 1905) Livingstone Notes. 18th November.

Bulawayo Chronicle (March 1930) Building the Highest Bridge in the World. 8th March.

Bulawayo Chronicle (November 1950) Falls Bridge. Letter from Mr Tiffen. 10th November.

Bulawayo Chronicle (March 1980) Victoria Falls bridge 'not scheduled for dismantling.' 21st March.

Burrett, R. and Murray, G. (2013) 'Iron Spine and Ribs' A brief history of the foundation of the railways of Zimbabwe and Zambia. Bulawayo.

Clark, P. M. (c.1911) Guide to the Victoria Falls. Undated, circa 1911.

Clark, P. M. (1936) Autobiography of an Old Drifter. Harrap, London.

Coillard, F. (1897) On the threshold of Africa - A Record of Twenty Years Pioneering among the Barotse of the Upper Zambezi. Hodder and Stoughton, London.

Conroy, D. (2003) The Best of Luck: In the Royal Air Force 1935-1946.

Creewel, J. (2004) A history of the Victoria Falls Hotel - 100 years 1904-2004. Edited and updated by Stan Higgins. (Originally published in 1994 as A history of the Victoria Falls Hotel - 90 Glorious Years 1904-1994).

Croxton, A. (1982) Railways of Zimbabwe. David and Charles (Publishers) Ltd.

[Originally published as Railways of Rhodesia, 1973].

Farrar, E. M. (1903) Impressions of a visit to the Victoria Falls. Unpublished manuscript, Bodleian Library, Oxford.

Fox, Sir. F. (1904) River, Road and Rail. J. Murray, London.

Fox, Sir. F. (1924) Sixty-three years of engineering, scientific and social work. J. Murray, London.

Fuller, B. (1954) Bid Time Return. De Bussy, Cape Town.

Girouard, Lieut-Col. Sir. P. (1906) The Railway of Africa, Scribner's Magazine, May 1906, p553-568. Charles Scribner's & Sons, New York.

Graetz, P. (1912) 'Im Motorboot quer durch Afrika, Vom Indischen Ozean zum Kongo.' Braunbeck & Gutenberg, Berlin.

Green, L. G. (1960) Great African Mysteries. Stanley Paul & Co. London.

Green, L. G. (1968) Full Many a Glorious Morning. Timmins. Cape Town.

Grogan, E. S. and Sharp, A. H. (1900) From the Cape to Cairo, Hurst and Blackett.

Harris, D. (1969) Victoria Falls Souvenir Guide Book.

Hang'ombe, K, Chabata, E. and Mamvura, Z (2019) *Syungu Namutitima* or Victoria Falls? Contest for place and place naming. Nomina Africana, Vol.33, No.1, p. 19-31.

Hensman, H. (1901) Cecil Rhodes A Study. William Blackwood and Sons.

Hill, C. W. (1911) Electric Crane Construction, Charles Griffin & Co, Ltd, London.

Hobson, G. (1907) The Victoria Falls Bridge. Institution of Civil Engineers, Session 1906-1907, Part IV, Section 1. Minutes of Proceedings 19th March (Paper No 3675). Volume 170, p.1-49.

Hobson, G. (1923) The Great Zambezi Bridge - The Story of a Famous Engineering Feat. [In Weinthal, L. (1923) Vol.II]

Honolulu Advertiser (1904) Particulars of the death of Mr Samuel T Alexander. 1st November. p.6. [Online source (subscription required): www.newspapers.com/image/259326721/]

Horner, J. G. [Editor] (1906) Cableways. Henley's Encyclopaedia of Practical Engineering and Allied Trades, Vol.3, p.107. New York.

Hutchinson, G. D. (1905) From the Cape to the Zambesi. J Murray, London.

Hyder Consulting (2007) Footprints on a Global Landscape - 100 years of improving the built environment. Hyder Consulting.

I.C.B.L, (2009) Landmine Monitor Report 2009, Special Ten-Year Review. International Campaign to Ban Landmines.

James, D. (1954) The Life of Lord Roberts. Hollis & Carter.

Lamplugh, G. W. (1905) Notes On The Geological History Of The Victoria Falls [in Sykes, F. W. (1905)].

Leen, D. (2018) Personal communication. June 2018.

Livingstone, D. (1857) Missionary travels and researches in South Africa. London.

Livingstone Mail (December 1906) Livingstone in 1906 - A Retrospect. Christmas Edition, December. [LMA]

Livingstone Mail (January 1907) Meeting with His Honour the Administrator, No.43. 19th January. [LMA]

Livingstone Mail (December 1907) Christmas Issue. December. [LMA]

Lloyd, C. (2013) Zambezi pioneers. 23rd January. [Online source: www. thenorthernecho.co.uk/history/memories/10180073.Zambezi_pioneers/]

London Daily News (May 1905) The Victoria Falls Bridge - Record Engineering Feat. 10th May.

Longbottom, C. (2018) Personal communication. June 2018.

McAdams, J. (1969) Birth of an Airline - Establishment of Rhodesian and Nyasaland Airways [Online source: www.rhodesia.nl/Aviation/rana.htm]

McGregor, J. (2003) The Victoria Falls 1900-1940: Landscape, Tourism and the Geographical Imagination, Journal of Southern African Studies, Vol.29, No.3, September 2003 , p.717-737.

McGregor, J. (2009) Crossing the Zambezi : The Politics of Landscape on an African Frontier. James Currey, Oxford & Weaver Press, Harare.

Mackintosh, C. W. (1922) The New Zambesi Trail; a record of two journeys to North-Western Rhodesia (1903 and 1920). Unwin, London.

Metcalfe, Sir C, and Richarde-Seaver, Major F. I. (1889) The British Sphere of Influence in South Africa. Fortnightly Review, Vol.267, p.351-63. London.

Metcalfe, Sir C. (c.1902-3) File note regarding visit to bridge site with George Pauling. Undated, circa 1902-3. [BRMA, unpublished].

Metcalfe, Sir C. (1903) File note regarding transport of bridge steelwork via Beira. 1903. [BRMA, unpublished].

Metcalfe, Sir C. (1904) Cape to Cairo Railway. Dawson Daily News, 29th September 1904.

Metcalfe, Sir C. (1923) The Kafue River Bridge. [In Weinthal, L. (1923) Vol.II]

Milner, V. G. M. (1951) My Picture Gallery, 1886-1901. J. Murray.

Molyneux, A. J. C. (1905) The Physical History of the Victoria Falls, Geographical Journal. Vol.25, No.1, p.40-55.

Morris, G. (2011) Personal Communication. February 2011.

Morwell Advertiser (October 1925) Victoria Falls, Rhodesia. 2nd October. [Online source: https://trove.nla.gov.au/newspaper/article/65903995]

Mubitana, K. (1990) The Traditional History and Ethnography. [In Phillipson D. W. [Editor] (1990) Mosi-oa-Tunya: a handbook to the Victoria Falls region.]

Munokalya, M. (2013) The Mukuni Royal Dynasty's Short History and the Munokalya Mukuni Royal Establishment's Ritual and Political Sovereignty.

Museo dell'emigrante, Roasio (2021a) Letter of Recommendation from Mr William Tower, 11th March 1905. Museo dell'emigrante, Roasio, Italy [unpublished].

Museo dell'emigrante, Roasio (2021b) Letter from District Commissioner's Office, Livingstone, to Mr Charles Beresford-Fox, 29th January 1905. Museo dell'emigrante, Roasio, Italy [unpublished].

Museo dell'emigrante, Roasio (2021c) Draft contract with Cleveland Bridge and Engineering Company and Giacomo D'Alberto regarding construction of concrete foundations, 4th July 1905 Museo dell'emigrante, Roasio, Italy [unpublished].

Muskett H. B. (1957) Steel Highway The Story of the Rhodesia Railways, 1897-1957. Rhodesian Graphic.

New York Times (October 1903) To Harness Victoria Falls. New York Times, 2nd October.

New York Times (March 1977) Podgorny Peers Into Rhodesia and Predicts 'Freedom' for the Blacks. 28th March.

New Zealand Herald (April 1902) The Cape to Cairo Railway. New Zealand Herald, 17th April. [Online source: https://paperspast.natlib.govt.nz/newspapers/NZH19020417.2.54]

New Zealand Herald (May 1906) To Harness The Zambesi. New Zealand Herald, 9th May. [Online source: https://paperspast.natlib.govt.nz/newspapers/NZH19060509.2.99.21]

New Zealand Herald (October 1907) Africa in 1957. New Zealand Herald, 26th October. [Online source: https://paperspast.natlib.govt.nz/newspapers/NZH19071026.2.88.45]

New Zealand Herald (December 1919) The Brontosaurus. British Hunter's Quest. 24th December. [Online source: https://paperspast.natlib.govt.nz/newspapers/NZH19191224.2.76]

Northern Rhodesia Journal (July 1951) Early Days in Kalomo and Livingstone. E. Knowles Jordan. Vol.1 No.4, p.16-23.

Northern Rhodesia Journal (January 1952) The Reminiscences of Arthur 'Ingeinyama' Davison. A F Davison. Vol.1 No.5, p.46-56.

Northern Rhodesia Journal (July 1952) The First Zambezi Regatta. Vol.1, No.6, p.64-65.

Northern Rhodesia Journal (July 1953a) Early Days Around the Copperbelt. A. E. Beech. Vol.2, No.2, p.41-48.

Northern Rhodesia Journal (July 1953b) Island Names. Vol.2, No.2, p.89.

Northern Rhodesia Journal (July 1954) Accident at the Building of the Victoria Falls Bridge. J. F. Sharp. Vol.2, No.4, p.116-7.

Northern Rhodesia Journal (January 1963) The Railway Reaches the Falls Bridge. W. Trayner. Vol.5, No.3, p.60.

Northern Rhodesia Journal (July 1964) The Livingstone Pioneer - The First Newspaper. P. Barnes. Vol.5, No.4, p.389.

Page, W. H. [Editor] (1905) Among the World's Wonders, The World's Work, Vol.9, No.4, February, p.5879. Page & Company, New York.

Paice, E. (2007) Tip and Run: The Untold Tragedy of the Great War in Africa. Weidenfeld & Nicolson.

Parsons, D. (1938) Harnessing the Victoria Falls, Discovery.

Pauling, G. (1926) Chronicles of a Contractor, Constable. [Reprinted 1969 Rhodesia Reprint Library Vol.4, Bulawayo (Edited by David Buchan)]

Phillipson, D. W. [Editor] (1990) Mosi-oa-Tunya: a handbook to the Victoria Falls region. Longman, Zimbabwe. (First Published, 1975. Second Edition, 1990)

Powell I. A. (1930) Building the highest bridge in the world. Bulawayo Chronicle, Saturday, 8th March.

Prahran Telegraph (July 1906) On The Zambesi. 28th July. [Online source: https://trove.nla.gov.au/newspaper/article/144511424]

Price, J. H. (1966) Behind the Headlines, Modern Tramway and Light Railway Review. Vol.29, No.338, p.48-49.

Prince, A. T. (1906) Bridging the gorge of the Zambezi. The World's Work, Vol.12, No.2, June 1906, p.7637-7647. Doubleday, Page & Company, New York.

Railway Magazine (1965) Spanning the Zambezi. Vol.3, No.775, p.621-625.

Ramboll (2016) Lifetime Of Historic African Steel Bridge Extended. March.

Rhodesia Herald (March 1957) Cabbages and Kings.

Rhodesia Railways (1905) Minutes of Ordinary General Meeting, London.

Rhodesia Railways (September 1906) Letter from Mr S. F. Townsend to Mr C. Corner regarding maintenance of the Bridge. [BRMA, unpublished]

Rhodesia Railways Bulletin (October 1926) Victoria Falls Bridge, No.21, p.9-11.

Rhodesia Railways Bulletin (November 1929) Victoria Falls Bridge: Strengthening and Reconstruction of Deck, No.34, p.6-8.

Rhodesia Railways Bulletin (July 1937) Inspection Gangways for Victoria Falls Bridge, No.126, p.10-11.

Rhodesia Railways Magazine (July 1953) Spectacular Model of the Victoria Falls Bridge. Vol.2, No.3, p.7.

Rhodesia Railways Magazine (December 1953) Attempt to Sabotage Falls Bridge. Vol.2, No.8, p.11.

Rhodesia Railways Magazine (December 1954) First Hotel Built in a Month. Vol.3, No.8, p.13.

Rhodesia Railways Magazine (July 1955) Fifty Years - The Story of a Bridge (Part 1). Vol.4, No.3, p.21-23.

Rhodesia Railways Magazine (August 1955) Fifty Years - The Story of a Bridge (Part 2). Vol.4, No.3, p.21-23.

Rhodesia Railways Magazine (September 1955) Fifty Years - The Story of a Bridge (Part 3). Vol.4, No.5, p.19-21.

Rhodesia Railways Magazine (September 1957) Railway History In The Leaves of A Circular. Vol.6, No.5, p.67.

Rhodesia Railways Magazine (November 1957) 'Cape To Cairo' Scheme Still A Dream, Vol 6, No 7, p.31.

Rhodesia Railways Magazine (July 1958) Some Reminiscences of The Early Days at the Falls. Vol.7, No.3, p.15.

Rhodesia Railways Magazine (March 1959) Falls Railway Bridge a 'Whispering Giant.' Vol.7, No.11, p.17.

Rhodesia Railways Magazine (March 1962) The Falls Fifty Years Ago. Vol.10, No.11, p.15-17.

Rhodesia Railways Magazine (August 1963) Famous Bridge is Having a 'Face Lift.' Vol.12, No.4, p.9.

Rhodesia Railways Magazine (October 1963) Falls Bridge - A Controversy. Vol.12, No.6, p.19.

Rhodesia Railways Magazine (May 1964) A railcar, A searchlight, A Blockhouse. Further Light On Falls Bridge Controversy. Vol.13, No.1, p.15.

Rhodesia Railways Magazine (January 1965) Old Timers Are Laid To Rest. Vol.13, No.9, p.15.

Rhodesia Railways Magazine (April 1965) Falls Bridge Renovated. Vol.13, No.12, p.19.

Rhodesia Railways Magazine (November 1965) Story of a Bridge 1905-1965, A Diamond Jubilee. Vol.14, No.7, p.11-13.

Rhodesia Railways Magazine (March 1967) Crossed the Falls by Blondin Cable, Vol.15, No.11, p.17.

Rhodesia Railways Magazine (July 1967) There was only one Jack Tar, Vol.16,

No.2, p.19.

Rhodesia Railways Magazine (August 1967) The bridge - Some reminiscences, Vol.16, No.4, p.19.

Rhodesia Railways Magazine (October 1967) A Message from the GM, Vol.16, No.6, Oct 1967, p.5.

Rhodesian National Tourism Board (1967) Victoria Falls. Publicity brochure.

Roberts, P. (2021a) Corridors Through Time - A History of the Victoria Falls Hotel. Third Edition. Zambezi Book Company / CreateSpace Independent Publishing. (First published 2015, The Jafuta Foundation, Zimbabwe).

Roberts, P. (2021b) Footsteps Through Time - A History of Travel and Tourism to the Victoria Falls. Second Edition. Zambezi Book Company / CreateSpace Independent Publishing. (First published 2017).

Roberts, P. (2021c) Life and Death at the Old Drift, Victoria Falls (1898-1905). Third Edition. Zambezi Book Company / CreateSpace Independent Publishing (First published 2018).

Rotberg, R. (1990) The Founder: Cecil Rhodes and the Pursuit of Power. Oxford University Press.

Scientific American Magazine (1905) Completion of the Victoria Falls Bridge. 22nd July, p.68-69.

Scientific American Supplement (1905) The Opening Of The Victoria Falls Bridge. Harold Shepstone. 4th November 1905. Vol.60, No.1557, p.24941-2.

Shepherd, G. (2008) Old Livingstone and Victoria Falls. Stenlake.

Shepherd, G. (2013) Old Frontier Life in North-Western Rhodesia. Stenlake.

Sir Douglas Fox and Partners (July 1903) Letter to Sir Charles Metcalfe regarding departure of Mr Imbault for the Falls. 10th July. Bulawayo Railway Museum. [BRMA, unpublished]

Sir Douglas Fox and Partners (January 1907) Letter to Chief Resident Engineer's Office, Rhodesia Railways regarding condition of Bridge paintwork. 25th January. [BRMA, unpublished]

Sir Douglas Fox and Partners (February 1907) Letter to Chief Resident Engineer's Office, Rhodesia Railways regarding rust on steelwork. 15th February. [BRMA, unpublished]

Sir Douglas Fox and Partners (March 1907) Letter to Chief Resident Engineer's Office, Rhodesia Railways regarding order of paint and materials. 8th March. [BRMA, unpublished]

South Africa Handbook, No.32 (1905) The Victoria Falls. Winchester House, London.

South Africa Magazine (April 1905) Zambesi River Bridged at Last, 8th April.

Southern Rhodesia Publicity Office (1938) The Victoria Falls of Southern Rhodesia. Government Stationery Office.

Stanley, H. M. (1898) Through South Africa - His Visit to Rhodesia, the Transvaal, Cape Colony, Natal.

Stirling, W. G. M. and House, J. A. (2014) They Served Africa with Wings. E-book Edition (First published 2002).

Strage, M. (1973) Cape to Cairo. Jonathan Cape.

Sydney Morning Herald (1929) Harbour Bridge Designer's Story. 11 March. [Online source: https://trove.nla.gov.au/newspaper/article/16537020]

Sykes, F. W. (1905) Official Guide to the Victoria Falls. Argus Printing & Publishing Co Ltd, Bulawayo.

Taylor, R. D. (2005) Bulawayo Victoria Falls Railway, Friends of the Bulawayo Railway Museum Newsletter, Volume 7, Issue 2, November.

Teede, J. and Teede, F. (1994) African Thunder - The Victoria Falls. Tutorial Press Ltd, Zimbabwe.

The Canberra Times (November 1976) Attack on Motel. Monday 1st November. [Online source: https://trove.nla.gov.au/newspaper/article/131793204]

The Canberra Times (December 1977) 8 people wounded in shelling. Tuesday 20th December. [Online source: https://trove.nla.gov.au/newspaper/article/110883647]

The Engineer (April 1905) The Victoria Falls Bridge. 7th April 1905. Vol.99, No.14. p.339-341. London.

The Engineering Record (May 1904) An African Cableway. 7th May 1904. Vol.49, No.19. p583. New York.

The Practical Engineer (February 1904) A Zambesi Cable Bridge. 05 February 1904. Vol.29, No.884. p.139. London.

Thornhill, J. B. (1915) Adventures in Africa. John Murray, London.

Thwaits, C. (1904) Notes from diary. [BRMA, unpublished].

Varian, F. H. (1953) Some African Milestones. George Ronald, Wheatley.

Victoria Falls Bits and Blogs (January 2012) Australian woman Erin Langworthy survives 111m bungee fall into the Zambezi River. 15th January. [Online source: www.vicfallsbitsnblogs.blogspot.co.uk/2012/01/australian-woman-erin-langworthy.html]

Victoria Falls Bits and Blogs (February 2016) Man survives Victoria Falls Bridge fall. 10th February. [Online source: www.vicfallsbitsnblogs.blogspot.co.uk/2016/02/man-survives-victoria-falls-bridge-fall.html]

Victoria Falls Bits and Blogs (July 2016) Suspended Uni-Visa facility to bounce back. 1st July. [Online source: www.vicfallsbitsnblogs.blogspot.co.uk/ 2016/06/ suspended-uni-visa-facility-to-bounce.html]

Victoria Falls Bits and Blogs (October 2017) Zim engages Zambia on one border post. 11th October. [Online source: www.vicfallsbitsnblogs.blogspot. com/2017/11/zim-engages-zambia-on-one-border-post.html]

Victoria Falls Bits and Blogs (December 2017) Vehicle Toll Fees for Victoria Falls Bridge. 15th December. [Online source: www.vicfallsbitsnblogs.blogspot. co.uk/2017/12/vehicle-toll-fees-for-victoria-falls.html]

Victoria Falls Bits and Blogs (September 2018) Chinese firm seeks to build new Victoria Falls Bridge. 11th September. [Online source: www.vicfallsbitsnblogs. blogspot.com/2018/09/chinese-firm-seeks-to-build-new-state.html]

Victoria Falls Bits and Blogs (January 2019) Land Shortage Hits Zimra's Victoria Falls Border Project. 28th January. [Online source: www.vicfallsbitsnblogs. blogspot.com/2019/01/land-shortage-hits-zimras-victoria.html]

Victoria Falls Bits and Blogs (February 2019) Human activities worry Vic Falls environmentalists. 19th February. [Online source: www.vicfallsbitsnblogs. blogspot.com/2019/02/human-activities-worry-vic-falls.html]

Victoria Falls Bits and Blogs (June 2019a) War over Vic Falls Zambezi bridge. 27th June. [Online source: www.vicfallsbitsnblogs.blogspot.com/2019/06/war-over-vic-falls-zambezi-bridge.html]

Victoria Falls Bits and Blogs (June 2019b) Zambia, Botswana to construct railway across Zambezi. 30th June. [Online source: www.vicfallsbitsnblogs.blogspot. com/2019/06/zambia-botswana-to-construct-railway.html]

Weinthal, L. [Editor] (1923) The Story of the Cape to Cairo Railway and River Route from 1887-1922. Pioneer Publishing Co. Vols I-V.

Wessels, H. (2015) A Handful of Hard Men: The S.A.S. and the Battle for Rhodesia. Casemate, Philadelphia and Oxford.

White, B. (1973) The Trailmakers, The Story of Rhodesia Railways. Supplement to Illustrated Life, Rhodesia, 31st May 1973.

Whitehead, D. (2014) Inspired by the Zambezi, Memories of Barotseland and a Royal River - the mighty Liambai. Goshawk, South Africa.

Williams, A. [Editor] (1909) Engineering Wonders of the World. The Great Zambesi Bridge. Vol.1, p.90-101. Thomas Nelson and Sons. London and New York.

Wonders of World Engineering (1937) The Victoria Falls Bridge. 1st June 1937. Part 14, p.411- 420. London.

Worthington, F. V. (1922) The Witch Doctor and Other Rhodesian Studies. The Field Press Ltd, London.

ALSO AVAILABLE:

TO THE BANKS OF THE ZAMBEZI AND BEYOND

RAILWAY CONSTRUCTION

FROM THE CAPE TO THE CONGO

(1893-1910)

A detailed study of railway construction in southern Africa, focussing on the development of the line north to the Victoria Falls and beyond, hailed at the time as the southern section of the envisaged, but eventually unrealised, Cape to Cairo Railway linking the length of the continent.

Fully illustrated with over 90 archive photographs.

LIFE AND DEATH
AT THE OLD DRIFT
VICTORIA FALLS
(1898-1905)

The Old Drift holds a pivotal place in the story of the modern development
of the Victoria Falls region, marking the main crossing point on the Zambezi
River above the Falls for travellers and traders heading north. Established
in 1898 the crossing became the focal point for the beginnings of a
small European community, before the development of the railway
and opening of the Victoria Falls Bridge in 1905 shifted the
focus of activity downstream.

With over 100 period photographs and illustrations.

New revised and extended third edition published September 2021.

CORRIDORS THROUGH TIME

A HISTORY OF
THE VICTORIA FALLS HOTEL

Established in 1904 the Victoria Falls Hotel has played a central role in the romance of a visit to the Falls for generations of travellers, its walls and gardens echoing with a rich history covering the development of a modern global tourism icon.

Fully illustrated with over 100 archive images and 30 modern photographs, 'Corridors Through Time' details the changing face of the 'Grand Old Lady of the Falls' and growth of tourism to the Victoria Falls, from humble beginnings to luxury five-star elegance, from the arrival of the railway to the age of aviation, and through colonial administration to political independence.

New revised and extended third edition published April 2021.

Footsteps Through Time

A History of Travel and Tourism to the Victoria Falls

Exploring over 150 years of travel and tourism to the Victoria Falls, 'Footsteps Through Time' charts the evolution of a global tourism attraction. Discover the human heritage of this famous natural wonder and the people who have carved their names in its history - from the arrival of Dr David Livingstone in 1855, the coming of the railway and opening of the Victoria Falls Bridge fifty years later, to the development of international air travel and transformation into the modern tourism destination we know today.

Fully illustrated with over 100 contemporary photographs and illustrations.

New revised and extended second edition published April 2021.

Printed in Great Britain
by Amazon

68131726R00133